CURRICULUM AND SCHOOL

CURRICULUM AND SCHOOL

DR. ISMAIL THAMARASSERI
DR. PUSHPITA RAJAWAT
ULFAT ALI LONE

KALPAZ

First Published, 2018

Published by

Kalpaz Publications
C-30, Satyawati Nagar,
Delhi – 110052
E-mail: kalpaz@hotmail.com
Ph.: 9212142040

Printed at: G. Print Process, Delhi

Cataloging in Publication Data—DK
Courtesy: D.K. Agencies (P) Ltd. <docinfo@dkagencies.com>

Thamarasseri, Ismail, author.
Curriculum and school / Dr. Ismail Thamarasseri, Dr. Pushpita Rajawat, Ulfat Ali Lone.
pages cm
ISBN 9789386397720

1. Education—Curricula—India. 2. Curriculum planning—India. I. Rajawat, Pushpita, author. II. Lone, Ulfat Ali, author. III. Title.

LCC LB1564.I4T43 2018 | DDC 375.000954 23

Contents

Preface

Knowledge and education are considered among the major factors contributing to the reduction of poverty, sustainable development and economic growth – and it is the curriculum that is increasingly viewed as foundational to educational reforms aimed at the achievement of high quality learning outcomes. The curriculum represents a conscious and systematic selection of knowledge, skills and values: a selection that shapes the way teaching, learning and assessment processes are organized by addressing questions such as what, why, when and how students should learn.

More broadly, the curriculum is also understood as a political and social agreement that reflects a society's common vision while taking into account local, national and global needs and expectations. The curriculum, in other words, embodies a society's educational aims and purposes. Contemporary curriculum reform and development processes therefore increasingly involve public discussion and consultation with a wide range of stakeholders. Curriculum design has evolved into a topic of considerable debate – with frequently conflicting perspectives – engaging policy-makers, experts, practitioners and society at large. The complexity of curriculum development processes and the range of issues informing the 'what' and the 'how' of teaching, learning and assessment present major challenges for policy-makers and curriculum developers. Since curriculum development processes are influenced both by local needs and by broader, transnational trends, a comprehensive international perspective on curriculum issues, trends and approaches is critical.

This book intends to support country efforts in mainstreaming challenging issues within the processes of curriculum renewal and development across different levels, settings and provisions of the education system. Also, they serve as reference materials for the capacity-development training on curriculum, learning and quality education – namely masters, diplomas, certificates and workshops –, to forge policy and technical dialogue involving a diversity of stakeholders and to support sustainable country field work. Given the essential role of curriculum in enabling quality learning and in articulating and supporting education that is relevant to holistic development, our purpose in this book is to identify what makes a quality curriculum, so as to support curricular innovation to the end of the realization of Sustainable Development Goals.

It is the curriculum that determines to a large extent whether education is inclusive, thus playing a significant role in ensuring that provision is equitable. It is the curriculum that provides the structure for the provision of quality learning, especially where teachers might be under-qualified and inexperienced, their classrooms under-resourced, and their students lacking the prior frameworks within which to situate their learning. And it is the curriculum that articulates both the competencies necessary for lifelong learning and the competencies needed for holistic development.

The curriculum is the sum total of the schools efforts to influence learning, whether in the classroom or in the playground, or out of school. K.G. Saiyidain says; "The curriculum is primarily an aid in the process of adjusting the child to the environment in which he functions from day to day and in the environment in which he will have to organize his activities late". The concept of the curriculum differs with different schools of philosophy. According to Idealism curriculum should stress on nature of the child, Curriculum should emphasize the higher values, Curriculum provides humanities a place of prominence, ethics, religion and arts find an important place. Idealism gives importance to physical education, hygiene, philosophy, physical skills, gymnastics, and athletics.

Recently all over India, the duration of B.Ed., programme enhanced to two academic years. The syllabus also re-framed accordingly. The National Council of Teacher Education (NCTE), India has laid down the new guidelines in framing the curriculum for the teachers training institutions at the national level. Most of the universities in India have adopted these new guidelines of devising the syllabi and others are in the process following the same. In the Bachelor of Education (B.Ed.) programme, there is a core course named as "*Curriculum and School*". The study of this course is essential for becoming an effective and successful teacher. The course intends to inform student-teachers that how curriculum-making plays a critical role in a heterogeneous and plural society like India. However, without a clear vision and understanding of curricular aims, schools tend to become rigid in their curricular practices, and uniformly imposed processes, meanings and values. This negates the ideals that they are expected to actualise. Therefore, the course aims at enthusing student-teachers to infuse dynamism in interpreting and transacting curriculum in the school, so that it becomes culturally sensitive in selection of knowledge, symbols and values, and child-friendly in pedagogy. Student teachers understand the evolving meanings of 'curriculum', when seen as a dynamic process. Within this broad field, conceptual linkages (and distinctions) between educational aims, curriculum framework, curriculum development, syllabus, teaching-learning materials, pedagogy as well as evaluation processes are recognised. The role of school organisation and culture, as well as of the teacher, in operationalising and developing a contextually responsive 'curriculum' and 'critical pedagogy' are explored. The scope for teachers to make curricular decisions, based on field realities is highlighted.

In preparation of this book the authors had to refer to the works of other authors and information sources. The authors extremely indebted to various writers, editors, educationists and scholars whose views and opinions are integrated in this book. The authors shall ever remain obliged to their teachers, parents, friends, colleagues, family members and students for their kind directions, guidance and assistance. The authors take this opportunity to express their sincere thanks to Prof. N.A. Nadeem, Prof. Nighat Basu, and all staff members of Central University of Kashmir for their valuable support. To them all, the authors offer their grateful thanks to ***M/s. Gyan Books Pvt Ltd. Delhi*** who came forward willingly undertakes the publishing of this book.

December, 2017
Srinagar, J&K

Dr. Ismail Thamarasseri
Dr. Pushpita Rajawat
Ulfat Ali Lone

Chapter - 1

Perspectives on Curriculum

Meaning of Curriculum

The term curriculum derives from the Latin word 'currere' which means a kind of route which the learner travels. All the activities going on the school or outside of the school is called curriculum. It is basic to the intellectual, physical, moral and emotional development of the child.

- "Curriculum comprises all the learning which is planned and guided by the school, whether it is carried on in groups or individually inside or outside of the school."- Kerr
- "Curriculum is the totality of experiences that pupils receive through the manifold activities that go in the school, in the classroom, library, laboratory, workshop, playground and in the numerous informal contacts between the teachers and pupils". - *The Secondary Education Commission, India (1952-1953)*
- "Curriculum is a tool in the hands of the Artist (Teacher), to mould his/her materials (Students), according to his/her ideals (objectives) in his/her studio (College/School)". - Cunningham.
- According to G. Hass, "The curriculum is all of the experiences that individual learners have in a programme of education whose purpose is to achieve broad goals and related specific objectives, which are planned in terms of a framework of theory and research or past and professional practice."
- According to Beans, "It is a process in which participants at many levels make decisions about what the purpose of learning ought to be, how these purposes might be carried out through teaching

learning situations and whether the purposes and means are both appropriate and effective."

- According to William M. Alexander of University of Florida, "the school curriculum has a framework or structure commonly called *design*, just as a building, a dress or an automobile has. Although less tangible (perceptible) and hopefully less fixed, the curriculum design provides a basis for classifying and organizing the curriculum opportunities offered by the school."
- A curriculum can be defined as a plan for action or a written document that includes strategies for achieving desired goals or ends. (Tyler, 1949).
- A curriculum usually contains a statement of aims and specific objectives. It indicates some selection and organization of content; it either implies or manifests certain patterns of learning and teaching... finally it includes a programme of evaluation of the outcomes. (Taba, 1962, p. 10).
- Curriculum is an organized set of formal education and/or training intentions. (Pratt, 1980).
- Curriculum is the planned experiences offered to the learners under the guidance of the school. (Wheeler, 1983).
- The curriculum consists of the ongoing experiences of children under the guidance of the school. It represents a special environment for helping children achieve self-realization through active participation within the school. (Shepherd & Ragan).
- The planned and guided learning experiences and intended outcomes, formulated through the systematic reconstruction of knowledge and experience, under the auspices of the school, for the learner's continuous and wilful growth in personal-social competence. (Tanner & Tanner).
- Curriculum is a plan for achieving intended learning outcomes, with what is to be learned and the results of instruction. (Unruh and Unruh, 1984).
- The curriculum of a school is the totality of the experiences that a school plans for its pupils. It is not restricted to courses; extracurricular activities and auxiliary services such as guidance and health services are also part of the curriculum. On the other hand the curriculum does not include everything the students learn in school. (Clarke and Starr, 1981)

- Curriculum is an explicitly and implicitly intentional set of interactions designed to facilitate learning and development and to impose meaning on experience. The explicit intentions usually are expressed in written curricula and in courses of study; the implicit intentions are found in the 'hidden curriculum' by which we mean the roles and norms that underlie interactions in the school. (Miller & Seller, 1985).
- The curriculum can be defined as a course of learning activities set out for the learner to perform to make him achieve certain goals prescribed by the educational system. The curriculum generally includes all subjects and activities over which the school has responsibility. It also defines the limits within which certain types of learning are to take place. It denotes those experiences and activities which are devised by the school or other institutions of learning for the purpose of changing a learner's behaviour, acquiring or reinforcing certain skills and preparing him to fit properly into his society. (Robinson,1983).
- A curriculum is considered the "heart" of any learning institution which means that schools or universities cannot exist without a curriculum. With its importance in formal education, the curriculum has become a dynamic process due to the changes that occur in our society. Therefore, in its broadest sense, curriculum refers to the "total learning experiences of individuals not only in school but society as well" (Bilbao et al., 2008).

The first known use in an educational context is in the *Professio Regia*, a work by University of Paris Professor Petrus Ramus published posthumously in 1576. The term subsequently appears in University of Leiden records in 1582. The word's origins appear closely linked to the Calvinist desire to bring greater order to education. The content of schooling in all of its forms (written and unwritten) is called the curriculum. This ancient Latin noun meant "a running, course" asin "conjiccere se in curriculum" or "a quick course at full speed, swiftly, hastily" (Andrews, 1854, p. 405).

It is content, programme of planned activities, intended learning outcomes, cultural preservation, experience, and agenda for social reconstruction. It is totality of all the learning to which students are exposed during their study in the school. It is a runway (one runs to reach the goal) or a race course referring to the course of deeds and experiences through which children grow and mature in becoming adults for success in adult society. It is totality of all the learning to which students are exposed during their study in the school. By the seventeenth century, the University of Glasgow also referred to its "course" of study as a "curriculum", producing the first known use of the term in English in 1633. By the nineteenth century, European universities routinely referred to their curriculum to describe both the complete course of study and particular courses and their content.

In some cases, people see the curriculum entirely in terms of the subjects that are taught, and as set out within the set of textbooks, and forget the wider goals of competencies and personal development. This is why a curriculum framework is important. It sets the subjects within this wider context, and shows how learning experiences within the subjects need to contribute to the attainment of the wider goals. A curriculum is considered the "heart" of any learning institution which means that schools or universities cannot exist without a curriculum. With its importance in formal education, the curriculum has become a dynamic process due to the changes that occur in our society. Therefore, in its broadest sense, curriculum refers to the "total learning experiences of individuals not only in school but society as well" (Bilbao et al., 2008).

Historical conception

"Action is response; it is adaptation, adjustment". - John Dewey

In the early years of the 20th century, the traditional concepts held of the "curriculum is that it is a body of subjects or subject matter prepared by the teachers for the students to learn." It was synonymous to the "course of study" and "syllabus". In *The Curriculum*, the first textbook published on the subject, in 1918, John Franklin Bobbitt said that curriculum, as an idea, has its roots in the Latin word for *race-course*, explaining the curriculum as the course of deeds and experiences through which children become the adults they should be, *for success in adult society*. Furthermore, the curriculum encompasses the entire scope of formative deed and experience occurring in and out of school, and not only experiences occurring in school; experiences that are unplanned and undirected, and experiences intentionally directed for the purposeful formation of adult members of society.

To Bobbitt, the curriculum is a social engineering arena. As per his cultural presumptions and social definitions, his curricular formulation has two notable features: (I) that scientific experts would best be qualified to and justified in designing curricula based upon their expert knowledge of what qualities are desirable in adult members of society, and which experiences would generate said qualities; and (II) curriculum defined as the deeds-experiences the student *ought to have* to become the adult he or she *ought to become.*

Hence, John Franklin Bobbitt defined the curriculum as an ideal, rather than as the concrete reality of the deeds and experiences that form people to who and what they are. Contemporary views of curriculum reject these features of Bobbitt's postulates, but retain the basis of curriculum as the course of experience(s) that forms human beings into persons. Personal formation via curricula is studied at the personal level and at the group level, i.e. cultures and societies (e.g. professional formation, academic discipline via historical experience). The formation of a group is reciprocal, with the formation of its individual participants.

Although it formally appeared in Bobbitt's definition, curriculum as a course of formative experience also pervades John Dewey's work (who disagreed with Bobbitt on important matters). Although Bobbitt's and Dewey's idealistic understanding of "curriculum" is different from current, restricted uses of the word, curriculum writers and researchers generally share it as common, substantive understanding of curriculum. Development does not mean just getting something out of the mind. It is a development of experience and into experience that is really wanted.

Robert M. Hutchins, President of the University of Chicago, regarded curriculum as "permanent studies" where the rules of grammar, rhetoric and logic and mathematics for basic education are emphasized. Basic education should emphasize 3 Rs and college education should be grounded on liberal education. On the other hand, Arthur Bestor as an essentialist believes that the mission of the school should be intellectual training; hence curriculum should focus on the fundamental intellectual disciplines of grammar, literature and writing. It should also include mathematics, science, history and foreign language.

This definition leads us to the view of Joseph Schwab that discipline is the sole source of curriculum. Thus in our education system, curriculum is divided into chunks of knowledge we call subject areas in basic education such as English, Mathematics, Science, Social Studies and others. In college, discipline may include humanities, sciences, languages and many more. Curriculum should consist entirely of knowledge which comes from various disciplines. To learn the lesson is more interesting than to take a scolding, be held up to general ridicule, stay after school, receive degrading low marks, or fail to be promoted.

Thus, curriculum can be viewed as a field of study. It is made up of its foundations (philosophical, historical, psychological, and social foundations); domains of knowledge as well as its research theories and principles. Curriculum is taken as scholarly and theoretical. It is concerned with broad historical, philosophical and social issues and academics. Under a starting definition offered by John Kerr and taken up by Vic Kelly in his standard work on the curriculum, curriculum is "all the learning which is planned and guided by the school, whether it is carried on in groups or individually, inside or outside the school. Four ways of approaching curriculum theory and practice.

- Curriculum as a body of knowledge to be transmitted.
- Curriculum as an attempt to achieve certain ends in students – products.
- Curriculum as a process.
- Curriculum as praxis

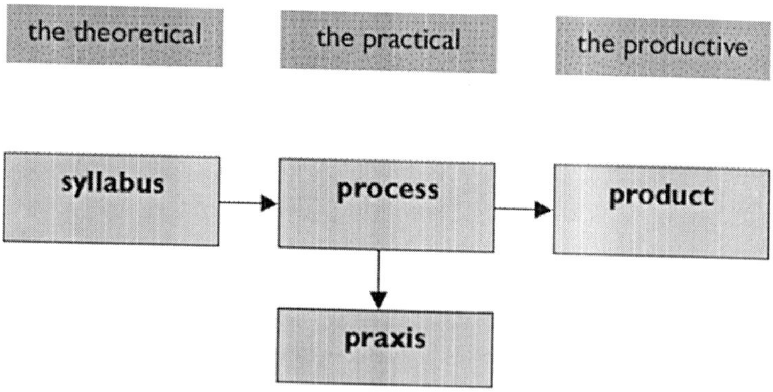

Figure 1.1: Ways of approaching Curriculum

In recent years the field of education, and therefore curriculum, has expanded outside the walls of the classroom and into other settings. Within these settings curriculum is an even broader topic, including various teachers such as other visitors, inanimate objects such as audio tour devices, and even the learners themselves. As with the traditional idea of curriculum, curriculum in a free choice learning environment can consist of the explicit stated curriculum and the hidden curriculum, both of which contribute to the learner's experience and lessons from the experience. These elements are further compounded by the setting, cultural influences, and the state of mind of the learner.

Nature of Curriculum

One of the most often repeated definitions of a curriculum are that curriculum is the total learning experience. This description implies that the crux of a curriculum is the different planned and unplanned activities which have been lived, acted upon or done by the learners with the guidance of the teacher.

Teaching as Process of Curriculum

Good teaching is difficult to agree upon. While it remains to be difficult to agree on what good teaching is, effective teaching can be demonstrated. Effective teaching is one that will bring about the intended learning outcomes.

Teaching and Learning in the Curriculum

The overflow of information in our midst and the different ways of retrieving them has become a challenge to both teaching and learning. Teaching and learning gives life and meaning to the curriculum. Each complements and supplements each other. The total learning experience provided by a school. It includes the content of courses (the syllabus), the methods employed (strategies), and other aspects, like norms and values, which relate to the way the school is organized.

It is the aggregate of courses of study given in a learning environment. The courses are arranged in a sequence to make learning subject easier. In schools, a curriculum spans several grades. Curriculum can refer to the entire program provided by a classroom, school, district, state, or country. A classroom is assigned sections of the curriculum as defined by the school.

Need of Curriculum in Schools

Every successful concept and project in life requires a proper framework and planning. This relates to all processes, including education. Whenever we embark on any new plan or procedure, we need to make sure that we have all the plans drawn up. What is on offer, what are the resources that we have, what are the steps, which we need to take and what are the goals that we need to achieve are some elements that need to be looked upon. A similar set of constraints when applied to education in schools and colleges gives birth to curriculum. A curriculum is a set of courses, including their content, offered at a school or university. The curriculum often contains a detailed list of subjects and the elements of teaching them. Having a curriculum provides several benefits, such as providing a structure for an educational course and having an end goal that teachers set for their students to reach. Curricula vary widely in structure and complexity, but are valuable for many different areas of education, including linguistics, mathematics and the sciences.

The Importance and Role of Curriculum

Our curriculum is who we are. It reflects the diversity of the disciplines that make up our college community, the myriad pedagogical philosophies we bring to the classroom each day, and the strengths of our education and training. Faculty are vested with the primary responsibility for the development of new courses and programs and the revision of existing courses and programs. The college's course outlines and degree and certificate programs reflect our own academic mission and philosophy. The course outline serves a number of purposes:

- It forms the basis for a contract among the student, instructor, and institution, identifying the expectations which will serve as the basis of the student's grade and giving the fundamental required components of the course which the student is guaranteed to receive from the instructor and institution.
- It is a document with defined legal standing which is read by many more eyes than just those of the instructor and student.
- It assists faculty in presenting their courses in a format which accurately reflects the quality instruction they are providing.
- It states the content and level of rigor for which students – across all sections of the course will held accountable.
- It states the prerequisites students need to advance successfully through a series of courses.

A curriculum is more than putting together a set of academically required subjects. It must consider all aspects of the student life, the learning needs of students, the time available for the sessions and the teachers' idea, capability and workload. Now that we know the constitution of a curriculum, let us study its importance in the lines that follow.

In Elementary Schools

In elementary schools, the curriculum is primarily drawn by the educational boards or some central society. They study the needs of the kids and all other feasibilities before selecting courses and drafting a curriculum. Here, the students have least choice in their subjects and study based on a universal curriculum, which works on all sections of the students' psyche and aid in the total development of the student. No area is left untouched. Hence, the curriculum aids in the proper development, while the child comes to terms with his or her own inclination. Therefore, at primary school levels, the curriculum aims at providing a structured platform, which gives every child an equal opportunity to excel.

In High Schools

At high school levels, teenagers can take their own liberty in choosing their path. Though complete autonomy does not rest with a student, a level of choice is very evident. This helps in the development of the teenager, with added importance of being given the field of his own choice. At this stage, the development is more focused and rampant, enhanced through a proper curriculum. Without an effective curriculum, a student would not be able to understand or meet the challenges of the society.

At College & Higher Education

At a higher stage of education, an unprecedented autonomy is provided to the students. The students can opt for a more focused curriculum, based on their choice of subjects. A student will graduate, post-graduate or attain a doctorate based on the choice of his subjects and the mode of his study, both or either one determined by him. The curriculum here is reduced to just a framework that is very flexible yet very important. The curriculum chosen by the student will go on to determine the shape of his/her career. A curriculum prepares an individual with the knowledge to be successful, confident and responsible citizens.

Components of curriculum

Curriculum (or curricula) is defined broadly to include four basic components:

- *Goals*: The benchmarks or expectations for teaching and learning often made explicit in the form of a scope and sequence of skills to be addressed;
- *Methods*: The specific instructional methods for the teacher, often described in a teacher's edition;
- *Materials*: The media and tools that are used for teaching and learning;
- *Assessment*: The reasons for and methods of measuring student progress.

Facets of Curriculum

Since curriculum reflects the models of instructional delivery chosen and used, some might indicate that curriculum could be categorized according to the common psychological classifications of the four families of learning theories "Social, Information Processing, Personalist, and Behavioural." Longstreet and Shane have dubbed divisions in curricular orientations as: child-centred, society-centred, knowledge-centred, or eclectic. The following represent the many different types of curricula used in schools:

- **Overt, explicit, or written curriculum:** Is simply that which is written as part of formal instruction of schooling experiences. It may refer to a curriculum document, texts, films, and supportive teaching materials that are overtly chosen to support the intentional instructional agenda of a school. Thus, the overt curriculum is usually confined to those written understandings and directions formally designated and reviewed by administrators, curriculum directors and teachers, often collectively.
- **Societal Curriculum (or Social Curricula):** As defined by Cortes (1981). Cortes defines this curriculum as: the massive, ongoing, informal curriculum of family, peer groups, neighbourhoods, churches, organizations, occupations, mass media, and other socializing forces that "educate" all of us throughout our lives. This type of curricula can now be expanded to include the powerful effects of social media: *YouTube*; *Facebook; Twitter; Pinterest*, etc and how it actively helps create new perspectives, and can help shape both individual and public opinion.
- **The Hidden or Covert Curriculum:** A hidden curriculum is a side effect of an education, "lessons which are learned but not openly intended" such as the transmission of norms, values, and beliefs conveyed in the classroom and the social environment.
- **Phantom Curriculum:** The messages prevalent in and through exposure to any type of media. These components and messages play a major part in the enculturation of students into the predominant meta-culture, or in acculturating students into narrower or generational subcultures.
- **Concomitant Curriculum:** What is taught, or emphasized at home, or those experiences that are part of a family's experiences, or related experiences sanctioned by the family. This type of curriculum may be received at church, in the context of religious

expression, lessons on values, ethics or morals, moulded behaviours, or social experiences based on the family's preferences.

- **Rhetorical Curriculum:** Elements from the rhetorical curriculum are comprised from ideas offered by policymakers, school officials, administrators, or politicians. This curriculum may also come from those professionals involved in concept formation and content changes; or from those educational initiatives resulting from decisions based on national and state reports, public speeches, or from texts critiquing outdated educational practices. The rhetorical curriculum may also come from the publicized works offering updates in pedagogical knowledge.
- **Curriculum-in-use:** The formal curriculum (written or overt) comprises those things in textbooks, and content and concepts in the district curriculum guides. However, those "formal" elements are frequently not taught. The curriculum-in-use is the actual curriculum that is delivered and presented by each teacher.
- **Received curriculum:** Those things that students actually take out of classrooms; those concepts and content that are truly learned and remembered
- **The Internal Curriculum:** Processes, content, knowledge combined with the experiences and realities of the learner to create new knowledge. While educators should be aware of this curriculum, they have little control over the internal curriculum since it is unique to each student. Educators can explore this curricula by using instructional assessments like "exit slips," reflective exercises, or debriefing discussions to see what students really remember from a lesson. It is often very enlightening and surprising to find out what has meaning for learners and what does not.
- **The Electronic Curriculum:** Those lessons learned through searching the Internet for information, or through using e-forms of communication. (Wilson, 2004) This type of curriculum may be either formal or informal, and inherent lessons may be overt or covert, good or bad, correct or incorrect depending on one's views. Students who use the Internet on a regular basis, both for recreational purposes (as in *blogs, wikis, chatrooms, listserves*, through instant messenger, on-line conversations, or through personal e-mails and sites like *Twitter, Facebook*, or *Youtube*) and for personal online research and information gathering are bombarded with all types of media and messages.

Principles Of Curriculum

Curriculum development is a comprehensive term, inside cover: planning, implementation and evaluation. Curriculum planning is the first step to build the curriculum when the curriculum workers to make decisions and take action to produce a plan that will be used by teachers and learners. Implementation of curriculum or curriculum implementation is also commonly referred to curriculum planning to transfer into operational action. Curriculum evaluation is the final step of curriculum development to determine how big the learning outcomes, level of achievement for programs that have been planned, and the results of the curriculum itself. In curriculum development, not only involve people directly associated with education alone, but it has involved many people, such as politicians, businessmen, parents of students, teachers, and elements - other elements of society who feel concerned with education. The main principles of curriculum construction may be mentioned as under:

- **Principle of Child Centeredness:** As modern education is child-centred the curriculum should also be child-centred. It should be based on the child's needs, interests, abilities, aptitude, age level and circumstances. The child should be central figure in any scheme of curriculum construction. In fact, curriculum is meant to bring about the development of the child in the desired direction so that he is able to adjust well in life.
- **Principle of Community Centeredness:** Though the child's development and growth is the main consideration of curriculum construction, yet his social behaviour is also to be suitably developed, both the individual development and the social development of the child deserve equal attention. He is to live in and for the society. Therefore, his needs and desires must be in conformity with the needs and desires of the society in which he is to live. The values, attitudes and skills that are prevailing in the community must be reflected in the curriculum. However, the society is not static. It is dynamic. Its needs and requirements are changing with the rapid developments taking place in all fields. While working for the development, this factor cannot be ignored.
- **Principle of Activity Centeredness:** The curriculum should centre round the multifarious activities of pupils. It should provide well selected activities according to the general interests and developmental stages of children. It should provide constructive, creative and project activities. For small children, play activities

should also be provided.! The purposeful activities both in the class-room and outside the class-room should be provided. It is through a net work of activities that the desired experiences can be provided and consequently desirable behavioural changes can be brought about in children.

- **Principle of Variety:** The curriculum should be broad-based so as to accommodate the needs of varied categories of pupils, so that they are able to take up subjects and participate in activities according their capacities and interests. The needs of pupils also change from place to place. For example, the pupils in rural areas, urban areas, and hilly areas will have different needs. The needs of boys and girls are also different. So these considerations should be reflected in the curriculum.
- **Principle of Co-ordination and Integration:** Of course, the pupils are to be provided with selected experiences through various subjects and activities but these must be well integrated. Various subjects and activities have to serve the same ultimate purpose, the achievement of the aims of education. The activities and subjects should not be put in after-tight compartments but these should be inter-related and well integrated so as to develop the whole child.
- **Principles of Conservation:** One of the main functions of education is to preserve and transmit our cultural heritage. This is essential for human progress. Culture consists of traditions, customs, attitudes, skills, conduct, values and knowledge. However, the curriculum framers must make a suitable selection of the elements of culture, keeping in view their educational value and the developmental stage of pupils.
- **Principle of Creativity:** The conservation of culture helps to sustain the society. The culture should not be simply transmitted but also enriched. There should be provision in the curriculum to develop the creative powers of the child so that s/he becomes a contributory member society. Raymont says, "In curriculum that is suited to the needs of today and of the future, there must be definitely creative subjects."
- **Principle of Forward Looking:** Education is to enable the child to lead a successful social life. So the curriculum should not cater to the present needs of the child alone. The needs of his future life should also be considered. The curriculum should also include

knowledge, skills, experiences, influences etc. which will develop in the child abilities and power to make effective adjustments in the later life.

- **Principle of Flexibility:** In our age, rapid developments are taking place in various fields. Consequently the needs of society are hanging. The content of curriculum cannot be same for all times to come. It should not be static. It must be dynamic and change with the changing times. It should reflect the latest trends in the field of education and psychology.
- **Principle of Balance:** The curriculum must maintain a balance between subjects and activities, between direct and indirect experiences, between academic and vocational education, between compulsory and optional subjects, between formal and informal education, between individual and social aims of education etc.
- **Principle of Utility:** Curriculum should be useful rather than ornamental. It should not only include subjects which owe their place in it to tradition. The curriculum must have practical utility for students. So there should be some provision for technical and vocational education in the curriculum.

The various principles of curriculum construction should be kept in mind. Various regional and national conditions should also be considered. It fact, all considerations which will help in achieving the aims of education should be given due consideration.

Four Perspectives On Curriculum: Traditionalists; Conceptual-empiricists; Re- Conceptualists; Social Constructivists

As educators, there are many approaches we take toward curricula. These approaches are based on sets of assumptions that we've made based on our education, experience, and other factors. Let us we will make an analysis of five curriculum perspectives including the major proponents and tenets of each. We will also discuss societal as well as political influences, major criticisms of each theory, and examples of ways these theories have been applied.

The Traditional Perspective (John Dewey, John Franklin Bobbitt, Edward. B. Taylor, Hilda Taba)

Traditionalists accept the schools and society as it is. The see the curriculum as comprised of the traditional academic subjects. The traditional perspective was a response to a contemporary problem during the nineteenth century (Posner, 2004). As society was becoming more diverse, schooling was not. The perspective is bent on preserving cultural heritage. That is, it takes the position that educational curricula's' primary goal is to transmit the accumulated knowledge of society. One of its major proponents was a humanities professor at the University of Virginia E.D. Hirsch, Jr. who suggested that the main purpose of education is to acculturate children (Hirsch, 1987). Its main criticisms come from progressive educators and those that adhered to another perspective, the experiential, who posit that this perspective does not take into account "...theories of learning, of motivation, of knowledge, or of school and society" (Posner, 2004, p. 47). They also suggest that the perspective does promote democratic values as it adopts an authoritative position regarding what the general knowledge of a given society is.

Pinar et al. (1995) state that the curriculum specialization was influenced by theorists such as Bobbitt, Harap, Charters, Dewey, and Thorndike who believed that education should be a science. According to Tanner and Tanner (1995), the quantitative and scientific method applied to curriculum construction is rooted in the positivistic paradigm. Bobbitt, Harap and Charters' traditionalist ideology, as well as Peters' and Snedden's was based on Taylor's scientific management as applied to schools and curricula, with the aim of maximum efficiency and utilitarianism (Eisner, 1985; Tanner & Tanner 1995; Kliebard 2000a). Bobbitt's (1913/1923) main point was: At a time when so much discussion is being given to the possibilities of 'scientific management' in the world of material production, it seems desirable that the principles of this more effective form of management be examined in order to ascertain the possibility of applying them to the problems of educational management and supervision. (p. 7)

Moreover, Bobbitt believed that the relatively new field of education was backward as compared to business and industry, and since these enterprises were flourishing in North America as never before, the sound management principles formulated by them would be ideal for education. Under this framework, the learning process was a unit of production, an assembly line analogy (Eisner, 1985). The educational process would be further atomized by identifying the goals and content, and the curriculum analyzed scientifically into mechanistic skills or behaviours based on the definitions of actions (Eisner 1985; Tanner & Tanner, 1995). Education or curriculum construction, therefore, became a series of specific activities, moving from larger to smaller units.

Harap also used the scientific-technological view which focused upon objectives, activities and social need analysis (Eisner, 1985). Besides the scientific method of curriculum, Thorndike applied behaviouristic (instrumental) psychology in sync with activity analysis (Thorndike, 1913; Tanner & Tanner 1995). Dewey also applied the scientific method to inquiry for informing educational practice, was usually ends means, linear and rational although he pointed out the limits of science in prescriptions for practice, and later he acknowledged the arts and human intelligence in human endeavour (Eisner, 1985). In other words, Dewey was both child-centred and progressive.

The Tyler Rationale

Tyler shared in this scientific mode of thinking with Dewey, Bobbitt and Charters, and he is considered to be a pre-eminent traditionalist. The Tyler Rationale, based on Basic Principles of Curriculum and Instruction became the most influential work in the field. Pinar et al. (1995) contend that Tyler was unopposed for 20 years, while Marsh and Willis (1995) state that his book was viewed as displaying common sense and clear thinking, and continues to be influential worldwide in curriculum planning. Jackson (1992) described Tyler's book as, "the Bible of curriculum making" (p. 24). Tyler (1975, p. 18) set out four questions, which he intended as a guide for curriculum planning, with the note that this was not meant to be theory, for it was "a practical enterprise:" According to Tyler (1949, p. 1), these steps are:

- What educational purposes should the school seek to attain?
- What educational experiences can be provided that are likely to attain these purposes?
- How can these educational experiences be effectively organized?
- How can we determine whether these purposes are being attained?

The main source of objectives would be gained from studies of students, schools, modern life, and from subject specialists. Tyler (1949) appeared to imply that conflict or class issues did not come into play, for the solution was for students to acquire a set of "knowledge, skills, attitudes, and the like" as outlined in objectives based on sociologists' findings of contemporary problems. School was viewed as "the agency" for empowerment to deal with those problems (p.5).

Tyler (1949) did not function independently. He referred to psychologists Prescott, Murray and Thorndike. Throughout the Rationale, references were made to altering students' behaviour based on the pre-set objectives, with the behaviour indicating success at meeting those objectives being determined in the process of evaluation. Tyler set out screens for deriving objectives, which were educational ends so as to prioritize and standardize them.

They were the schools' "Educational and Social Philosophy" (Tyler, pp. 35-36) and psychology of learning. Hence his thinking became known as having an ends-means focus. Tyler's viewpoint was shaped by the post positivist movement that emerged from his predecessors, but he was a pragmatist. In the late 1940s Tyler was embedded in the thinking of the post positivist paradigm. Tyler was a post positivist method-wise for having guiding questions to conduct his studies. As opposed to the earlier traditionalists who broke down jobs and tasks to write curricula, Tyler (1975) sought for multiple areas of input, and called for constructive participation in curriculum development, or a group procedure. Tyler also described teaching as an art, as opposed to a science, arguing against so-called teacher-proof and rigid curricula, and called for teacher participation in the curriculum building plan. Although a post positivist in practice, he moved away from the post positivist conception of teachers as workers, and Tyler was influenced by progressive-experimentalist thought that included problem-solving and societal values (Hlebowitsh, 1992). Tyler called his approach pragmatic, for he acknowledged limited resources for curriculum development and implementation. He sought to use the available information at each of the four step process, as opposed to a totalizing comprehensive curriculum.

Tyler's concepts are still influential with the focus on objectives or purposes, the designing of effective curricula and evaluation. However, there is movement to standardization across communities as opposed to localized curricula as espoused by Tyler, with a national curriculum in the UK, the US No Child Left Behind Act, and government-produced achievement exams in Canadian provinces.

Conceptual-Empiricists Perspective (Benjamin S. Bloom, J.S. Bruner, Berliner, Posner, Stake, Walberg)

Conceptual Empiricists bring the content of Psychology, Anthropology, Philosophy etc to the practice of curriculum work. The structure of the discipline movement, with focus on the structure of content, came to the fore in 1959 after the Woods Hole Conference, influenced by cognitive psychologist Jerome Bruner. Eventually, the conceptual-empiricist camp replaced traditionalists in curriculum (Giroux, Penna & Pinar 1981; Pinar et al. 1995), and continued to have some influence in education into the

1960s, using the scientific and mathematical paradigm. The curriculum field faced prospects of re-invention in the late 1960s as the traditional curriculum influence waned. As Schwab (1978) stated, "The field of curriculum is moribund" (p. 288). This condition was due to its inability to advance education any further. The field had over-depended on theory, which became increasingly disconnected with social changes and practice in schools, and Schwab proposed a solution for curriculum specialists to operate in the modes of "the practical, the quasi-practical, and the eclectic". Such pronouncements and the sidestepping by the US government towards curriculum research meant the decline of the traditionalists. Schwab (1962) argued for curriculum building based, in particular, on the structure of the sciences and their theories. Schwab called this deep knowledge, as such curricula were built on truth. Pinar et al. (1995) categorized the conceptualist-empiricist movement. This group consisted of post-positivist scientific thinkers who were professional educators in their field, and the movement was pro-discipline. Professional educators and students were not consulted in curriculum shaping, imposing a structure on students and teachers. It was the disciplines themselves – the subject matter and their underlying structures and methods of inquiry, mediated through the subject experts – that would determine the shape of curricula (Hampson, 1975). Prevalent views and practice had swung away from progressive education, to social efficiency in the form of life adjustment education as characterized by the Tyler Rationale, to a subject-centred education, and then to Re-conceptualization (Pinar et al., 1995). Substantive theorizing is designed to highlight appropriate content for the curriculum. Analysis of current situations and suggest alternatives to current patterns of content and experiences.

Re- Conceptualists Perspective / Critical Theorists (Michael Apple, Huebner)

Pinar et al. (1995) called the group emerging from the traditionalists, re-conceptualists, as they challenged traditional views and were influenced by postmodernism. As Pinar (1999) explained, after the 1960s national (USA) curriculum movement, curriculum professors were asked to be bureaucrats, to relay to teachers how to fulfil politician, businessperson and arts and science professors' objectives, to keep the curriculum intact except to transmit curricula more efficiently in the name of accountability. The re-conceptualists sought to understand curriculum from a theoretical, research-based, and historically oriented basis, as opposed to the practical development and management of educational processes. Discontent with the Tyler Rationale, the use of other traditions such as psychoanalytic theory, phenomenology, existentialism, hermeneutics, literary criticism, as well as predominantly leftist Marxist and neo-Marxist thought, with focus on inequalities, among others, characterized re-conceptualists (Jackson, 1992). In summary, Pinar (1999a) called "the project of understanding" a form of praxis, leading to "history, politics, race, gender, phenomenology, postmodernism, autobiography, aesthetics, theology, the institution of schooling, the world" (p. 366). For practitioners, the Tylerian influence is still evident (Jackson, 1992) as curriculum development is no longer the purview of curriculum specialists, but of subject specialists. With re-conceptualized curriculum, understanding is of interest. The end of the traditional paradigm occurred with re-conceptualization and with it the questioning of the place of theory in the field (Pinar et al., 1995). As Pinar (1999b) stated, The term Re-conceptualists described individuals whose scholarship challenged this tradition-that is, suggested that the function of curriculum studies was not the development and management but the scholarly and disciplined understanding of educational experience, particularly in its political, cultural, gender, and historical dimensions. During the past two decades the field of curriculum has been re-conceptualized from an exclusively practice-oriented field to a more theoretical, historical, research-oriented field. (p. 484)

Greene (1971), influenced by existentialism and phenomenology, analysed curriculum through literary criticism, espousing a view that centred on the necessity of consciousness in learning as opposed to the mere habitual. Humanities, especially literature, could help students overcome meaninglessness brought on by the primacy of science. She argued that curriculum should develop a propensity of thought below the surface and raise self-consciousness, internalization of knowledge, and encourage questioning and the linking of themes and disciplines (Greene, 1971). Furthermore, students need to understand their roots, underlying self-concepts and make a connection between what was previously known and new learning through reflection to add meaning. To Greene, this required a conscious process based on rationality and developing networks of relationships in order to prepare students for an ever-changing world in order to problem solve.

Huebner, an intellectual founder of re-conceptualization in the 1970s, wrote of moving beyond scientific and empirical language (Pinar et al., 1995). Huebner (2000) argued that curriculum is often incoherent and lacks precision. So-called scientific curriculum theories had not advanced the field and had created an artificial breach between theory and practice. For Huebner, curriculum involved the interaction of three elements: research, practice, and language. However, language must be seen as contextualized within time, place, and culture, and open to interpretation. Curriculum research is often language oriented giving sense and structure to the collected information. Huebner (1966) maintained that because language is not fixed, approaches to curriculum that impose a set language of means and outcomes (e.g. the Tyler Rationale) are flawed in their perspectives (Pinar et al., 1995). Macdonald (1971/2000) conceived of the curriculum as operating within the framework of two levels of decision making, both of which reflect fundamental values. First is the structural level, which Macdonald saw as incorporating the basic tenets of faith that underlie educational norms and beliefs and which provide direction for education. The second level, termed rational values, details these fundamental values at the plane of curriculum design, thus demonstrating the application of the essential structural principles. Within this framework operate three perspectives as outlined by Macdonald: the technical, interpretive, and emancipatory, each reflecting a set of beliefs underpinning education and the world and each belief calling for its own curriculum design. Thus, the technical reflects the scientific, empirical, expert, designed curriculum approach of the structural empiricists. The interpretative perspective seeks consensus and follows the ends-means methodology of Tyler, while the emancipatory breaks with previous curriculum theory in seeing curriculum as a means of raising self-consciousness amongst individuals and as a liberating force through individually centred, reflective practice and dialogue.

Essentially, Macdonald (1971/2000) doubted the possibility of a neutral curriculum, instead arguing for the pervasiveness of fundamental values in all aspects of curriculum at the theoretical and applied stages. This emphasis on values and beliefs as the foundation of curriculum became a major force within the re-conceptualist movement and would prove influential in elucidating a view of curriculum that sought the purpose of curriculum in the transformation of society through critical awareness, empowerment, and self-knowledge. The re-conceptualists later viewed curriculum and school affairs as being in a state of conflict as opposed to earlier proponents of structural functionalism, which entailed the view of consensus in society, with the different parts contributing to society in equilibrium, in interdependence, and harmony, with orderly evolutionary processes (Gingrich, 1999). Conflict theories were a reaction to this consensual view of society.

Critical Pedagogy and Neo-Marxism.

Amongst the re-conceptualists, one important frame of thought has been a critical pedagogic, neo-Marxian, analysis of the undergirding structures of the curriculum process, involving political curriculum analysis. Apple (1971), a critical theorist and Marxist (Pinar, 1999b), was influenced by the Frankfurt school, which viewed society as being asymmetrical and under the hegemony of power groups based on wealth, race, and gender (Grace, in press), and used culture generally, not only material productions and the economy, to analyse society (Pinar et al., 1995). One can implicitly read in this Marxian analysis a critique of the empirical conceptualists, who placed curriculum in the hands of specialists (Schwab, 1962) and of Tyler, (1949) whose objectives could be viewed as replicating the goals of society's controlling interests.Apple indicated the importance of understanding the societal norms that lie behind educational activities and denounced the underlying cultural transmission of the hegemonic groups in society. Apple (1990) regarded textbooks as being an instrument to increase the legitimated knowledge within society, the beliefs and values of the dominant cultural group, as opposed to neutral sources of knowledge. The New Right, by attempting to enforce a centralized, regimented curriculum, has sought to perpetuate the cultural domination of a pro-capitalist, pro-Western, neo-liberal tradition that has allowed the exploitation of the curriculum by multinational corporations with a globalization agenda. In opposition, Apple responded with a call for a new framework for curriculum that promoted a non-Western, non-capitalist, and non-gender biased democratized education that sought a diversity of curricula and opened the way for multiple readings that break the knowledge monopoly of entrenched interests and empowers and respects all individuals. Smith (2003) in describing the effects of globalization on schooling and the influence of the neo-liberal economic system on society and youth, where youth becomes an inconvenience for adults, called for humanistic solutions that promote social and cultural harmony.

Freire, (1970/1989) an emancipatory theorist, wrote of the goal of social justice through egalitarian praxis. Like Apple, Freire wrote about overcoming domination by the elite at the core. In dialectical fashion, Freire drew out the opposing forces in society such as domination that have to be reigned in, partly through real education involving reflection, praxis leading to cognitive awareness. In his banking concept of education, which is the teacher centred approach to learning, the teacher pours information into the empty vessel student, who recounts it in robotic fashion. The transmission of knowledge is static, and often not relevant to the students' lives.

To Friere (1970/1989), such education meets the needs of the oppressor and he called for the individual to be provided with the freedom to create their own understanding. Freire advocated empowerment through knowledge building, critical dialogue, education and action that was based on a true, reciprocal partnership between student and teacher. By focussing on formal education, educators deprived their students of a true learning experience, promoted passive thinking, denied students their individual humanity and contribution to the world, and upheld the status quo.

For Friere, education's goal (1970/1989) is seen as ending this stagnation by developing learners with the ability and appetite for critical inquiry and original and diverse thought through a mutuality of learning between educators and students. The hub of such pedagogy is dialogical problem posing, whereby dialoguers actively participate in critical thinking. This type of thinking views reality as a transformative and liberating process through action and reflection (praxis). Authentic education is founded upon both parties in the educative act mediating with each other and with the world around them, constructing fresh viewpoints. Such educative processes emphasize the true humanness of each student (1970/1989). As Wardekker (2004) wrote, curriculum planning involves cultural politics centred on the issue of whose knowledge is being taught, and is therefore divisive. In this view, schooling seeks to express and perpetuate the values and norms of a middle class, capitalistic, society and continuing societal stratification (McLaren, 1989). McLaren wrote of culture as a field of discourse (Pinar et al., 1995) and noted that curriculum "assumes that the social, cultural, political and economic dimensions are the primary categories for understanding contemporary schooling" (McLaren 1989, p. 185) and propagates, in the form of a concealed curriculum, the patterns of dominance and subordination since "knowledge is socially constructed" (p. 169). In consequence, education should be regarded as a force of domination; however, education also contains the seeds of opposition and liberation.

Since the re-conceptualization, Pinar (2004a) labelled the field as the post-reconceptualization era whereby the progressive curriculum research project consists of authoring the synoptic textbooks for teachers which consist of reconstructed school and interdisciplinary subjects in nature to create views such as montages otherwise unseen in subject curriculum that centre around standardized exams. The task of this post-re-conceptualized project is to mitigate the subjective in society and academic knowledge with autobiographical and cultural research, that includes speaking to "students' subjectivity and to their lived understanding and experiences of society" for social reconstruction (p. 17). In this process, the intellectual work provides subjective meaning and the autobiographical and cultural studies give social significance. The research methods are "work-like" and "documentary," synoptic, "critical and transformative" that leads teachers and students to original texts and moves to the subjective social self-formation (p. 18). The aim is to educate the public and to elevate teachers to intellectuals from "colleagues not clients, working in educational institutions, not academic businesses" (p. 18). Hence, the progressive curriculum project has moved from bureaucratic efficiency and oversight over schools and curricula implementation to research school subjects, the disciplines, with a focus on the interdisciplinary, using cultural reading to produce the synoptic text that moves those involved with this intellectual endeavour from original content into subjective reading of it and articulation of society. The Curriculum Field and Corresponding Movements in the Research Arena The three camps of the curriculum field have parallel movements in the research arena. Philosophically, parallels exist in the social sciences and curricular studies which have foundations in similar paradigms. For example, philosophical similarities exist in the traditionalist movement in curriculum studies and the positivistic/post-positivistic movement in the social sciences. The conceptual-empiricist movement was, in turn, influenced by the post-positivist movement. Furthermore, the re-conceptualist movements are related to the constructivist and critical movements in the behavioural sciences. Usually, the post-positivist research methods are commensurable with quantitative, constructivist method with qualitative, and pragmatism with mixed methods (Creswell, 2009). These social science paradigms will be described briefly, and then compared to the curriculum movements to demonstrate that these two fields have shared philosophical foundations.

Social Constructivists

According to Guba and Lincoln (2005), social constructivists/constructionists sought meaning formation, community consensus regarding what was "real", useful and with meaning effecting action. Therefore, social phenomena involved meaning making which was central to social constructionists/constructivists since meaning making effects action. Falling within the constructivist or constructionist paradigm were critical theories. Both constructionists and critical theories critiqued socio-economic structures and interrogated power relations within society, thereby with the goals of transforming and constructing new social relations and structures. Education, and by implication curricula became tools for the betterment of society, whether to ameliorate inequality, classism, sexism, homophobia, racism, or cultural hegemony.

Denzin and Lincoln (2005) identify two periods in qualitative research. The first was the **traditional period**, which began at the beginning of the twentieth century, and which lasted until World War II. Qualitative researchers wrote "objective" descriptions of field experiences of the "Other," in line with the positivist scientist paradigm such as ethnographic field work in anthropology. This traditional qualitative research was concerned with a "valid, reliable and objective interpretation in their writings" (Denzin & Lincoln, 2005, p. 15). However, objectivism was questioned since ethnographies did not produce timeless truths, as was believed with other, more scientific approaches.

The Constructivist Perspective suggests that curriculum should be based on the tenet that educators should develop curriculum to provide opportunities for students to make sense of the newly acquired knowledge in their personal ways. Indirectly, its primary proponent was the eminent psychologist Jean Piaget who asserted that students assimilate information, as opposed to acquire it. They then accommodate new knowledge by reorganizing information so that it may fit into their existent thought structures. The constructivist perspective is currently under attack in American education as it promotes inquiry-based learning which can be time consuming (Mayer, 2004). In an increasingly accountable age, science and math teachers are shying away from the perspective in building their curricula. However, the perspective is alive in elementary schools using the Montessori method. Because learning is adapted to a child's developmental level, the constructivist approach is a prime way to create curricula for students to absorb knowledge.

The perspectives above can be viewed as a veritable timeline of the development of curricular movements in education. The traditional perspective promotes a return to the mastery of basic literacy skills and the diffusion of common values. The experiential perspective promotes the need to incorporate all aspects of a student's life in developing the curriculum he will learn. The disciplines perspective promotes the development of intellectual capabilities by focusing on the thought structures of given content areas. The behavioural perspective promotes the setting of learning objectives and the focusing of curriculum to meet the needs of students as they acquire those objectives. Finally, the constructivist perspective promotes the notion that educators should devise curricula so that students may personalize their learning by reorganizing their thought structures around what they learn in school. All five perspectives provide vantage points that augment varying visions of modern education.

Core Curriculum

Educators define "core curriculum" as the knowledge and skills expected to be learned by a student by high school graduation. Generally, the core curriculum consists of knowledge and skills related to academic subjects. Mastery of the core curriculum is what both parents and teachers stress as essential for academic success in school, and later in life. In most states, opportunities are provided for students to meet other criteria in cases when those students cannot meet the academic demands of the core curriculum. The Core Curriculum is the name given to a set of courses designed to give you the fundamentals of education. Every public institution of higher education has a Core Curriculum. The Core is designed to provide a solid foundation for your education.

There are many versions of the core curriculum. Each state assumes responsibility for minimum standards for high school graduation. This core curriculum becomes the foundation for almost all learning, from kindergarten through high school. The Core Curriculum is designed to meet the goals of a liberal arts education. It gives students a perspective and an informed acquaintance with the major branches of learning: the humanities; the physical and biological sciences and mathematics; and the social sciences. The Core is designed to develop critical thinking skills, to challenge students intellectually, to promote an appreciation for diverse cultures and to increase moral and civic awareness. The Core integrates Writing across the Curriculum to strengthen students' writing ability in all disciplines. The Core Curriculum is the set of common courses required of all undergraduates and considered the necessary general education for students, irrespective of their choice in major. The communal learning - with all students encountering the same texts and issues at the same time - and the critical dialogue experienced in small seminars are the distinctive features of the Core. Begun in the early part of the 20th century, the Core Curriculum is one of the founding experiments in liberal higher education. Not only academically rigorous but also personally transformative for students, the Core seminar thrives on oral debate of the most difficult questions about human experience.

The learning objectives of the Core include "global objectives" that cut across different disciplines. The three global objectives articulate the expectation that upon completion of the core, students will be able to:

- Communicate effectively in writing.
- Demonstrate the ability to use logical reasoning to support conclusions.
- Demonstrate competence in information literacy by selecting, utilizing and documenting appropriate sources.

Basis of the pattern of Core Curriculum

There are three aspects of the rationale underlying core theory:

- It was John Dewey's philosophy of experimentalism that gave the core theory of curriculum. Three concepts which John Dewey upheld, have had significant influence upon the development of core curriculum ideas: (I) Focus of learning upon fundamental human activities, (II) learning viewed as continuous reconstruction of experiences, and (III) problem-solving emphasized as an important part of learning.
- Basic democratic values and the dynamic changes in political and social ideas in the world. Theses cultural factors have contributed towards the nature of core proposals.
- Acceptance of cognitive theories of learning. There is an increased recognition of the role of cognition in human learning. Increased attention is being paid to learning as dynamic, organic process rather than only to the end product of learning. There is recognition of the breadth or totality of learning, including not only verbal and motor responses, but also attitudes and emotional aspect of behaviour. There is also recognition of the interrelatedness of these many aspects of learning.

What are the characteristics of core curriculum?

- It utilizes the problems of personal and social development common to all youth.
- It develops these problems without reference to the traditional subject-matter fields.
- It encourages the use of the problem-solving technique to attack problems.
- It has a provision for individual and group guidance.
- The core programme provides means for developing social competence.

What are the benefits of the Core Curriculum?

- **It saves the time:** With seven colleges, there's one near your home or workplace. Class times on days, evenings, weekends and online ensure that everyone can find time to earn college credit.
- **It's guaranteed to transfer:** You can complete your general education requirements for college, and transfer of completed credits to any public college or university is guaranteed. However, please check with the institution you want to attend to make sure the courses you select will be applicable to the major/main subjects you want to pursue when you transfer.
- **It shows accomplishment and educational attainment:** You can achieve a goal that builds your self-esteem, résumé and job-seeking abilities on your way to a college degree! With only three or four more courses beyond the Core, you can earn an associate degree!

Elements of Core Curriculum

- It is the general education aspect of all teaching, regardless of social status or vocational choice of the students, all the students can benefit by it.
- The core pattern is problem-centred. There can, of course, be many kinds of problems, but the aim here is to focus on the common problems of the learners.
- The process of learning is important. It is assumed that in preparation for living in a democratic society, the learners should get first-hand experience in the fundamental processes of democratic living.
- The core pattern is oriented towards guidance and counselling. There is focus on the problems of the learner, for which guidance is needed.

Hidden Curriculum

The term 'hidden curriculum' was invented by **Philip Jackson**. Jackson was influenced by the educational psychology of French philosopher Emile Durkheim who had "the most philosophically and scientifically comprehensive, clear, and workable approach to moral education. Jackson invented the term 'hidden' or 'unstudied curriculum' refers to ninety percent of what goes on in classrooms, the curriculum of obligatory instruction. The hidden curriculum of the educational system reproduces the basic structure of the culture. The school's function of socialisation is represented by three central characteristics of school life which teach the student to fit into a society of the same three characteristics - the crowds, the praise, the power. In school the student learns to be treated as a member of a crowd of same-age, same-status others and thus to fit into a world of impersonal authority in which a relative stranger gives orders and wields power.

A **hidden curriculum** can be defined as the lessons that are taught informally, and usually unintentionally, in a school system. These include behaviours, perspectives, and attitudes that students pick up while they're at school. This is contrasted with the formal curriculum, such as the courses and activities students participate in. The hidden curriculum begins early in a child's education. Students learn to form opinions and ideas about their environment and their classmates. For example, children learn 'appropriate' ways to act at school, meaning what's going to make them popular with teachers and students. They also learn what is expected of them; for example, many students pick up on the fact that year-end test scores are what really matter. These attitudes and ideas aren't taught in any formal way, but kids absorb and internalize them through natural observation and participation in classroom and social activities.

Areas of hidden curriculum in our schools that mould perspectives of students deal with issues such as gender, morals, social class, stereotypes, cultural expectations, politics, and language. Gender roles, for example, become very apparent in early grades when socializing becomes divided into boys and girls. Many books at this young age support the ideas of gender separation, which, in turn, encourages these norms in early years. The importance of boy's athletics used to be a clear example of hidden curriculum, but since the passage of Class IX, many school districts have strived for a greater balance for girls and boys teams. Hidden curriculum is often found within the formal curriculum of a school; this may be partially in what is not taught. For example, if an English class only assigns reading material with the main characters or with stories set in that particular country only. This may teach students, including English learners, that our school systems don't appreciate other cultures and languages. The influence of this can lead to a negative self-image or a hatred for reading.

Definitions of Hidden Curriculum

- "The hidden curriculum highlights the importance and impact of structural factors on the learning process. Focusing on this level and type of influence draws our attention to, among other things, the commonly held 'understandings,' customs, rituals, and taken-for-granted aspects of what goes on in the life-space we call education." (Hafferty 1998, p. 404).

- "Hidden curriculum is defined as a set of influences that function at the level of organizational structure and culture". (Hafferty, 1998).

Features of Hidden Curriculum

- Privileges and responsibilities given to older students (prefects/ class captain/member of student council.
- School rules, detention and suspension, rewards like merit, awards, prizes, good marks, etc.
- Males and females often play different sports, have different dress rules and are slotted in different subjects, education courses and career. Teachers' expectation about boys and girls are different. Boys are treated differently and are given different attention
- Respecting the authority of teachers, regardless of what they say or do. Pupils always have to justify where they are going and why, and have to do as they are told.
- Punctuality (being on time) belonging to the school and not to the pupil.
- Concentrating on school work whether it is boring or not and whether the student is willing to do it or not.

Components of the Hidden Curriculum

- Rules and Guidelines.
- Policy development/implementation.
- Role models.
- Resources.
- Peer interactions.
- Faculty and staff interactions.
- Physical environment.
- Patient population/interactions.
- Institutional slang.

Processes Attributable to the Hidden Curriculum (Lempp & Seale, 2004)

- Loss of idealism.
- Adoption of a ritualized professional identity.

- Emotional neutralization.
- Change of ethical integrity.
- Acceptance of hierarchy.
- Learning of less formal aspects.

Uncovering the Hidden Curriculum Requires:

- Collective commitment among students and educators.
- Understanding of the plurality of values, beliefs, and cultures.
- Recognition of that which is external to the formal curriculum.
- Community education.

How Hidden Curriculum Can Affect Learning: Some Examples

- **Physical Conditions of the Classroom or School Environment**: Is the classroom conducive to learning? Is it well-lighted and well-ventilated? Are there enough chairs and tables for students? Is there enough space for students to do group activities or online activities? Is there always electricity in the place or is brown-out or power outage frequent? If the answer to these questions is no, then learning among students will be more difficult. An uncomfortable classroom will make students uneasy thus affect their academic performance. The physical environment is not conducive to learning.
- **The Mood of the Teachers or Students:** Are the teachers always on the mood to deliver the lesson? Are they given teaching loads and schedules that are fair? As human beings, no matter how teachers hide their emotions or feelings from the students, they are affected by the strains and stresses that may come along. However, many will argue that teachers must leave their problems at home and pretend like actors and actresses in the classroom.
- Students may also be in a bad mood. They may be hungry, or emotionally affected due to their parents' lack of time or financial support, or they have misunderstandings with their friends, or loved ones. While ideally the mood of teachers and students should be right for effective interaction, this is not always the case. Bad moods will hinder learning to take place.
- **The Teacher-Learner Interaction:** Having a limited background on the needs of the students, their interests and learning styles, the teachers may find it hard to interact well with the students. They

should have a good repertoire of strategies or activities in order to implement the instructional objectives and reach the learning outcomes. More often than not, the mood of the students and teachers may also affect their interaction.

- **Peer Influence:** Students learn more with their friends. For example, Liza is interested in studying or learning during that day; but if many of her friends are noisy due to stress, she will be affected and influenced to be noisy too. So, the success of the lesson can be determined when the learning outcomes have been achieved by the students.

Classroom Implications of Hidden Curriculum

Knowing some of the examples of hidden curriculum will help the department chairpersons, course directors and course coordinators to be more humane in giving loads, and in rating the performance of their teachers through classroom observations. They should also consider the hidden factors that may affect the learning outcomes. But of course, recognition of the hidden curriculum should not be used as an excuse to cover up the teachers' inefficiency in class. Instead, teachers should be creative, flexible and positive in teaching the students in spite of their personal problems and anxieties in life. To the administrators, they should ensure that the school environment and learning resources are conducive for teaching and learning. They should figure out ways to combat the hidden curriculum. In conclusion, the lessons may not be implemented as planned. Many teachers may write excellent lesson plans or syllabi but when they are already in class, they would realize that there are aspects in the lesson plans that cannot be implemented due to hidden curriculum.

Spiral Curriculum / Spaced Or Distributed Approach

The Spiral Curriculum is predicated on cognitive theory advanced by Jerome S Bruner (1960), who wrote, "We begin with the hypothesis that any subject can be taught in some intellectually honest form to any child at any stage of development." In other words, even the most complex material, if properly structured and presented, can be understood by very young children. Key features of the spiral curriculum based on Bruner's work are: (1) The student revisits a topic, theme or subject several times throughout their school career; (2) The complexity of the topic or theme increases with each revisit; and (3) New learning has a relationship with old learning and is put in context with the old information. The benefits ascribed to the spiral curriculum by its advocates are: (1) The information is reinforced and solidified each time the student revisits the subject matter; (2) The spiral curriculum also allows a logical progression from simplistic ideas to complicated ideas; and (3) Students are encouraged to apply the early knowledge to later course objectives. Although there is no clear empirical evidence of the overall effects of the spiral curriculum on student learning, "features" of that curriculum have been linked to improved learning outcomes. In addition, the spiral curriculum incorporates many research-based approaches from cognitive science that have been linked, individually, to improved student performance as well.

Spiral curriculum is an approach to education that introduces key concepts to students at a young age and covers these concepts repeatedly, with increasing degrees of complexity. This approach is also known as also known as a "spaced" or "distributed" approach. It contrasts with "blocked" or "massed" curricula, which do not introduce difficult concepts until the student has reached a higher level of education. Nearly any subject can be taught with spiral curriculum. Such curricula break down key concepts into "strands," ideas that are taught year after year, adding to the depth of knowledge each year. For example, Everyday Mathematics, a curriculum designed with the spiral approach, organizes its lessons around six broad categories (strands) of mathematical concepts that are taught in multiple units each year. Rather than waiting until students have mastered addition, subtraction, multiplication and division, Everyday Mathematics introduces algebraic concepts as early as kindergarten, when students are taught to recognize patterns and find rules governing specific mathematical functions. The curriculum returns to these ideas frequently, adding new information each year and setting higher comprehension goals for each grade level as students gain mastery of the subject.

The idea of spiral curriculum is attributed to Jerome S Bruner, who discussed it in his 1960 book, "The Process of Education." Proponents of spiral curriculum say that the approach helps students score better on tests and retain information longer than students who learn from curricula that take a massed approach.

The spiral curriculum is a popular model based on the theory that any content can be learned by any person if presented effectively. The basic components of a spiral curriculum are:

- Learners revisit topics several times throughout the program.

- The complexity of the material increases with each revisit.
- New concepts build on previous learning.

Spiralling supports comprehensive learning where connections are made over time. In the renewed curriculum, systems and themes will spiral through the program. The curriculum will build from fundamental content such as basic terms to more complicated concepts to complex analysis and application of knowledge. This is a big contrast from the current structure where learning is concentrated in blocks.

The following example shows how a system could start spiralling through the first two years of courses. Introduction to Educational Psychology ! Advanced Educational Psychology. This is just one example. All of the systems and themes will be similarly spiralled with primary and secondary content integrated throughout the program.

The spiral approach is a technique often used in teaching where first the basic facts of a subject are learned, without worrying about details. Then as learning progresses, more and more details are introduced, while at the same time they are related to the basics which are reemphasized many times to help enter them into long-term memory.

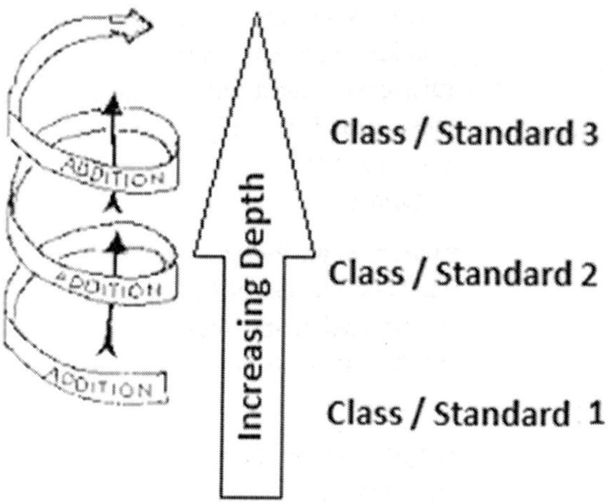

Figure 1.2: Spiral Curriculum

Roles of Spiral Approach in Teaching

- A sequencing strategy
- A teaching strategy
- Basic idea behind spiral progression approach - to expose the learners to a wide variety of concepts/topics, skills and attitudes that are deemed of "continual concern of everyone" until they are mastered.
- A spiral curriculum design is one in which "key concepts are presented repeatedly throughout the curriculum, but with deepening layers of complexity."
- After a mastery of the initial topic, the student "spirals upwards" as the new knowledge is introduced in next lessons, enabling him/her to reinforce what is already learned. In the end, a rich breadth and depth of knowledge is achieved.
- With this procedure, two purposes are served: 1. The previously learned concept is reviewed hence improving its retention 2. The topic may be progressively elaborated when it is reintroduced leading to a broadened understanding and transfer of learning.
- The Spiral Curriculum was proposed by Bruner, 1977 In structuring a course, certain prerequisite knowledge and skills must be first mastered which in turn provides linkages between each lesson as the students "spirals upwards" in a course of study.
- In Grade 3 Grade 4 Grade 5 Grade 6 students are studying the *Characteristics of Living Things*. It follows a Spiral approach viz., Parts and Functions of Living Things, a. Human b. Animals c. Plants, Interaction of Living Things with the Environment Humans, Major Organs of the Body Care for them Diseases, Animals, Plants, Terrestrial Aquatic Life Cycles, Interactions: Beneficial Harmful Stages of Growth and Development, Development of Secondary Sex differences in modes of reproduction in Human, Animals, Plants, Flowering plants Non-flowering Plants, Human Body System, Musculoskeletal System, Digestive System, Circulatory System Humans, of Animals and Plants, Respiratory System Characteristics of Vertebrates and invertebrates and Economic importance Caring for animals.
- The Learning Spiral is a curriculum design framework which will help science teachers construct lessons, activities or projects that target the development of thinking skills and dispositions which do not stop at identification, instead facilitate implementation of the desired performance.

- It is a curriculum design tool which will help develop concrete and practical thinking-centred lessons that make students performances of understanding explicit. It may be used to structure an entire project which can readily fit into the regular curriculum and can help design thinking centred lessons.
- The learner-centred approach is characterized by: Learn with focus on the learners, and learning in a real situation as the teachers facilitate their students to learn from experience, activities and work, leading to the development of learners in all aspects physical, mental, emotional, social and intellectual.
- In adopting the spiral approach, the teachers will been enriched with varied experiences in preparing every science lesson and curriculum a proper blending of concepts, skills and values from the natural and physical sciences and appropriately sequenced from a start upward according to the level of difficulty.
- One should always remember that one keeps moving upward, but keeps returning to the fundamentals through reviews but adding more.

Jerome S Bruner emphasized the gains that can be acquired by developing students powers of analysis, judgment and memory in order to increase capacity to transfer lcarning His idea was that transfer of thinking processes from one context to another required students to learned the fundamental principles of subjects and to explore ideas on a deeper level rather than just mastering facts and rote learning procedures. In the spiral progression approach, the first basic facts of a subject are learned without worrying about details. In spiral teaching, teacher moves upward but keeps returning to the fundamentals.

Integrated Curriculum

An integrated curriculum is described as one that connects different areas of study by cutting across subject-matter lines and emphasizing unifying concepts. Integration focuses on making connections for students, allowing them to engage in relevant, meaningful activities that can be connected to real life. Have you ever wondered what and how an integrated curriculum works? Learn about this hot topic that is shaping how teachers teach and students learn in the classroom.

Generally learning in the classroom and being taught subjects in isolation. For example, it was only taught reading comprehension in reading class or math in mathematics class but never in other subjects. It is often wondered why some math concepts weren't taught in science since they somehow seemed to have a relationship. Has that ever happened to you?

Today, there is a focus on an integrated curriculum. Can you imagine how an integrated curriculum can benefit your students? Understanding the benefits and how to effectively integrate curriculum can help teachers and students become more successful in the classroom.

Benefits of Integrated Curriculum

Do you wonder why it is important to integrate curriculum? Think about how much you could learn in a classroom where you learn math, science and reading all in one lesson or teaching a theme-based unit that focuses on cultural diversity and incorporates core content area topics. If we taught through an integrated curriculum, the students showed higher signs of retention at an increased rate than when an integrated curriculum was not implemented. The reason for this is because they were able to more closely relate to content and make real world connections in integrated curriculum approaches.

Students not only connect and create more real world connections in integrated classrooms, but they are also more actively engaged. Creating an integrated curriculum means that teachers are charged with having to create challenging, fun, meaningful tasks that help students connect to information. Creating a solar system unit that also requires oral language development and practice, reading comprehension skills and mathematics, can engage students far more than just a lesson on the solar system alone. Integration helps to achieve retention and engagement in classrooms, which yields higher mastery of content standards.

One final key benefit of an integrated curriculum is the ability for students to see skills multiple times. Instead of teaching comprehension strategies in just reading, teaching those strategies across multiple disciplines can give students an opportunity to see and implement it more often. The repetition of the skills being taught creates a higher level of understanding and retention of information for students in the classroom.

Examples of Integrated Curriculum

Think about the idea of integration as either a multidisciplinary approach or an interdisciplinary approach. A multidisciplinary approach focuses primarily on the disciplines. Teachers who use this approach organize standards from the disciplines around a theme. In an interdisciplinary approach, teachers organize the curriculum around common learnings across disciplines. They chunk together the common learnings embedded in the disciplines to emphasize interdisciplinary skills and concepts.

To create multidisciplinary integrated curriculum, develop a central theme focused on social studies and teach History, Geography, Economics and Government in that thematic based unit. You may also achieve this by creating a mathematics thematic unit that teachers the relationship between fractions, percents, decimals and ratios. This will help students make connections to many disciplines.

Thinking about an interdisciplinary unit can be just as fun. Focus on creating a lesson on sculpting or singing while still teaching math and communication concepts. Try having your students make wind or rain machines while still teaching the interdisciplinary skills of numeracy and communication of ideas. The idea of an interdisciplinary approach is to have students learn more than just the immediate content being taught. They can learn interdisciplinary skills such as thinking skills or research skills that are integrated among all disciplines.

Defining Integrated Curriculum

What exactly is integrated curriculum? In its simplest conception, it is about making connections. What kind of connections? Across disciplines? To real life? Are the connections skill-based or knowledge-based? Defining integrated curriculum has been a topic of discussion since the turn of the 20th century. Over the last hundred years, theorists offered three basic categories for interdisciplinary work; they defined the categories similarly, although the categories often had different names. Integration seemed to be a matter of degree and method. For example, the National Council of Teachers of English (NCTE) offered the following definitions in 1935:

- Correlation may be as slight as casual attention to related materials in other subject areas . . . a bit more intense when teachers plan it to make the materials of one subject interpret the problems or topics of another.

Fusion designates the combination of two subjects, usually under the same instructor or instructors. Integration is the unification of all subjects and experiences. The debate on Integration started in the early '90s. At the time, we were unaware of the long history of educators with similar concerns. We defined three approaches to integration - *multidisciplinary, interdisciplinary, and trans-disciplinary*. We noticed that people seemed to approach integrating curriculum from three fundamentally different starting points. In looking back, we see that our definitions closely aligned with the definitions proposed by other educators over the decades. The three categories offer a starting point for understanding different approaches to integration.

Multidisciplinary Integration

Multidisciplinary approaches focus primarily on the disciplines. Teachers who use this approach organize standards from the disciplines around a theme. Figure 1.3 shows the relationship of different subjects to each other and to a common theme. There are many different ways to create multidisciplinary curriculum, and they tend to differ in the level of intensity of the integration effort. The following descriptions outline different approaches to the multidisciplinary perspective.

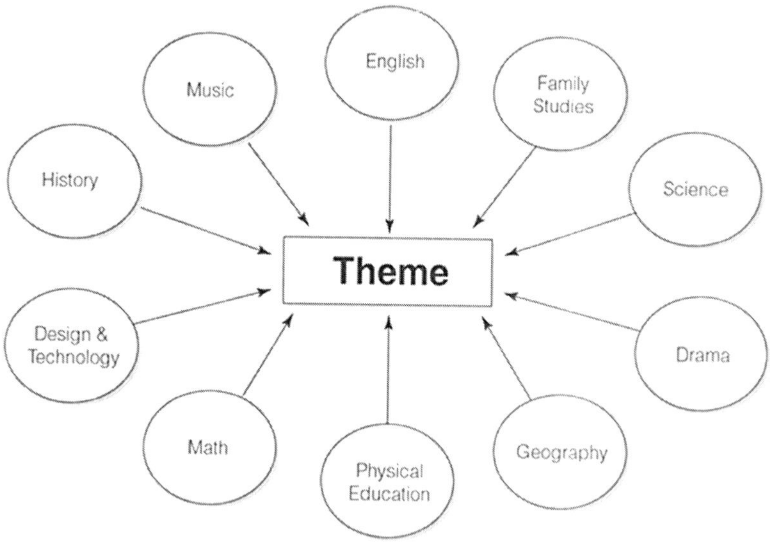

Figure 1.3. The Multidisciplinary Approach

Intra-disciplinary Approach. When teachers integrate the sub-disciplines within a subject area, they are using an intra-disciplinary approach. Integrating reading, writing, and oral communication in language arts is a common example. Teachers often integrate history, geography, economics, and government in an intra-disciplinary social studies program. Integrated science integrates the perspectives of sub-disciplines such as Biology, Chemistry, Physics, and Earth/Space Science. This type of intra-disciplinary program is usually offered for middle schools. Through this integration, teachers expect students to understand the connections between the different sub-disciplines and their relationship to the real world. The program reports a positive impact on achievement for students who participate.

Fusion: In this multidisciplinary approach, teachers fuse skills, knowledge, or even attitudes into the regular school curriculum. In some schools, for example, students learn respect for the environment in every subject area. At Mount Rainier Elementary in Washington State, teachers incorporate the theme of peace into every thread of the school's curriculum (Lester, 2001). Students begin each week promising to be peaceful, respectful, and responsible. They follow a list of responsibilities and learn about peace in their classes. In reading, for example, students analyze positive characteristics of people in stories; in social studies, they learn the importance of cultures working together. The school records the number of days without a fight as "peace days"; teachers write the accumulated number of peace days on the blackboard in every classroom. Teachers wear peace signs, and students greet each other with the peace sign.

Fusion can involve basic skills. Many schools emphasize positive work habits in each subject area. Educators can fuse technology across the curriculum with computer skills integrated into every subject area. Literacy across the curriculum is another example of fusion. The November 2002 issue of *Educational Leadership* featured the theme of "Reading and Writing in the Content Areas" and focused on how to fuse literacy into the curriculum.

To prepare students for the compulsory 10th grade literacy test, 9th grade teachers at North Park Secondary School in the Peel District School Board in Ontario developed subject-specific tasks for literacy skills. For example, students practiced skills related to developing supported opinions on disposal of hazardous waste in science, immigration policies in geography, correct approaches to problem solving in math, the influence of peer pressure in family studies, and part-time employment and its impact on teens in business studies. Teaching literacy skills across the curriculum facilitated a low-risk environment for the eventual testing in the next year (Patten, 2001).

Service Learning: Service learning that involves community projects that occur during class time falls under the category of multidisciplinary integration. At Spring Valley School in Columbia, South Carolina, more than 1,200 Spanish-language students engaged in service learning projects.

In one project, they distributed 20 tons of food, clothing, medicine, and household products to needy new arrivals in the area with the fastest-growing Hispanic population (Glenn, 2001). At Topa Topa Elementary School at Ojai, California, 5th and 6th grade students created pamphlets on the pros and cons of pesticides to explain how crop pickers can protect themselves against the substances. Students passed out the brochure, written in Spanish and English, to workers and consumers throughout the Ojai Valley. Through the project, students fulfilled state-required standards for language arts, science, and social studies (Ragland, 2002).

Glenn (2001) found that more than 80 percent of the schools that integrate service learning into the classroom report an improvement in grade point averages of participating students. For example, when teachers integrated service learning into the curriculum in a Springfield, Massachusetts, high school, the dropout rate dropped from 12 percent to 1 percent, the number of students going to college increased by 22 percent, and those achieving a grade point average of 3.0 or higher increased from 12 percent to 40 percent. According to Glenn, such programs foster a lifelong commitment to civic participation, sharpen "people skills," and prepare students for the work force.

Learning Centres/Parallel Disciplines: A popular way to integrate the curriculum is to address a topic or theme through the lenses of several different subject areas. In an elementary classroom, students often experience this approach at learning centres. For example, for a theme such as "patterns," each learning centre has an activity that allows the students to explore patterns from the perspective of one discipline - Math, Language, Science, or Social Studies. As students move through the learning centres to complete the activities, they learn about the concept of patterns through the lenses of various disciplines.

In the higher grades, students usually study a topic or theme in different classrooms. This may take the form of parallel disciplines; teachers sequence their content to match the content in other classrooms. Students often experience American literature and American history as parallel disciplines. They study a particular period of history and read literature from that period. For example, students read *The Red Badge of Courage* in English while studying the Civil War in history. Students usually must make the connections themselves.

Theme-Based Units: Some educators go beyond sequencing content and plan collaboratively for a multidisciplinary unit. Educators define this more intensive way of working with a theme as "theme-based." Often three or more subject areas are involved in the study, and the unit ends with an integrated culminating activity. Units of several weeks' duration may emerge from this process, and the whole school may be involved. A theme-based unit involving the whole school may be independent of the regular school schedule. At Fitch Street School in the District School Board of Niagara in Ontario, Ellie Phillips and four of her colleagues collaborated on a two-week, cross-grade curriculum unit on the Olympic Games. Curriculum planning required eight half-hour sessions. Teachers grouped students into five multi-age classes representing grades 4, 5, 6, and 7. The multi-age groups met for one hour daily for nine days. In these groups, students devised a performance task that they presented on the final day of the unit. The teachers observed numerous benefits, such as the following:

- Students exhibited excellent on-task behaviour.
- Students worked collaboratively.
- Multi-age teams formed within the multi-age classes.
- Students were engrossed both as presenters and as the audience for the half-day performance task presentations.
- Students used a wide range of presentation products, such as video, debate, sculpture, and so on.
- Students demonstrated depth of understanding of topics as a result of their sustained interest around various questions (e.g., Are the Olympics relevant today? Does the Olympic creed stand the test of time?).
- Fewer recess problems occurred during this two-week period.
- Teachers enjoyed the process and the results.

Other thematic programs may involve teachers across the same grade. Charles Jervis, Jerry Sauter, and Steve Bull of Auburn High School in Riner, Virginia, have collaborated for many years to teach thematic units in grade 11. They have done this without the luxury of common planning time. One topic they have developed is Exploring a Local Ecosystem from Multiple Perspectives. Students explore the Pandapas Pond from the different disciplinary lenses of science (Earth Sciences, Biology, Chemistry, and Physics), English (genre readings, analyses, and communication skills), and Math (data analysis tools and techniques). The teachers carefully connect the activities to the standards in each discipline. Over time, they have developed a long list of possible culminating activities. They update their Web site continually and use it as a teaching tool with students.

Interdisciplinary Integration

In this approach to integration, teachers organize the curriculum around common learnings across disciplines. They chunk together the common learnings embedded in the disciplines to emphasize interdisciplinary skills and concepts. The disciplines are identifiable, but they assume less importance than in the multidisciplinary approach. Figure 1.4 illustrates the interdisciplinary approach.

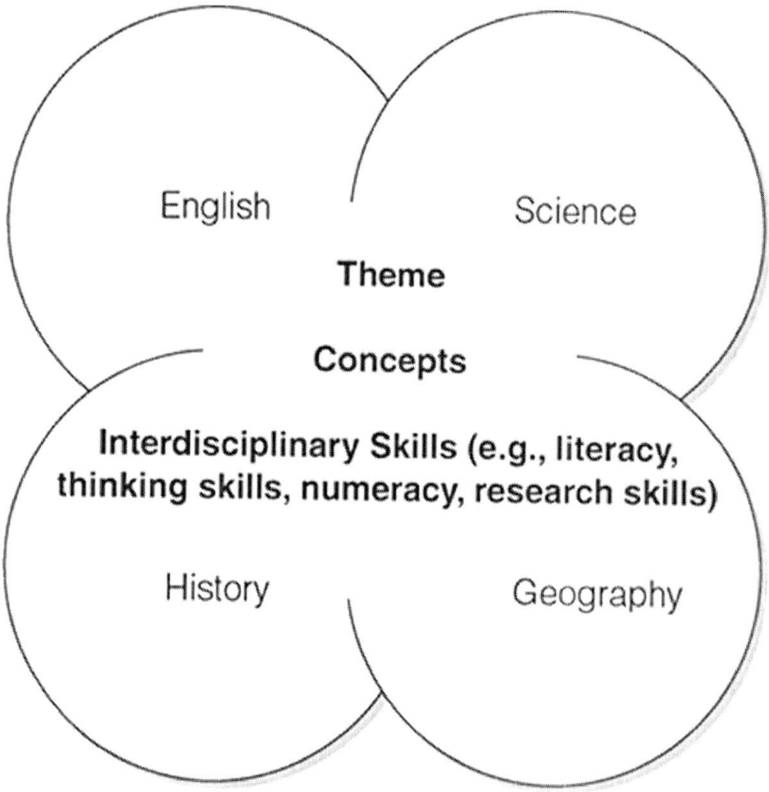

Figure 1.4. The Interdisciplinary Approach

The children in Florida making wind and rain machines while learning language skills are experiencing interdisciplinary curriculum. They are learning the interdisciplinary skill of communication (thinking and writing in a structured and coherent way). The teacher also focuses on "big ideas" in the concepts of evaporation, condensation, and thermal energy. These concepts transfer to other lessons beyond wind and rain machines; thus, the lesson develops a higher level of thinking than if students simply focused on the wind and rain machines.

Is the example of students learning math and core curriculum through clogging and the arts an interdisciplinary one? Yes, if students are learning skills and concepts beyond the immediate lesson. In *Learning Through the Arts*™, for example, students learn math and science concepts and skills while singing, sculpting, painting, and dancing. Artists from the community collaborate with teachers to create integrated lessons that focus on standards. A three-year study of more than 6,000 elementary students participating in this program showed an 11-point increase in math scores among students in 170 schools across Canada. Literacy scores remained the same; however, students reported being happier going to school, and researchers found that students were more engaged in their lessons (Upitis & Smithirin, 2002).

At Mott Hall Academy in New York City, students work on interdisciplinary projects that integrate laptop computers. Mott Hall is a math, science, and technology academy for students in grades 4 through 8 who are primarily Hispanic. Every student and teacher has a laptop computer. Teachers integrate computer use into the curriculum, rather than adapting curriculum to the use of computers. In Sandra Skea's 5th grade class, for example, students constructed handmade kites from material such as paper, straws, aluminium foil, skewers, and string. To engage students' imagination, Skea began by reading a story about kites. Students studied such diverse topics as electromagnetism and the use of kite flying in celebrations. They developed a deep understanding of principles of ratio and proportion as they designed and refined their kites - first on the computer and then by hand. Students also wrote poetry and prose about kites. Skea used the projects as evidence that students not only met, but also exceeded, the standards. She used rubrics to show students how the projects related to grade-level standards and provided the criteria for evaluation. Beyond the academic content, these students learned generic skills related to working together, research, writing, and design and construction (Furger, 2001).

Trans-disciplinary Integration

In the trans-disciplinary approach to integration, teachers organize curriculum around student questions and concerns (see Figure 1.5). Students develop life skills as they apply interdisciplinary and disciplinary skills in

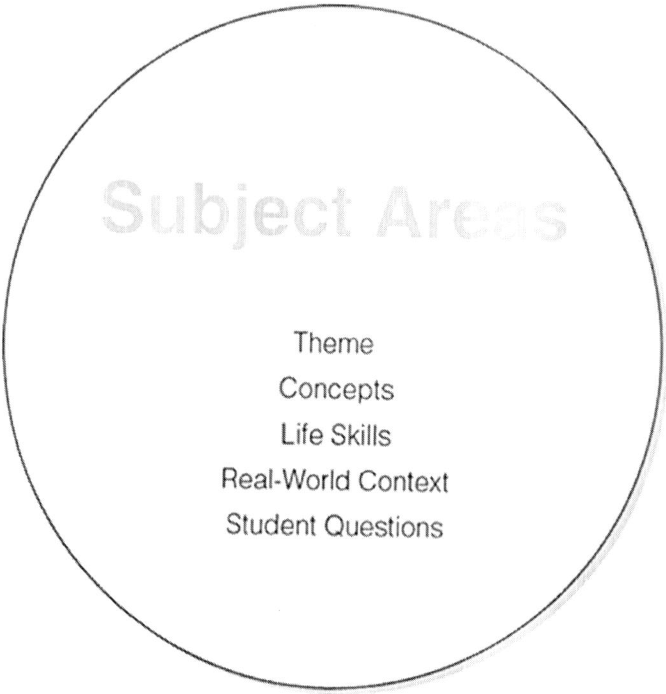

Figure 1.5. Trans-disciplinary Approach

a real-life context. Two routes lead to trans-disciplinary integration: project-based learning and negotiating the curriculum.

Project-Based Learning

In project-based learning, students tackle a local problem. Some schools call this problem-based learning or place-based learning. According to Chard (1998), planning project-based curriculum involves three steps:

- Teachers and students select a topic of study based on student interests, curriculum standards, and local resources.
- The teacher finds out what the students already know and helps them generate questions to explore. The teacher also provides resources for students and opportunities to work in the field.
- Students share their work with others in a culminating activity. Students display the results of their exploration and review and evaluate the project.

Studies of project-based programs show that students go far beyond the minimum effort, make connections among different subject areas to answer open-ended questions, retain what they have learned, apply learning to real-life problems, have fewer discipline problems, and have lower absenteeism (Curtis, 2002). Newsome Park Elementary School in Virginia, described in Chapter 9, successfully embraces the project method. At Grand River Collegiate Institute in the Waterloo Region District School Board in Ontario, 11th grade students took on the problem of improving the city image (Drake, 2000). This project did not originate in any subject area; students completed project work in a separate time slot scheduled into the school day. After extensive research, students wrote proposals to renew or enhance the city's image and presented the proposals to a group of external evaluators. Student assessment considered teamwork, critical thinking skills, problem solving, and time management. Interestingly, more than one proposal received serious consideration by the city council.

Negotiating the Curriculum: In this version of the trans-disciplinary approach, student questions form the basis for curriculum. Mark Springer of Radnor, Pennsylvania, negotiated an integrated curriculum with students (Brown, 2002). Springer led the nationally known Watershed program for 11 years. His current curricular program is Soundings. In Soundings, 8th grade students develop their own curriculum, teaching methods, and assessments around areas of interest to them. Themes that students have developed include Violence in Our Culture, Medical Issues Affecting Our Lives, and Surviving Alien Environments.

The Soundings program is based on the work of James Beane (1997), who advocates theme studies revolving around personal growth and social issues. On standardized tests, Soundings students perform about the same as students who have not participated in the program. Parents are overwhelmingly positive about the program, and high school teachers report that Soundings graduates appear to discuss topics at a more sophisticated level than students who have not been in the program.

How the Three Approaches Connect with Each Other

When Susan led a provincial team in developing an integrated curriculum, she noticed how her team suddenly shifted into deeper and deeper levels of connection (Drake, 1991). The boundaries of the disciplines seemed to dissolve abruptly. During the early '90s, Ontario mandated integrated curriculum for kindergarten through grade 9. Susan interviewed others who were developing integrated curriculum and reported similar experiences of dissolving the boundaries (Drake, 1993). As soon as they made one set of connections, another set appeared. In Rebecca's context, she found the same dissolving of the boundaries (Burns, 1995).

Describing her experiences to a colleague, Susan discovered there were academic terms for this phenomenon: multidisciplinary, interdisciplinary, and trans-disciplinary. The essential difference between the three approaches was the perceived degree of separation that existed between subject areas. Given our experiences at the time, both of us believed that the three approaches fit on an evolutionary continuum. Other theorists have also offered continuums (Fogarty, 1991; Jacobs, 1989).

Standards-based approaches further blur the boundaries of these categories. Multidisciplinary integration might remain somewhat distinct because the procedures of the disciplines are dominant. Current thinking, however, suggests that even intra-disciplinary projects should include math and literature/media to be rich and vibrant (Erickson, 1998). Interdisciplinary approaches offer an excellent fit for standards when educators approach them through a backward design process. Although teachers might organize trans-disciplinary curriculum around a real-world context, the reality of covering the standards and grading in distinct subject areas quickly brings them back to the disciplines.

Is there an evolutionary continuum? We suspect that obvious differences will continue to exist in the extent to which educators choose to integrate and for how long. We believe that educators will continue to experience deepening connections as they become more experienced in this area. In an era of standards and accountability, no one approach seems preferable. Indeed, they seem more and more alike as teachers integrate standards-based planning with effective teaching and learning practices. The multidisciplinary, interdisciplinary, and trans-disciplinary perspectives offer different maps to begin the design process. Teachers can use any of the approaches at any level of education, in a single classroom or in a team approach.

Table 1.1 shows the relationships among the three different approaches. Some differences in intent are apparent. We found, however, that the educators who actually implement integrated approaches are the same educators who are interested in the most effective ways to teach. They are the ones who constantly ask, "How can I engage all of my students in this learning?" They also are the ones who use the most effective planning strategies, such as a backward design process, and are concerned with authentic assessment practices. Therefore, despite some differences in the degree and the intent of integration, the three approaches share many similarities. The centrality of standards and the need for accountability bring the three approaches closer together in practice.

Table 1.1.
Comparing and Contrasting the Three Approaches to Integration

	Multidisciplinary	*Interdisciplinary*	*Trans-disciplinary*
Organizing Centre	Standards of the disciplines organized around a theme	Interdisciplinary skills and concepts embedded in disciplinary standards	• Real-life context· • Student questions
Conceptionof Knowledge	• Knowledge best learned through the structure of the disciplines • A right answer • One truth	• Disciplines connected by common concepts and skills • Knowledge considered to be socially constructed • Many right answers	• All knowledge interconnected and interdependent • Many right answers • Knowledge considered to be indeterminate and ambiguous
Role of Disciplines	• Procedures of discipline considered most important • Distinct skills and concepts of discipline taught	Interdisciplinary skills and concepts stressed	Disciplines identified if desired, but real-life context emphasized
Role of Teacher	• Facilitator • Specialist	• Facilitator • Specialist/generalist	• Co-planner • Co-learner· • Generalist/ Specialist
Starting Place	Disciplinary standards and-procedures	Interdisciplinary bridge KNOW/DO/BE	• Student questions and concerns • Real-world context
Degree of Integration	Moderate	Medium/intense	Paradigm shift
Assessment	Discipline-based	Interdisciplinary skills/conce-pts stressed	nterdisciplinary skills/ concepts stressed
NOW?	Concepts and essential understandings across disciplines	Concepts and essential understandings across disciplines	Concepts and essential understandings across disciplines
DO?	• Disciplinary skills as the focal point· • Interdisciplinary skills also included	• Interdisciplinary skills as the focal point • Disciplinary skills also included	Interdisciplinary skills and disciplinary skills applied in a real-life context

Disadvantages of Integrated Curriculum:

- The fundamentals of a discipline may be neglected
- some topics may be omitted
- teachers may be less enthusiastic and less comfortable when not teaching in their own discipline
- discipline based teaching may be cheaper
- students may develop a clearer picture of a discipline as a career in the discipline based method

Curriculum Framework-need And Importance; Ramification Of Curriculum Framework Into Curriculum, Syllabus And Textbooks

A curriculum framework is an organized plan or set of standards or learning outcomes that defines the content to be learned in terms of clear, definable standards of what the student should know and be able to do. A curriculum framework is part of an outcome-based education or standards based education reform design. The framework is the first step, defining clear, high standards which will be achieved by all students. The curriculum is then aligned to the standards, and students are assessed against the standards. As compared with traditional education which is concerned only about delivering content, a standards based education reform system promises that all will succeed if all are held to high expectations. When the standards are reached, there will be no achievement gap where some groups are allowed to score lower than others, or the disabled are offered different opportunities than others. All will meet world class standards and be qualified for good colleges and trained for good jobs which pay good wages. In a traditional education system, the curriculum was defined by those who created textbooks rather than government bodies which assembled groups of stakeholders to create standards based on consensus of what students should know and be able to do.

A curriculum framework describes the educational environment in which syllabuses (or subject specific outlines of objectives, outcomes, content and appropriate assessment and teaching methodologies) can be developed. A curriculum framework is most commonly developed at a national level, but a form of curriculum framework could be developed at international level by a group of countries with similar goals and educational environments. One function of a curriculum framework is to define a set of 'curriculum standards' that enable a range of curricula to co-exist, on the proviso that each curriculum complies with specific criteria. A curriculum framework is therefore a very useful mechanism for allowing flexibility and diversity among countries within an affiliation of some kind or ethnic groups within a single state. Each individual system can maintain the 'identity' of its own curriculum while ensuring consistency and quality through compliance with a set of agreed standards expressed in the framework.

Common Elements of a Curriculum Framework

- **Introduction**: Current Context describes the social and economic environment in which educational policy is made and in which teaching and learning occur.

- **Educational Policy**: Statements describes the Government's goals for education, such as universal literacy and numeracy, the development of skills needed for economic prosperity and the creation of a stable and tolerant society
- **Statement of Broad**: Learning Objectives and Outcomes / standards for each level / cycle describe what students should know and be able to do when they complete their school education. Outcomes should be expressed in a range of domains, including knowledge, understanding, skills and competencies, values and attitudes
- **Structure of the Education System** describes the school system within which the curriculum framework is to be applied. It should specify: (1) Number of years of schooling, including compulsory schooling (2) Stages (or cycles) of schooling and their durations (3) Number of weeks in the school years, hours / teaching periods in the school week
- **Structure of curriculum content,** learning areas and subjects describes the organization of content within the framework and the extent to which schools and students can make choices. It might describe: (1) The pattern of Subjects or Learning Areas to be studied in each stage or cycle (such as core, elective and optional subjects) (2) The number of hours to be assigned to each subject or Learning Area in each stage or cycle.
- **Standards of resources required** for implementation describes standards as they apply to: (1) Teachers – qualifications, teaching load (number of classes per week) (2) Students – number per class in each subject (3) Materials – textbooks, computers, other equipment; facilities – classrooms, furniture, fittings.
- **Teaching Methodology** describes the range of teaching approaches that might be employed in the implementation of the framework.
- **Assessing and Reporting** student achievement describes. The importance of assessing the extent to which students achieve the outcomes of each subject, and recommends or prescribes types of assessment strategies.
- How achievement will be certified.

Significance of Curriculum in School Education

Give the centrality of a curriculum for school education; the Curriculum Framework should be more extensively discussed in public. A curriculum framework has to address educational programmes as well as acquainting society with what the next generation is being taught and why. At the present point in the history of India, curriculum framework has a more than routine relevance. It has to concern itself with how we can prevent the hijacking of the curriculum of the kind that we experienced under the previous government.

Differentiating between curriculum and syllabus;

When it comes to education, the two concepts which pop up in our mind is syllabus and curriculum. People are quite confused between these two, although the fact is that there is a difference. If we talk about the syllabus, it is focused towards a particular subject. Unlike curriculum, which is related to the all round development of a student. In the same way, there are a number of differences between the syllabus and curriculum which has been presented in this article excerpt. The main difference between a syllabus and a curriculum is that a curriculum is a more generalized or an overview of the subjects or topics that the students are meant to learn. However, a syllabus is a more detailed overview of the subject of study. For example: a math curriculum may list basics of algebra, basics of geometry and basics of trigonometry. While, the class syllabus will list what topics will be covered under each of the basic topics, what will be the concepts that students may understand by the end of each topic, and it may even list what exercises or problems in the textbook will be covered during class. Hence, it can be said that syllabus is a subset of curriculum.

Table 1.2:
Difference between Syllabus & Curriculum

Basis for Difference	***Syllabus***	***Curriculum***
Meaning	Syllabus is the document that contains all the portion of the concepts covered in a subject.	Curriculum is the overall content, taught in an educational system or a course.
Origin	Syllabus is a Greek term.	Curriculum is a Latin term.
Set for	A subject	A course
Nature	Descriptive	Prescriptive
Scope	Narrow	Wide
Set out by	Exam board	Government or the administration of school, college or institute.
Uniformity	Varies from teacher to teacher	Same for all teachers.
Term	For a fixed term, normally a year.	Till the course lasts.

Notion of Textbook

- A textbook is a collection of the knowledge, concepts, and principles of a selected topic or course. It's usually written by one or more teachers, college professors, or education experts who are authorities in a specific field. Most textbooks are accompanied by teacher guides, which provide you with supplemental teaching materials, ideas, and activities to use throughout the academic year.
- Textbook is a teaching tool (material) which presents the subject matter defined by the curriculum. A university textbook is required to contain the complete overview of the subject, including the theories, as well as to be of a more permanent character. A text-book is probably the cheapest and most reliable source of information. It also serves as a reference book for the teacher.
- A text-book is a concise source of material for reviews. It helps the students to acquire the required information with speed. While revising his lessons pupils can work independently making use of text-books at his disposal.
- A text-book helps these students in thoroughly understanding the subject matter. It also helps the students to make up his deficiency because of his failure to attend certain classes due to unavoidable reasons.
- A teacher can make use of the text-book to give home-work and assignments to the pupils.
- The text-bode specifies the standards expected to be attained by a particular class. It also gives suggestion about the use of various teaching aids and activities to be undertaken. A text-book also helps the teachers in teaching and correlating the subject with other things. It lays down the order of procedure.
- In lower classes text-books with coloured illustrations provide an incentive to learning and they provide attraction for the young learner. That is why a text-book for every child has become essential equipment.
- Teacher may use any of the methods of teaching he feels a necessity of text-books. The work of the teacher does not end in the class-room he has to see that the pupil can readily apply the knowl-edge gained by him in the class-room. For this it is desirable to provide the student with a record of class-work and also some ques-tions for practice. This record can be had, by the pupil, by taking notes in the class, but these lengthy dictation and

notes may prove to be most-time consuming. A good text-book saves the times of the teacher as well as of the taught.

Definition of Textbooks

- A textbook is a printed and bound artefact for each year or course of study They contain facts and ideas around a certain subject. (Encyclopedia of Education, 2008b).
- Textbooks are not like other books. Today, textbooks are assembled more than they are written. They are not usually written by a single author, nor are they a creative and imaginative endeavour. They are, in fact, usually specially made by a corporation to follow a set standard curriculum for a school system or larger organization, such as a province (Encyclopedia of Education, 2008b)
- Textbooks are as universal as formal schooling and almost as old. They have been used to aid teaching, and in some cases, to be the teacher for centuries. Textbooks are not just teaching and learning objects but are political documents that hold content that reflects the vision of a specific group (Encyclopedia of Education, 2008a).
- Ac-cording to Dr. D.S. Kothari, "The question of text-books is the most important and urgent one for our country. Energetic on State and National basis is required to progress the preparation of high quality school text-books"

Advantages of textbooks in Teaching & Learning

- Textbooks are especially helpful for beginning of teachers. The material to be covered and the design of each lesson are carefully spelled out in detail.
- Textbooks provide organized units of work. A textbook gives you all the plans and lessons you need to cover a topic in some detail.
- A textbook series provides you with a balanced, chronological presentation of information.
- Textbooks are a detailed sequence of teaching procedures that tell you what to do and when to do it. There are no surprises—everything is carefully spelled out.
- Textbooks provide administrators and teachers with a complete program. The series is typically based on the latest research and teaching strategies.
- Good textbooks are excellent teaching aids. They are a resource for both teachers and students.

Conclusion

Curriculum organisation is a scientific process which involves basic principles on which its credibility exists. It is not just collection of topics, because it reflects ethos (philosophy / culture) of the society: themes of the subject and learning variability. The curriculum is the totality of experiences that the child gains through the multifarious activities in the school. The review of the present curriculum is reveal that it is subject oriented, examination ridden, not in conformity with the aims and objective of the teaching science, rigid and outfits the different age group. So, it is imperative that the present curriculum should be reorganized in the light of the Perspectives on Curriculum.

Model Questions

Very Short Answer type Questions. To be answer in about 20 words each.

1. Define Curriculum.
2. Enlist the principles of Curriculum Construction.
3. What are the characteristics of Core Curriculum?
4. Justify the need of Curriculum in Schools.

Short Answer type Questions. To be answer in about 150 words each.

5. How curriculum vary at Elementary, Secondary and Higher Education level? Illustrate.
6. Are you think curricula become a tool for the betterment of society? Substantiate.
7. How Hidden Curriculum can affect Learning?
8. Describe the four Perspectives on Curriculum.

Multiple Choice Questions

9. The term 'hidden curriculum' was invented by ____________.

   (a) John Dewey

   (b) Philip Jackson

   (c) John Bobbit

   (d) Paulo Friere

10. The ____________ is predicated on cognitive theory advanced by Jerome Bruner.

   (a) Hidden Curriculum

   (b) Spiral Curriculum

(c) Core Curriculum

(d) Integrated Curriculum

11. The first known use of the term *Curriculum* in an educational context is in the *Professio Regia*, a work by ———— published posthumously in 1576.

(a) William M. Alexander

(b) John Franklin Bobbitt

(c) Cunningham

(d) Professor Petrus Ramus

12. ———— is usually confined to those written understandings and directions formally designated and reviewed.

(a) Societal or social curricula

(b) The hidden or covert curriculum

(c) Rhetorical curriculum

(d) Overt or explicit curriculum

Answer Key

9:b

10:b

11:d

12:d

Reference

Dushi, G. *The main principles of curriculum construction*. retrieved on 8-4-2017 from

http://www.preservearticles.com/2012010920286/the-main-principles-of-curriculum-construction-may-be-mentioned-as-under.html

http://www.ccet.ua.edu

http://www.mcps.org/pandapas/

http://www.ltta.ca.

Sharma, A. *Characteristics of core curriculum* . retrieved on 8-4-2017 from http://www.preservearticles.com/2012030825872/what-are-the-characteristics-of-core-curriculum.html

Gupta, D, *Curriculum- Basic Concept*. retrieved on 9-10-2012 from http://www.slideshare.net/deepati1/curriculum-basic-concept?related=1 on 5-11-2015.

Goslin, G. *The History of the Textbook Research Project for ETEC* 540 retrieved on 25-3-2016 from http://courses.educ. ubc.ca/etec540/May08/goslina/researchtopic/ Definition%20of%20textbooks.html

Memaine, *Nature, concepts and purposes of curriculum.* retrieved on 7-3-2013 from http://www.slideshare.net/memaine_027/nature-concepts-and-purposes-of-curriculum 17023484 on 5-11-2015.

Cortes, C.E. (1981) The societal curriculum: Implications for multiethnic educations. in Banks, J.A (ed.) *Educations in the 80's: Multiethnic education*. National Education Association.

Eisner, E.W. (1994). *The Educational Imagination: On design and evaluation of school programs.* (3rd. ed) New York: Macmillan.

Boutelier, S. *Lesson Transcript* retrieved on 30-04-16 from http://study.com/academy/lesson/hidden-curriculum-in-education-definition-examples-quiz.html

Longstreet, W.S. & Shane, H.G. (1993) Curriculum for a new millennium. Boston: Allyn and Bacon.

Oliva, P. (1997) *The Curriculum: Theoretical dimensions*. New York: Longman.

Anglin, R. (1999). *An Introduction to Curriculum Development.* Stephenson's Press.

Bowler, M. (1999). *Feeling Power: Emotions and Education*. New York: Routledge.

Hafferty, F. & Franks, R. (1994) The Hidden Curriculum, Ethics Teaching, and the Structure of Medical Education. *Academic Medicine* 69: 861-71.

Hafferty, F. (1998) Beyond curriculum reform: confronting medicine's hidden curriculum. *Academic Medicine*, 73(4): 403-407.

Bilbao, P. P., et.al. (2008). *Curriculum Development.* Philippines: Lorimar Publishing, Inc.

Kigali, R. *Guidelines for Constructing a Curriculum Framework for Basic Education* retrieved from http://www.ibe.unesco.org/ fileadmin/user_upload/COPs/ News_ documents /2007/0709Kigali/Curriculum_ Framework_ Guidelines.pdf

S. Surbhi. *Difference Between Syllabus and Curriculum*. retrieved from http://keydifferences.com/difference-between-syllabus-and-curriculum.html on 05-05-2016

Pungur, L. & Buck, G.H. *A pragmatic approach to curriculum.* retrieved on 8-4-2017 from http://lib-ocs.lib.sfu.ca:8087/ fedcan/index.php/ csse2009/csse2009/ paper/viewFile/1968/627

Ahangarzadeh, E. *Five Theoretical Perspectives on Curriculum*. retrieved on 8-4-2017 from http://www.emilahangarzadeh. com/single-post/2014/12/22/ Five-Theoretical- Perspectives-on-Curriculum

Lawrence, A. *Principles of Curriculum Construction*. retrieved on 8-4-2017 from https://www.academia.edu/1745090/Principles_of_Curriculum_Construction

Pemikiran. *Curriculum Development Principles*. retrieved on 8-4-2017 from http://ariefsugianto503.blogspot.in/2010/09/curriculum-development-principles.html

Drake, S.M. & Burns, R.C. *Meeting Standards Through Integrated Curriculum*. retrieved on 8-4-2017 from http:// www.ascd.org/ publications/books/103011/chapters/What-Is-Integrated-Curriculum%C2%A2.aspx

Integrated Curriculum: Definition, Benefits & Examples. retrieved on 8-4-2017 from http://study.com/academy/lesson/integrated-curriculum-definition-benefits-examples.html

What is the definition of spiral curriculum? . retrieved on 8-4-2017 from https://www.reference.com/education/definition-spiral-curriculum-331ff5861fa7c9de#

Howard, J. *The Spiral Curriculum. Research into Practice.* retrieved on 8-4-2017 from https://eric.ed.gov/?id=ED538282

Hatuina, R. *Spiral Curriculum*. retrieved on 8-4-2017 from https://www.slideshare.net/lavirchameiram/the-spiral-curriculum

Chapter - 2

Concept of Curriculum

Curriculum Framework

A curriculum framework is an organized plan or set of standards or learning outcomes that defines the content to be learned in terms of clear, definable standards of what the student should know and be able to do. A curriculum framework is part of an outcome-based education or standards based education reform design. The framework is the first step, defining clear, high standards which will be achieved by all students. The curriculum is then aligned to the standards, and students are assessed against the standards. As compared with traditional education which is concerned only about delivering content, a standards based education reform system promises that all will succeed if all are held to high expectations. When the standards are reached, there will be no achievement gap where some groups are allowed to score lower than others, or the disabled are offered different opportunities than others. All will meet world class standards and be qualified for good colleges and trained for good jobs which pay good wages. In a traditional education system, the curriculum was defined by those who created textbooks rather than government bodies which assembled groups of stakeholders to create standards based on consensus of what students should know and be able to do.

A curriculum framework describes the educational environment in which syllabuses (or subject specific outlines of objectives, outcomes, content and appropriate assessment and teaching methodologies) can be developed. A curriculum framework is most commonly developed at a national level, but a form of curriculum framework could be developed at international level by a group of countries with similar goals and educational environments. One function of a curriculum framework is to define a set of 'curriculum standards' that enable a range of curricula to co-exist, on the proviso that each curriculum complies with specific criteria. A curriculum framework is therefore a very useful mechanism for allowing flexibility and diversity among countries within an affiliation of some kind or ethnic groups within a single state. Each individual system can maintain the 'identity' of its own curriculum while ensuring consistency and quality through compliance with a set of agreed standards expressed in the framework.

Common Elements of a Curriculum Framework

- **Introduction**: Current Context describes the social and economic environment in which educational policy is made and in which teaching and learning occur.
- **Educational Policy**: Statements describes the Government's goals for education, such as universal literacy and numeracy, the development of skills needed for economic prosperity and the creation of a stable and tolerant society
- **Statement of Broad**: Learning Objectives and Outcomes / standards for each level / cycle describe what students should know and be able to do when they complete their school education. Outcomes should be expressed in a range of domains, including knowledge, understanding, skills and competencies, values and attitudes.
- **Structure of the Education System** describes the school system within which the curriculum framework is to be applied. It should specify: (1) Number of years of schooling, including compulsory schooling (2) Stages (or cycles) of schooling and their durations (3) Number of weeks in the school years, hours / teaching periods in the school week.
- **Structure of curriculum content**, learning areas and subjects describes the organization of content within the framework and the extent to which schools and students can make choices. It might describe: (1) The pattern of Subjects or Learning Areas to be studied in each stage or cycle such as core, elective and optional subjects. (2) The number of hours to be assigned to each subject or Learning Area in each stage or cycle.
- Standards of resources required for implementation describes standards as they apply to: (1) Teachers – qualifications, teaching load viz. number of classes per week (2) • Students – number per

class in each subject (3) Materials – textbooks, computers, other equipment; facilities – classrooms, furniture, fittings.

- Teaching methodology describes the range of teaching approaches that might be employed in the implementation of the framework.
- Assessing and reporting student achievement describes.
- The importance of assessing the extent to which students achieve the outcomes of each subject, and recommends or prescribes types of assessment strategies.
- How achievement will be certified.

Significance of curriculum in school education

Give the centrality of a curriculum for school education; the Curriculum Framework should be more extensively discussed in public. A curriculum framework has to address educational programmes as well as acquainting society with what the next generation is being taught and why. At the present point in the history of India, curriculum framework has a more than routine relevance. It has to concern itself with how we can prevent the hijacking of the curriculum of the kind that we experienced under the previous government.

Differentiating between Curriculum and Syllabus

When it comes to education, the two concepts which pop up in our mind is syllabus and curriculum. People are quite confused between these two, although the fact is that there is a difference. If we talk about the syllabus, it is focused towards a particular subject. Unlike curriculum, which is related to the all round development of a student. In the same way, there are a number of differences between the syllabus and curriculum which has been presented in this article excerpt.

The main difference between a syllabus and a curriculum is that a curriculum is a more generalized or an overview of the subjects or topics that the students are meant to learn. However, a syllabus is a more detailed overview of the subject of study. For example: a math curriculum may list basics of algebra, basics of geometry and basics of trigonometry. While, the class syllabus will list what topics will be covered under each of the basic topics, what will be the concepts that students may understand by the end of each topic, and it may even list what exercises or problems in the textbook will be covered during class. Hence, it can be said that syllabus is a subset of curriculum.

Basis for Difference	*Syllabus*	*Curriculum*
Meaning	Syllabus is the document that contains all the portion of the concepts covered in a subject.	Curriculum is the overall content, taught in an educational system or a course.
Origin	Syllabus is a Greek term.	Curriculum is a Latin term.
Set for	A subject	A course
Nature	Descriptive	Prescriptive
Scope	Narrow	Wide
Set out by	Exam board	Government or the administration of school, college or institute.
Uniformity	Varies from teacher to teacher	Same for all teachers.
Term	For a fixed term, normally a year.	Till the course lasts.

Notion of textbook

A textbook is a collection of the knowledge, concepts, and principles of a selected topic or course. It's usually written by one or more teachers, college professors, or education experts who are authorities in a specific field. Most textbooks are accompanied by teacher guides, which provide you with supplemental teaching materials, ideas, and activities to use throughout the academic year. Textbook is a teaching tool (material) which presents the subject matter defined by the curriculum. A university textbook is required to contain the complete overview of the subject, including the theories, as well as to be of a more permanent character. A text-book is probably the cheapest and most reliable source of information. It also serves as a reference book for the teacher.

A text-book is a concise source of material for reviews. It helps the students to acquire the required information with speed. While revising his lessons pupils can work independently making use of text-books at his disposal. A text-book helps these students in thoroughly understanding the subject matter. It also helps the students to make up his deficiency because of his failure to attend certain classes due to unavoidable reasons.

A teacher can make use of the text-book to give home-work and assignments to the pupils. The text-bode specifies the standards expected to be attained by a particular class. It also gives suggestion about the use of various teaching aids and activities to be undertaken. A text-book also helps the teachers in teaching and correlating the subject with other things. It lays down the order of procedure. In lower classes text-books with coloured illustrations provide an incentive to learning and they provide attraction for the young learner. That is why a text-book for every child has become essential equipment.

Teacher may use any of the methods of teaching he feels a necessity of text-books. The work of the teacher does not end in the class-room he has to see that the pupil can readily apply the knowl-edge gained by him in the class-room. For this it is desirable to provide the student with a record of class-work and also some ques-tions for practice. This record can be had, by the pupil, by taking notes in the class, but these lengthy dictation and notes may prove to be most-time consuming. A good text-book saves the times of the teacher as well as of the taught.

Definition of Textbooks

The definitions for Textbooks are wide and varied. One common definition is that a textbook is a printed and bound artefact for each year or course of study (Encyclopaedia of Education, 2008). They contain facts and ideas around a certain subject. Textbooks are not like other books. Today, textbooks are assembled more than they are written. They are not usually written by a single author, nor are they a creative and imaginative endeavour. They are, in fact, usually specially made by a corporation to follow a set standard curriculum for a school system or larger organization, such as a province (Encyclopaedia of Education, 2008).

Textbooks are as universal as formal schooling and almost as old. They have been used to aid teaching, and in some cases, to be the teacher for centuries. Textbooks are not just teaching and learning objects but are political documents that hold content that reflects the vision of a specific group. Ac-cording to Dr. D.S. Kothari, "The question of text-books is the most important and urgent one for our country. Energetic on State and National basis is required to progress the preparation of high quality school text-books"

Importance of textbooks in teaching learning

Textbooks provide several advantages in the classroom:

- Textbooks are especially helpful for beginning of teachers. The material to be covered and the design of each lesson are carefully spelled out in detail.
- Textbooks provide organized units of work. A textbook gives you all the plans and lessons you need to cover a topic in some detail.
- A textbook series provides you with a balanced, chronological presentation of information.
- Textbooks are a detailed sequence of teaching procedures that tell

you what to do and when to do it. There are no surprises—everything is carefully spelled out.

- Textbooks provide administrators and teachers with a complete program. The series is typically based on the latest research and teaching strategies.
- Good textbooks are excellent teaching aids. They are a resource for both teachers and students.

Core Curriculum

Educators define "core curriculum" as the knowledge and skills expected to be learned by a student by high school graduation. Generally, the core curriculum consists of knowledge and skills related to academic subjects. Mastery of the core curriculum is what both parents and teachers stress as essential for academic success in school, and later in life. In most states, opportunities are provided for students to meet other criteria in cases when those students cannot meet the academic demands of the core curriculum. The Core Curriculum is the name given to a set of courses designed to give you the fundamentals of a college education. Every public institution of higher education has a Core Curriculum. The Core is designed to provide a solid foundation for your college education and is guaranteed to transfer as a block of credit between and among Texas institutions of higher education.

There are many versions of the core curriculum. In our country, each state assumes responsibility for minimum standards for high school graduation. This core curriculum becomes the foundation for almost all learning, from kindergarten through high school. The Core Curriculum is designed to meet the goals of a liberal arts education. It gives students a perspective and an informed acquaintance with the major branches of learning: the humanities; the physical and biological sciences and mathematics; and the social sciences. The Core is designed to develop critical thinking skills, to challenge students intellectually, to promote an appreciation for diverse cultures and to increase moral and civic awareness. The Core integrates Writing across the Curriculum to strengthen students' writing ability in all disciplines. The Core Curriculum is the set of common courses required of all undergraduates and considered the necessary general education for students, irrespective of their choice in major. The communal learning—with all students encountering the same texts and issues at the same time—and the critical dialogue experienced in small seminars are the distinctive features of the Core. Begun in the early part of the 20th century, the Core Curriculum is one of the founding experiments in liberal higher education in the United States and it remains vibrant as it enters its tenth decade. Not only academically rigorous but also personally transformative for students, the Core seminar thrives on oral debate of the most difficult questions about human experience.

The learning objectives of the Core include "global objectives" that cut across different disciplines. The three global objectives articulate the expectation that upon completion of the core, students will be able to:

- Communicate effectively in writing.
- Demonstrate the ability to use logical reasoning to support conclusions.
- Demonstrate competence in information literacy by selecting, utilizing and documenting appropriate sources.

Basis of the Pattern of Core Curriculum

There are three aspects of the rationale underlying core theory:

1. It was John Dewey's philosophy of experimentalism that gave the core theory of curriculum. Three concepts which John Dewey upheld, have had significant influence upon the development of core curriculum ideas: (I) Focus of learning upon fundamental human activities, (II) learning viewed as continuous reconstruction of experiences, and (III) problem-solving emphasized as an important part of learning.
2. Basic democratic values and the dynamic changes in political and social ideas in the western world. Theses cultural factors have contributed towards the nature of core proposals.
3. Acceptance of cognitive theories of learning. There is an increased recognition of the role of cognition in human learning. Increased attention is being paid to learning as a dynamic, organic process rather than only to the end product of learning. There is recognition of the breadth or totality of learning, including not only verbal and motor responses, but also attitudes and emotional aspect of behaviour. There is also recognition of the interrelatedness of these many aspects of learning.

What are the Characteristics of Core Curriculum?

The characteristics of core curriculum are as follows:

- It utilities the problems of personal and social development common to all youth.

- It develops these problems without reference to the traditional subject-matter fields.
- It encourages the use of the problem-solving technique to attack problems.
- It has a provision for individual and group guidance.
- The core programme provides means for developing social competence.

What are the benefits of the Core Curriculum?

It saves the time. Class times on days, evenings, weekends and online ensure that everyone can find time to earn college credit. It's guaranteed to transfer. You can complete your general education requirements for college, and transfer of completed credits to any public college or university in Texas is guaranteed. However, please check with the institution you want to attend to make sure the courses you select will be applicable to the major you want to pursue when you transfer. It shows accomplishment and educational attainment. You can achieve a goal that builds your self-esteem, résumé and job-seeking abilities on your way to a college degree! With only three or four more courses beyond the Core, you can earn an associate degree!

Elements of Core Curriculum

- It is the general education aspect of all teaching, regardless of social status or vocational choice of the students, all the students can benefit by it.
- The core pattern is problem-centred. There can, of course, be many kinds of problems, but the aim here is to focus on the common problems of the learners.
- The process of learning is important. It is assumed that in preparation for living in a democratic society, the learners should get first-hand experience in the fundamental processes of democratic living.
- The core pattern is oriented towards guidance and counselling. There is focus on the problems of the learner, for which guidance is needed.

Curriculum Planning In Indian Context

The main thrust in curriculum planning that may be mentioned during the period immediately before independence as well as during the post-independence decades in India are stated briefly under:

The Basic Education Curriculum:

Mahatma Gandhi was deeply affected by the limitations of the contemporary system of education. He realised the urgent need for the reform of that system. The rigid lifeless, meaningless curriculum had to be replaced by a vital, dynamic purposeful curriculum related to the life and experience of the Indian pupil. The Basic Education Scheme, also called Wardha Scheme was designed by dedicated, patriotic, highly experienced and enlightened educators, and was put into operation in many schools in rural areas. It was a work-oriented curriculum with learning through productive work, which was not only creative but also socially useful. This was totally new and revolutionary concept of productivity, introduced as a part of education in India, from 1937 gradually in many rural areas. Gandhiji's idea of socially useful productive work in the curriculum has now become a part of educational thinking and planning in the decades after independence by the various commissions and reports on Education.

In order to realise the objectives Gandhiji had in mind, free compulsory education was to be made available to all children in the age group of 7-14 years. For the development of the whole man and his intellectual, physical and spiritual powers there would be (I) A Basic Craft in accordance with local conditions and needs (II) The Mother Tongue (III) Arithmetic (IV) Social Studies (V) General science including native study, Botany, Zoology, physiology, Hygiene and physical education (VI) Art (VII) Music (VIII) Home Science. These subjects would form part of a correlated activity curriculum, taught cohesively, and centering round the basic craft. No subject would be taught in isolation.

The Secondary Education Commission of 1952-53

This was called the Mudaliar Commission. In keeping with the needs and aspirations of the people of free India, the previous pattern of 5+3+2, or 10 years at school was considered unsatisfactory. Henceforth, schools were to follow 5+3+2 pattern. Schools became Higher Secondary and Multipurpose schools. A great diversity of courses and streams were offered, clusters of subjects were made in the academic, vocational and commerce as well as fine arts streams. The mother-tongue and regional languages were strongly represented in the curricula. Other subjects stressed democratic citizenship, vocational efficiency, personality and leadership qualities through theory and practice activities in the school.

The Kothari Commission 1964-66

School education and its availability had greatly expanded in the decades after independence. However, the quality of education was not perceived as being satisfactory.

- The commission emphasized the right type of vocational training-students were to be exposed to a variety of traders and occupations, not only traditional occupations, but to new fields and jobs related to the advances in science and technology. The entire structure and function of vocational education was recognized to meet the needs of agriculture, science and industry. This also had to be related to work experience as, well as socially useful productive work.
- Scientific and Technological Education was given great importance. Modern laboratories in which real experiments relating to scientific and technological developments would be performed on physics, chemistry and biological sciences.
- Social and National Service programmes would be developed and promoted in all the schools.

The 5+5+2 or 12 years of schooling provided under the proposed Kothari Education Scheme made it possible to include programmes for citizenship, national integration socially useful productive work in all schools. The pattern of 12 years schooling was introduced in 1973 and gradually by the end of 1977-78 it spread all over the country. The curriculum was enriched and strengthened by this plan in the Fifth Five-Year plan period.

The National Policy on Education 1986

Prime Minister Rajiv Gandhi (1985) announced that a new education policy would be started which should "promote national cohesion and the work ethic", so that the country would be scientifically and economically equipped to enter the 21st century. Accordingly in 1986, a national education policy was made. Under this NPE the curricular content and processes of education would be enriched and enhanced by:

- Cultural content of Fine Arts, Music, Folklore
- Value Education
- Language, Books and Libraries
- Use of Media and Technology
- Environmental Studies
- Work Experience

- Mathematics and Science teaching
- Physical Education

Curriculum in The Ramamurti Report 1990

The curriculum recommendations embedded in the Ramamurti Report do not differ greatly from those in the National Policy on Education of 1986. The outstanding difference is the policy, the administrative measure and the organizational structures suggested, some of which may at some stage have some effect on the curriculum.

- Value Education
- Mother Tongue as language
- Science, Mathematics and Computer Education
- Media and Technology
- Work Experience
- Environmental Education
- Physical Education
- An Activity Curriculum
- Self-Sufficiency
- School and Community relationship

Meaning And Concerns Of 'Hidden' Curriculum

The term 'hidden curriculum' was invented by **Philip Jackson**. Jackson was influenced by the educational psychology of French philosopher Emile Durkheim who had "the most philosophically and scientifically comprehensive, clear, and workable approach to moral education. Jackson invented the term 'hidden' or 'unstudied curriculum' refers to ninety percent of what goes on in classrooms, the curriculum of obligatory instruction. The hidden curriculum of the educational system reproduces the basic structure of the culture. The school's function of socialisation is represented by three central characteristics of school life which teach the student to fit into a society of the same three characteristics - the crowds, the praise, the power. In school the student learns to be treated as a member of a crowd of same-age, same-status others and thus to fit into a world of impersonal authority in which a relative stranger gives orders and wields power.

A **hidden curriculum** can be defined as the lessons that are taught informally, and usually unintentionally, in a school system. These include behaviours, perspectives, and attitudes that students pick up while they're at school. This is contrasted with the formal curriculum, such as the courses and activities students participate in.

The hidden curriculum begins early in a child's education. Students learn to form opinions and ideas about their environment and their classmates. For example, children learn 'appropriate' ways to act at school, meaning what's going to make them popular with teachers and students. They also learn what is expected of them; for example, many students pick up on the fact that year-end test scores are what really matter. These attitudes and ideas aren't taught in any formal way, but kids absorb and internalize them through natural observation and participation in classroom and social activities.

Areas of hidden curriculum in our schools that mould perspectives of students deal with issues such as gender, morals, social class, stereotypes, cultural expectations, politics, and language. Gender roles, for example, become very apparent in early grades when socializing becomes divided into boys and girls. Many books at this young age support the ideas of gender separation, which, in turn, encourages these norms in early years. The importance of boy's athletics used to be a clear example of hidden curriculum.

Hidden curriculum is often found within the formal curriculum of a school; this may be partially in what is not taught.

"The hidden curriculum highlights the importance and impact of structural factors on the learning process. Focusing on this level and type of influence draws our attention to, among other things, the commonly held 'understandings,' customs, rituals, and taken-for- granted aspects of what goes on in the life-space we call education." (Hafferty 1998, p. 404) "Hidden curriculum is defined as a set of influences that function at the level of organizational structure and culture". (Hafferty, 1998).

Features of Hidden Curriculum

- Privileges and responsibilities given to older students (prefects/ class captain/member of student council.
- School rules, detention and suspension, rewards like merit, awards, prizes, good marks, etc.
- Males and females often play different sports, have different dress rules and are slotted in different subjects, education courses and career. Teachers' expectation about boys and girls are different. Boys are treated differently and are given different attention

- Respecting the authority of teachers, regardless of what they say or do. Pupils always have to justify where they are going and why, and have to do as they are told.
- Punctuality (being on time) belonging to the school and not to the pupil.
- Concentrating on school work whether it is boring or not and whether the student is willing to do it or not.

Components of the Hidden Curriculum

- Rules and Guidelines.
- Policy development/implementation.
- Role models.
- Resources.
- Peer interactions.
- Faculty and staff interactions.
- Physical environment.
- Patient population/interactions.
- Institutional slang.

Processes Attributable to the Hidden Curriculum (Lempp and Seale, 2004)

- Loss of idealism.
- Adoption of a ritualized professional identity.
- Emotional neutralization.
- Change of ethical integrity.
- Acceptance of hierarchy.
- Learning of less formal aspects of "good doctoring.

Uncovering the Hidden Curriculum Requires:

- Collective commitment among students and educators.
- Understanding of the plurality of values, beliefs, and cultures.
- Recognition of that which is external to the formal curriculum.
- Community education.

How Hidden Curriculum Can Affect Learning: Some Examples

- *Physical Conditions of the Classroom or School Environment: Is* the classroom conducive to learning? Is it well-lighted and well-ventilated? Are there enough chairs and tables for students? Is there enough space for students to do group activities or online activities? Is there always electricity in the place or is brown-out or power outage frequent? If the answer to these questions is no, then learning among students will be more difficult. An uncomfortable classroom will make students uneasy thus affect their academic performance. The physical environment is not conducive to learning.

- *The Mood of the Teachers or Students:* Are the teachers always on the mood to deliver the lesson? Are they given teaching loads and schedules that are fair? As human beings, no matter how teachers hide their emotions or feelings from the students, they are affected by the strains and stresses that may come along. However, many will argue that teachers must leave their problems at home and pretend like actors and actresses in the classroom. Students may also be in a bad mood. They may be hungry, or emotionally affected due to their parents' lack of time or financial support, or they have misunderstandings with their friends, or loved ones. While ideally the mood of teachers and students should be right for effective interaction, this is not always the case. Bad moods will hinder learning to take place.
- *The Teacher-Learner Interaction:* Having a limited background on the needs of the students, their interests and learning styles, the teachers may find it hard to interact well with the students. They should have a good repertoire of strategies or activities in order to implement the instructional objectives and reach the learning outcomes. More often than not, the mood of the students and teachers may also affect their interaction.
- *Peer Influence:* Students learn more with their friends. For example, Mary is interested in studying or learning during that day; but if many of her friends are noisy due to stress, she will be affected and influenced to be noisy too. So, the success of the lesson can be determined when the learning outcomes have been achieved by the students.
- *Classroom Implications:* Knowing some of the examples of hidden curriculum will help the department chairpersons, course directors and course coordinators to be more humane in giving loads, and in rating the performance of their teachers through classroom observations. They should also consider the hidden

factors that may affect the learning outcomes. But of course, recognition of the hidden curriculum should not be used as an excuse to cover up the teachers' inefficiency in class. Instead, teachers should be creative, flexible and positive in teaching the students in spite of their personal problems and anxieties in life.

To the administrators, they should ensure that the school environment and learning resources are conducive for teaching and learning. They should figure out ways to combat the hidden curriculum. In conclusion, the lessons may not be implemented as planned. Many teachers may write excellent lesson plans or syllabi but when they are already in class, they would realize that there are aspects in the lesson plans that cannot be implemented due to hidden curriculum.

References

Anika Sharma characteristics of core curriculum http://www.preservearticles.com/2012030825872/what-are-the-characteristics-of-core-curriculum.html

Glenn Goslin The History of the Textbook Research Project for ETEC 540http://courses.educ.ubc.ca/etec540/May08/goslina/researchtopic/Definition%2 0of%20textbooks.html March 25, 2016.

Cortes, C.E. (1981) The societal curriculum: Implications for multiethnic educations. In Banks, J.A (ed.) Educations in the 80's: Multiethnic education. National Education Association.

Eisner, E.W. (1994) The educational imagination: On design and evaluation of school programs. (3rd. ed) New York: Macmillan.

Stefani Boutelier Lesson Transcript retrieved from http://study.com/academy/lesson/hidden-curriculum-in-education-definition-examples-quiz.html on 30-04-16.

Longstreet, W.S. and Shane, H.G. (1993) Curriculum for a new millennium. Boston: Allyn and Bacon.

Oliva, P. (1997) The curriculum: Theoretical dimensions. New York: Longman.

Wilson, L. O. (1990, 2004, 2006) Curriculum course packets ED 721 & 726.

Anglin, R. (1999) An Introduction to Curriculum Development, Stephenson's Press.

Bailey, B. and Yussuf-Khalil, Y. (1998) Principles of Curriculum Development and Management.

Aultman, J. (2005) Uncovering the Hidden Medical Curriculum through a Pedagogy of Discomfort, Advances in Health Sciences Education, 10:263-273.

Bowler, M. (1999) Feeling Power: Emotions and Education New York: Routledge.

Hafferty, F. and Franks, R. (1994) The hidden curriculum, ethics teaching, and the structure of medical education. Academic Medicine 69: 861-71.

Hafferty, F. (1998) Beyond curriculum reform: confronting medicine's hidden curriculum. Academic Medicine, 73(4): 403-407.

Hafferty, F. (2000) In search of a lost cord: Professionalism and medical education's hidden curriculum. IN D. Wear and J. Bickel (Eds.) Educating for

Professionalism: Creating a Culture of Humanism in Medical Education. Iowa City: University of Iowa Press.

Fins, J. J., and Rodriquez del Pozo, P. (2011). The hidden and implicit curricula in cultural context: New insights from Doha and New York, Academic Medicine 86(3): 321-325.

Mossop, L., Dennick, R., Hammond, R. and Robbe, I (2013) Analysing the hidden curriculum: use of cultural web. Medical Education 47: 134-143.

Bilbao, P. P., Lucido, P. I., Iringan, T. C., Javier, R. B., (2008). Curriculum development. Philippines: Lorimar Publishing, Inc.

Ken Brown (1998) Introduction to sociology http://vcampus.uom.ac.mu/soci1101/851_features_of_the_hidden_curriculum.html.

Bhatia &Bhatia, (2007,) The Philosophical & Sociological Foundations of Education, Doaba Publications House.

Kigali, Rwanda – September 2007 Guidelines for Constructing a Curriculum Framework for Basic Education retrieved from http://www.ibe.unesco.org/fileadmin/user_upload/COPs/News_documents/2007/0709Kigali/Curriculum_Framework_Guidelines.pdf

Deepty Gupta, Oct 09, 2012, Curriculum- Basic Concept. retrieved from http://www.slideshare.net/deepati1/curriculum-basic-concept?related=1 on 5-11-2015.

Memaine, Mar 07, 2013, Nature, concepts and purposes of curriculum retrieved from http://www.slideshare.net/memaine_027/nature-concepts-and-purposes-of-curriculum 17023484 on 5-11-2015.

S.Surbhi November 23, 2015 Difference Between Syllabus and Curriculum retrieved from http://keydifferences.com/difference-between-syllabus-and-curriculum.html on 05-05-2016.

Chapter - 3

Types of Curriculum

Meaning & Definition Of Curriculum

In ancient Greece, Socrates argued that education was about drawing out what was already with the student. (The word education comes from the Latin word 'educere' meaning "to lead out"). There is a dangerous tendency to assume that when people talk about education they mean the same thing. It is for this reason that a definition for education is important to explore. No single definition or meaning however can be assigned to the term education. Similarly to become educated is a complex process, which cannot be sufficiently explained as an event. Thus, you should be clear from the outset that without understanding the meaning of the term "education" you can be in no position to explain, assess or evaluate what our institutions of education are doing. Similarly without the conception of what education is, empirical research into educational effectiveness of programmes and strategies cannot begin. Thus, the understanding of education is key to the study of curriculum since curriculum is the means of achieving educational goals.

- Farrant (1980) Education is the total process of human learning by which knowledge is acquired, faculties trained and skills developed.
- Mbiti (1981) defines education as a deliberate attempt to acquire and to transmit the accumulated, worthwhile skills, attitudes, knowledge and understanding from one human generation to the next. He further asserts that education includes all activities which are worthwhile and which can be taught or learned through a variety of meaningful ways.

- Fafunwa (1984) defines education as "the aggregate of all the processes by means of which a person develops abilities, skills and other forms of behaviour of positive and sometimes of negative value to the society in which he lives.

It is important that you bear in mind that these are just but some of the definitions that can help you to have a clear understanding of what education is all about. Admittedly, they are many scholars who have defined education. However, no matter what the definition of education may be, it is vital to note that education is always a positive process. It is all about the acquisition of worthwhile or desirable skills, attitudes, knowledge and values. Thus, we can finally say that; Education is a process of acquiring, developing and transmitting desirable accumulated and new knowledge, wisdom, values, attitudes and skills as a result of growth, maturation and learning which can be best utilized for life in a changing society.

Over the past decades many definitions of a curriculum have been provided but because key players in education represent a diversity of values and experience, it is difficult to get wide public or professional consensus. Educators define curriculum in different ways in part because they bring to that task different perceptions of what curriculum should be. Paradoxically, the term 'curriculum' has a long history despite its apparently recent common usage. Curriculum was considered by writers on education such as Plato, Aristole, J.A. Comenius and Friedrich Froebel, although the usage of the term has not been popularised until this century.

To define a curriculum as 'what is taught in schools' is of course, very vague. Persons often talk about 'school curriculum' in this general way and they tend to mean by this the range of subjects taught and the amount of instruction time given to each in terms of hours or minutes.

A curriculum defined as 'content' is an interesting emphasis and brings into question another term, namely the 'syllabus'. A 'syllabus' is usually a summary statement about the content to be taught in course or unit, often linked to an external examination. It is typically a list of content areas. A syllabus is clearly a subsection of curriculum and as such is subsumed within the broader concept. This emphasis on what content to be taught is a critical element of a syllabus but a curriculum includes more than this. Characterizing curriculum as subject matter is the most traditional image of curriculum which depicts it as the combining of subject matter to form a body of content to be taught. Such content is the product of accumulated wisdom, particularly acquired through the traditional academic disciplines. You will discover that most teachers when asked to describe their school's curriculum they provide a litany of subjects or subject matter taught to students.

Defining a curriculum as a 'set of performance objectives' or student learning is a very practical orientation of curriculum. This approach focuses upon specific skills or knowledge that it is considered should be attained by learners. Proponents of this approach argue that if a teacher knows the targets which learners should achieve, it is much easier to organize elements to achieve this end. The strength of this approach is that it focuses upon the learners who are after all the ultimate beneficiaries. You should also understand that this approach can lead to an overemphasis upon behavioural outcomes and objectives. Also a curriculum document which is simply a listing of objectives would have to be very large.

To define a curriculum as 'that which is taught both inside and outside school, directed by the school' indicates that all kinds of activities that occur in the classroom, playground and community, comprise the curriculum. This emphasis has merit in that it demonstrates that school learning is not just confined to the classroom. However, you will realise that it seems to indicate that the only important learning experiences are those which are directed by school personnel.

To define a curriculum in terms of 'what an individual learner experiences as a result of schooling' is an attempt to widen the focus. The emphasis here is upon the student as a self-motivated learner.

The definition which refers to a curriculum as 'everything that is planned by school personnel' is yet another orientation which emphasizes the planning aspect of curriculum. Few would deny that classroom learning experiences for students need to be planned although some unplanned activities will always occur (and these can have positive or negative effects).

Educators and Scholars define curriculum in different ways, in part because they bring to that task different perceptions of what curriculum should be. As seen in the previous paragraphs some educators see the curriculum as a list of subjects to be studied, while others see it as entire course content. Still others perceive curriculum as a set of planned learning experiences offered by teachers. Another group state that curriculum is a written plan of action. The following are some of the well-known definitions that we can consider. The term curriculum is derived from the Latin word *currere*, which means to run or to run the course. Based on this origin, some authorities have defined curriculum as a course of study subject matter. This definition has been found limiting and many authorities have modified it. The following are some of the definitions of curriculum that you will find very useful by renowned scholars in curriculum studies and education.

The word "curriculum" as it is defined from its early Latin origins means literally "to run a course." If one thinks of a marathon with mile and direction markers, signposts, water stations, and officials and coaches along the route, this beginning definition is a metaphor for what the curriculum has become in the education of our children. Here are multiple definitions of curriculum, from Oliva (1997); Curriculum is:

- That which is taught in schools
- A set of subjects.
- Content
- A program of studies.
- A set of materials
- A sequence of courses.
- A set of performance objectives
- A course of study
- Is everything that goes on within the school, including extra-class activities, guidance, and interpersonal relationships.
- Everything that is planned by school personnel.
- A series of experiences undergone by learners in a school.
- That which an individual learner experiences as a result of schooling.

Some Other Definitions

- Ralph Tyler (1949): -'All the learning of students which is planned by and directed by the school to attain its educational goals.
- Taba (1962): -'a plan for learning."
- D. K. Wheeler (1978): -'the planned experiences offered to the learner under the guidance of the school.'
- Kerr (1968): -'all the learning, which is planned and guided by school whether it is carried on in groups or individually.'
- E. Eisner (1985): -'a course, or a classroom can be conceived of as a series of planned events that are intended to have educational consequences for one or more students.'
- G. Saylor (1981): -'a plan for providing sets of learning opportunities for persons to be educated.'

- Oluoch (1982): -'all that is planned to enable the students acquire and develop the desired knowledge, skills and attitudes.
- M. Skilbeck (1984): -'the learning experiences of students, in so far as they are expressed or anticipated in goals and objectives, plans and designs for learning and the implementation of these plans and designs in school environments.'
- Glatthorn (1987): -'plans made for guiding learning in schools usually represented in retrievable documents of several levels of generality and the actualization of those plans in the classroom as experienced by the learners and as recorded by an observer; those experiences take place in a learning environment which also influence what is learned.'
- J. Wiles & J. Bondi (1989): -'a goal or set of values, which are activated through a development process culminating in classroom experiences for student.
- M. Print (1993): -'all the planned learning opportunities offered to learners by the educational institution and the experiences learners encounter when the curriculum in implemented.

Classification Of Curriculum

Obviously the answer to this question is subject to interpretation. Since curriculum reflects the models of instructional delivery chosen and used, some might indicate that curriculum could be categorized according to:

- The common psychological classifications of the four families of learning theories: **Social, Information Processing, Personalist, and Behavioral.**
- Longstreet and Shane have dubbed divisions in curricular orientations as: **Child-centred, Society-centred, knowledge-centred, or eclectic**.
- Common philosophical orientations of curriculum parallel those beliefs espoused by different philosophical orientations: **Idealism, Realism, Perennialism, Essentialism, Experimentalism, Existentialism, Constructivism, Reconstructivism** and the like.

Types of Curriculum

There are many types of curriculum design, but here we will discuss only the few. Types or patterns are being followed in educational institutions.

- Subject Centred curriculum
- Teacher centred curriculum
- Learner centred curriculum
- Activity/Experience curriculum
- Integrated curriculum
- Core curriculum
- Broad field curriculum
- Hidden curriculum

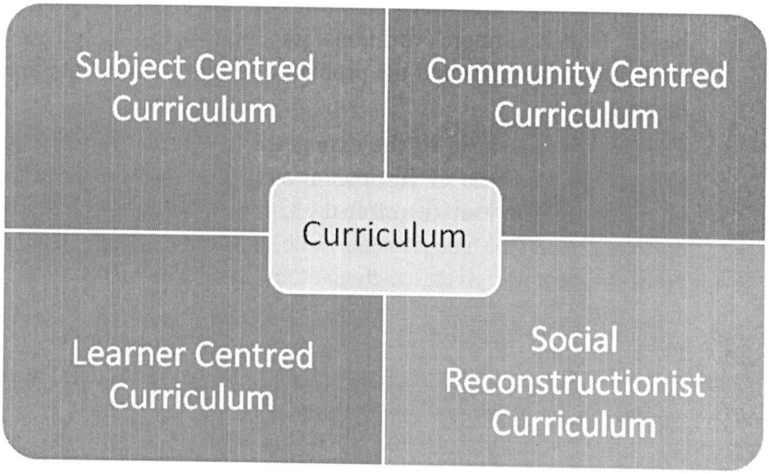

Fig: 3.1 Types of Curriculum

Subject Centred Curriculum

Subject matter is the most used and accepted curriculum Design, it is also the oldest curriculum Design. We see the earliest example in the medieval era in the Middle Ages the monastery and Cathedrals and the organizations of the seven liberal arts in the schools of ancient Greece and Rome. The seven liberal arts were consisted of two divisions:

- Trivium
- Quadrivium

These subjects were broad. In the modern period the *Trivium* was further divided to include literature and history and the *quadrivium* to include algebra, trigonometry, geography, botany, zoology, physics and chemistry. In this manner subjects added one after the other so much so that in 1930 there were over 300 different subjects.

After centuries the curriculum design of the seven liberal arts are still the nucleus of the subject curriculum. In a subject base curriculum every subject is separate unit. In this kind of curriculum four or five subject are placed in curriculum and each subject has a separate teacher. Every teacher try to teach his own subject, no one intervene in the subject of other teacher

Characteristics of Subject Curriculum

- **Information for future use:** Importance is given to acquire knowledge and information for future use, only those subjects are considered important which have a value and the individual have benefit from it in future (vocational importance). Adult problems are given importance and the problems of children in youth are ignored
- **Progress is measured to the extent the students learned the subject:** In this type of curriculum subject matter is the most important thing to learn therefore the learning is measured by how much and well the subject matter has been mastered by the pupil. Frequent tests are given to students to check the degree of the achievement in the subject.
- **Pre- determined uniform standard of knowledge:** There is a uniform standard for all the students to pass the subject else they well have to repeat the subject therefore the experts of the subject centred approach strongly support the minimum standards for examination so all achieved the set standard and qualify the examination. The teacher tries to help the weak students and to bring him to the set standard and pass the exam or repeat a grade.
- **Each subject is a separate entity (unit) with a logical organization of its own:** Importance is given to the acquisition of skills, facts and information for vocational purpose in different logically organized subjects. The teaching staffs teaches different subjects and they do not discuss or plan subject together.
- **Practice in skills is emphasized:** The main aspect of subject base curriculum is the continuous practice or drill in a specific skill, it is one of the typical characteristics of the subject base curriculum. For this purpose multiple methods are used; evaluations, Exercise session, tutoring classes are often dedicated to such type of practices and all the students are given equal opportunities to participate.
- **Subject matter is selected by adults/experts for teaching learning situation:** The content of the subject is selected in

advance before the teaching learning process; the subject matter is logically organized from simple to complex with the help of the experts, specialists, teacher's supervisors, planners, writers and administrators.

- **Learning subject matter is an end in itself:** The main focus of the teachers, administrators and students are to complete the subject matter, to cover all the topics which are provided in the course out line by Listening to lectures, studying the recommended textbook. It is all preparation for examination on the part of students and teachers and it shows the influence of the subject centred approach. For the teacher to finish the textbook on time is a great accomplishment.

Requirements for the Operation of Subject centred Curriculum

- Trained Teachers with mastery in a subjects and expert in methodology are required to teach.
- A separate classroom for each subject and each level.
- A fixed time table is required for different subjects according to importance of the subjects and age in curriculum.
- Special arrangements for guidance physical education, Indoor and outdoor activities, tours and examinations etc.
- Need of Text books and guide books for subject centred curriculum.

Criticism on Subject Centred Curriculum

Teacher has the control over pupil experiences, Learning activities and conduct. The teacher follows the decision of others in the planning and evaluation process. The teacher and headmaster formulate the rules for the classrooms management. They demand a very stern discipline and they want a quite classroom atmosphere, teacher thinks it is the best situation for teaching learning process.

- **It is compartmentalized and fragmentary:** The critics believed that there is no unity and continuity in the subject base matter. The subject is learned in parts. Every teacher is specialist in one subject and he feel pride to have the knowledge of his own subject and teaching and denying any responsibility for any other subject. Here they say that the learner acquire scraps of information not actual knowledge.
- **Subject centred curriculum ignores the interest and activities of the learner.** The critics think that the arrangement of the

course content is useless and inefficient and not suitable for teaching learning process. The subjects are logically organized.

- The critics also have a viewpoint that the fact is the students know about the history what a few men had done in the past but they do not know about the current situation in their own country and what are the hopes and desires of Pakistani people and what are the social problems they have today here.
- The critics also said that subject base curriculum fails to develop habits of effective and critical thinking. This curriculum gives importance to mastery of conclusions of thought (the end result) rather than the process through which that conclusion were derived. Which support this conclusion that it lead to uncritical thinking? The traditional assumption is that anybody who has learned the facts and information can think effectively, but the evidence does not support this assumption.

Defences of Subject Centred Curriculum

- The supporter of the subject base curriculum rejects the claim that it did not develop child's thinking. They argue that it is the most suitable method for the development of critical thinking in an individual but if one can't then the problem lies in the instruction not in the curriculum itself. A vast majority of countries select this method and they are producing botanist, doctors and geologist and so on.
- The other claim that it is fragmentary and compartmentalized is also not true about subject base curriculum alone because no one can study one subject in one session at once in any kind of curriculum. They use the principle of selection in the selection of course contents. In a sense anything that is learnt is a fragment and is a part of some larger unit.
- It gives the teacher the idea what to teach and the student what he suppose to learn and how much time they have to cover the course of the subject. This provides them with a constant source of security and a self evaluation process through which they know how much course they have cover and how to complete.
- Subject base curriculum use a logically sound framework for the organization of subject matter, it used the cause and effect principle in science and the chronological order of the historical events but they assumed an order and are reliable for learning experiences.

- The evaluation of subject base curriculum is easy. It use the achievement based testing in the evaluation to find the mastery of the subject matter in the individual.
- It has a bright future. Subject approach is useful for specialization in any branch of knowledge. It is more effective.

Learner-centred Curriculum

The supporters of learner-centred Curriculum give importance to individual development and they wants to organize the curriculum according to the needs and interest of learners, there are fundamental differences in this approach and the subject-centred design. This movement from the traditional curriculum towards a programme that stresses the interests and needs of students, This approach was used by Rousseau in the education of *Emile*, then Dewey in his laboratory School in 1896-1904. it is believed that all of these twentieth-century efforts reflect, the influence of Dewey.

It is a fundamental principle of education that the beginning of each instruction it shall be connected with the previous experience of learners. The purpose is that the experience and the capacities that have been developed in early lessons, it should provide a starting point for further learning. The current importance given to student-centred programmes may not always acknowledge the Dewey's philosophy and influence on the movement to incorporate more student-serving learning opportunities into the curriculum.

The association for the Advancement of Progressive Education formed in 1919, had its aim "The development of the individual, based upon the scientific study of his mental, physical, spiritual, and social characteristics and needs". The views of this association, later called the Progressive Education Association (PEA), were compatible with the ideas of Dewey's as indicated by their principles:

- Freedom to develop naturally.
- Interest is the motive of all work.
- The teacher is a guide, not a task-master.
- Scientific study of pupil development.
- Greater attention to all that affects the child's physical development.
- Co-operation between school and home to meet the needs of child-life.
- The progressive school a leader in educational movement.

The aim of using the learner-centred curriculum on the part of curriculum planners to interpret the needs and interests design as one based on common needs and interests of learners rather than on those of the particular population to be served. Reflected in curriculum plans, this interpretation could and sometimes did, become the rationale for teaching. Research on learner centred curriculum in recent years made it possible for curriculum planners to develop a better learner-centred curriculum. Modern learning theories and dissatisfaction of students and parents from the old curriculum are moving curriculum and instruction toward a design that focus on real student needs and interests.

Characteristics

The curriculum design on the needs and interests of student has these characteristic and features.

- The curriculum plan is based on knowledge of learner's needs and interests in general and diagnosis the specific needs and interests of the population served by the plan.
- The curriculum plan is flexible, to accept new modification to conform to the needs and interests of particular learner's. In fact, in some curriculum designs the learner may develop his or her own curriculum plan with the guidance of a teacher.
- The learner is consulted and tutored individually at difficult points in the curriculum and instructional process.

Learner centered approach is an example of the applications of needs and interests (activities) approach. Subject obstacles were lowered or removed as teachers combined subjects to study social problems identified by students. Students in the experimental schools were more successful in college. This practice has ever lasting effect on secondary education.

Applications of learner Centred Curriculum:

If the learning opportunities are not based on the needs and interests of the learners then there is no assurance that the learners well equipped with the skills to participate effectively in social activities; students as adults and good citizens. Therefore we see that the needs and interests design as especially appropriate for the personal development, but not for the social competence domain. The most common approach to meet the needs and interests of learners is the grouping of students for special programmes believed by the planners to match the needs and interests of the students concerned.

The major use of the needs and interests design in curriculum planning is in the provision of options for individual students. For example, the middle schools provide many special interests activate, exploratory courses and other experiences aimed at giving each student opportunities to explore his own interest.

Currently the movement in higher education and expansion of it by "Open University" arrangements illustrates the feature of the needs and interests design. Drunker (1969) argues for continuing education which assumes "that the more experience in life and work people have, the more eager they will be to learn and the more capable they will be of learning.

Curriculum plans emphasizing the option concept:

- The options are based on knowledge of learner characteristic.
- Scheduling and other arrangements facilitate, selection and choice of options, with counselling services available to help students.
- Students are actively involved in planning and evaluating the options in general and for themselves in particular.

Community Centred Curriculum

The Community-Centred Curriculum is meant to reach out beyond the classroom and into the community where the world can be changed by students and teachers. The curriculum is based on societal issues, and the goal of the curriculum is to explore and solve those issues. This is very much an activist model, where students are encouraged to be leading activists in their community where life problems, community affairs, and real-world problems exist. The foundation of the community centred curriculum is built on real-world problems, and the content is various social issues. In the community centred curriculum, students are agents of change seeking to make a difference in their community.

Characteristics of the Community-Centred Curriculum

The main Characteristics of the community centred curriculum is the group and group action. The community centred curriculum is a problem-solving curriculum, and these problems are to be solved through the participation and efforts of the whole group. Students work to find the social relevance of their efforts and how they can improve their citizenship by the projects they take on. The experiences that the students participate in the real world are alive, organic, real, and life changing. Students are consistently working to make the world a better place. "young people are at a formative, idealistic stage of their life, and they need to learn that they can and should make a difference in the world" (ellis, 74).

Teacher's role in the community-centred curriculum

In the community centred curriculum teachers have a very important role. They serve as facilitator: organizing group efforts, showing students that they are in this together, that they need each other, and that they have to have a group to do this. Some often question why this role is so important. We need to realize that children are not born with all the necessary social skills to work together as a group. Therefore, the teacher helps children develop their social skills and create a climate for collaboration and team building. These skills and this environment are essential for success within the community centred curriculum. The teacher is responsible for turning their class into a problem-solving unit. They help their unit solve their community based problems by planning and coordinating trips into the community. They are also responsible for making connections with community members who will further help the students with their projects. Since teamwork is such a large part of this curriculum, teachers often work with teachers throughout the school in order to help students achieve their goals.

Student's role in the community-centred curriculum

The students' role in the community centred curriculum is perhaps the most important. They do not sit at their desk with textbooks doing never ending class work. Students are responsible for being aware of the world around them and the issues that impact their life. It is from these life issues and problems that the community centred curriculum is developed. Students' goal is to leave the world a better place than they found it through group efforts. The *esprit de corps* (the common spirit) is a focal point of the curriculum and developed as the students work together in group projects. Students are to engage in the culture and become involved in the community that lies beyond their school and to make a difference in that community. Participation if the true key of the community centred curriculum, and students must work together if they wish to succeed. Students start their learning process with a driving question. They then take this question and explore it through inquiry using applied knowledge. Students then engage with their peers, teachers, and community members in collaborative activities. The students' project learning can be scaffold by various supports including technology. Finally, students create tangible projects that will address their driving question.

Learning environment of the community-centred curriculum

The community centred curriculum requires a classroom like any other school. Students come together to discuss community issues and decide where their course of study should go. Therefore, the classrooms and schools that participate in the community centred curriculum are like a democracy. Students make many of the key decisions. While there are the traditional grade levels based mostly on age, cross-grade level activities are very common place. Students must work together to solve particular issues, and sometimes that requires other grade levels. Since the community centred curriculum focuses on the real world, the real world is the community centred curriculum's learning laboratory. Students spend much of their time outside of the classroom and school, and in the community investigating. The community centred curriculum has integrated studies where students and teachers work backwards from the problem, trying to find out how they can be of help.

Assessments in the community-centred curriculum

Assessments in the community centred curriculum usually focus around the students' efforts and outcomes. In the community centred curriculum students are working to solve problems within their community, and part of their assessment focuses on the outcomes of their efforts to solve the problem. Therefore, students are also assessed on their ability to apply their knowledge and skills when trying to solve the particular problem at hand. The community centred curriculum also allows for students to develop their citizenship and leadership abilities, as well as fostering their social growth. A group reflection takes place after a project has been completed where students can get together and share any and all thoughts about the project and what the next steps should be. Types of community centred curriculum assessment include: written work, observations, presentations, informal discussions and questions, project designs, and final products. Teachers are not the only ones involved in the assessment process, students and peers are also actively involved. Students are given the chance to create their own rubric which the teacher can use to assess their learning.

Advantages of a Community-Centred Curriculum

- **Increases students awareness of social issues and current events:** One of the benefits of the community-centred curriculum is that social issues are the foundation of the curriculum. Instead of spending their day at a desk reading textbooks and doing seatwork, students are called to participate in real world activities.

The focus of the curriculum is on real life problems that are occurring in the classroom, the local community and around the world.

- **Fosters positive social interactions:** In the community centred curriculum, students are constantly interacting with one another, and team building, collaborative effort, and cooperative learning are all a large part of the school experience. Group projects dominate the curriculum, which requires frequent collaboration and fosters the social skills that are necessary for participation in a group. The principles of democracy, participation and citizenship are stressed.

Social Re-constructionist Curriculum

Social Re-constructionist are interested in the relationship between curriculum and the social, political and economic development of society. Social Re-constructionist are convinced that education can effect social change, citing, for example, literacy campaigns that have contributed to successful political revolutions.

Aspects of re-constructionism appeared in American curriculum thought in the 1920s and 1930s. Harold Rugg was concerned about the values for which the school should work. He tried to awaken his peers to the "lag" between the curriculum, a " lazy giant" and the culture, with its fast-paced change and resultant staggering social dislocations. Rugg's textbooks, teaching and professional leadership had one overriding quality- the spirit of social criticism. He wanted learners to use newly emerging concepts from social sciences and aesthetics to identify and solve current problems.

In early 1950s, the late Theodore Brameld outlined the distinctive features of social reconstructionism: First, he believed in a commitment to building a new culture. Brameld was infused with the conviction that people are in the midst of a revolutionary period from which the common people will emerge as controllers of the industrial system, public services, and of cultural and natural resources.

Second, Brameld felt that the working people should control all principal institutions and resources if the world is to become genuinely democratic. Teachers should ally themselves with the organised working people. A way should be found to enlist the majority of people of all races and religions into a great democratic body with power to enforce its policies. Third Brameld believed that the school should help the individual, not only to develop socially, but to learn how to participate in social planning as well. There are many premises of social reconstruction and the different directions taken by different social re-constructionist such as revolution, critical inquiry, and futurism. A distinction is also made between a curriculum of reconstruction, which attempts to change the social order, and a curriculum of social adaptation, which helps students fit into a world they never made.

Purpose of the social Re-constructionist curriculum

The primary purpose of the social Re-constructionist curriculum is to confront the learner with the many severe problems that humankind faces. Social Re-constructionist believe that these problems are not the exclusive concern of 'Social studies, but of every discipline, including economics, aesthetics, chemistry and mathematics. Now it is a critical period where the crisis is universal, and the widespread nature of the crisis must be emphasized in the curriculum.

The social Re-constructionist curriculum has no universal objectives and content. For example, the first year of such a curriculum might be devoted to formulating goals for political and economic reconstruction. Activities related to this objective might include the following:

- A critical survey of the community (for example , one might collect information on local patterns of savings and expenditures)
- A study relating the local economy to national and worldwide situations
- A study treating the influence of historic causes and trends on the local economic situations
- An examinations of political practices in relation to economic factors
- A consideration of proposals for change in political practices
- A determination of which proposals satisfies the needs of the most people

Objectives in later years of the curriculum might include the identification of problems, methods, needs, and goals in science and art; the evaluation in the relationship between education and human relations; and the identification of aggressive strategies for effective change.

Role of the Teacher

Teachers must relate national, world and local purposes to the students' goals. Students thus use their interests to help find solutions to the social problems emphasized in their classes. If a community wants to encourage participation of different ethnic groups in public meetings, for example , a foreign language class could help facilitate this participation by interpreting. Such a Programme provides an opportunity for students to use their special skills and interests to promote community goals in discussion groups, general assemblies, and other local organizations.

The teacher stresses cooperation with the community and its resources. For e.g. Students may spend time away from the school participating in community health projects (for science classes) or in community acting, writing or dance programs (for arts and literature classes). Even the arts must be integrated with other concerns in the programme. The interconnection between arts & science and arts & economics, for e.g., might be strengthened as the arts students looks at art in home and city planning, contrasts unhealthy communities with "ideal garden cities" and attempts to see the desire for business profits affects the quality of life.

Also, as a resource person and catalyst, the teacher seeks opportunities for youth to work as equals with adults in social projects and political activities. For e.g. the school project like channels funds to students who, with adults, make grants to deserving neighbourhood undertaking such as attempting to clean up surroundings and serving meals to homeless children. However, more than encouraging social service, the teacher should challenge the beliefs of students and develop their critical consciousness.

Social re-constructionist hold that all teachers are political persons who must choose either to serve whoever is in power (Conservatives) or present options to those in power (Social re-constructionist). This is not to say that the teacher neglects course content simply to politicize students but that students learn to recognize that content is never neutral and it is in the favour of community.

Basis for selecting learning opportunities

For the social Re-constructionist a learning opportunity must fulfil three criteria:

- It must be real
- It must require action
- It must teach values

Learners must focus on an aspect of the community which they believe they can change and to which they will devote their efforts. Passive study, simulations and role playing do not meet this criterion. Learners must have the opportunity to recognize the real importance of what they are to do. Learners must act on an issue or problem, not merely study it. Responsible action on matter of public concern may include working with community groups, informing people about social problems, and taking a stand on controversial issues. Learners must form a coherent system of values.

Organisation

A social Re-constructionist organizes learning activities around such questions like:

- Can the ordinary human being fulfil his or her own capabilities in the face of depersonalised forces?
- Can neighbourhoods learn to work together to solve their own problems?
- Can the economic and political establishments be rebuilt so that people everywhere have access to environmental and cultural resources?

Instructional sequence typically follows these stages

- Stage 1: Identifying issues that appear most problematic.
- Stage 2: Examining the realities of the student's lives, including constraints and root causes of their problems.
- Stage 3: Linking issues to institutions and structures in the larger society.
- Stage 4: Relating social analysis to the visions and ideals students have for their world, community and themselves and
- Stage 5: Taking some responsibility (action) for putting the realities more in accordance with the ideal.

Evaluation

Evaluation covers a broad spectrum of students' abilities-articulation of issues, generation of possible solutions, redefinition of their world views, willingness to take action toward an ideal. Students are expected also to evaluate their own learning and to reflect as group about the actions they have taken. Social Re0constructionist are also interested in the effect of the curriculum upon the community. Factors to be weighed include the growth of community consensus, increased political power of the working class, and an improved quality of life.

Model Questions

1. Give the different perspective for categorisation of curriculum.

2. Explain two main characteristics of subject centred curriculum.
3. Explain the criticisms about the subject centred curriculum.
4. What is the main focus of community centred curriculum? Discuss.
5. What are the teacher's roles in the Society-Centred Curriculum?
6. Explain Social Re-constructionist curriculum with reference to Characteristics, students role and purpose.
7. Differentiate the subject centred curriculum and learner centred curriculum.
8. Write down the principles of learner centred curriculum according to PEA (Progressive Education Association).
9. What is the main focus of community centred curriculum? Discuss.
10. What are the teacher's roles in the Society-Centred Curriculum? Discuss.

References

Bob Moon and Patricia Murphy (Ed) (1999); Curriculum in Context; Paul Chapman

http://blog.saffronart.com/2012/07/31/intothefutureartseducationinindia/

http://portal.unesco.org/culture/en/files/27030/11164964493artisticeducweb.p df/artisticeducweb.pdf

http://www.indiaifa.org/programmes/kalikalisu.html

http://www.ncert.nic.in/departments/nie/deaa/publication/Print/pdf/1.pdf

http://www.ncert.nic.in/html/pdf/ncf_qna.pdf

http://www.ncert.nic.in/new_ncert/ncert/rightside/links/pdf/focus_group/Indian_Languages.pdf

NCERT, (1988), *Guidelines and Syllabi for Secondary Stage (Class IX, X),* New Delhi: NCERT. Publishing, London

Tanner, D., and Tanner, L. (1995).*Curriculum Development: Theory into Practice* (3rd ed.). Englewood Cliffs, NJ: Merrill

Tyler, R. W. (1949) *Basic Principles of Curriculum and Instruction*. Chicago:

UNESCO (1996) *Learning: the treasure within*. Paris: UNESCO.

University of Chicago Press.

www.coreknowledge.org/curriculum/

www.jstor.org/stable/1492888

Chapter - 4

Philosophical Basis of Curriculum

Introduction

Curriculum as a field of study is relatively young. Most place its birth during the second or third decade of this century, often with the publication of Franklin Bobbitt's. In 1918, Denver superintendent Jesse Newlon's suggested use of teachers in curriculum development. It is important to note that the study of curriculum did not begin as an addition to an extant field, say as a subfield of psychology or philosophy. Rather, it began in administrative convenience: professional responsibility for curricular matters. They came from every academic background imaginable. This means different kinds of thinking from the scientific to the artistic have emerged in the curriculum field.

Curriculum as a field includes curriculum theory, development, implementation (that is, instruction), and evaluation. Traditional, conceptual-empiricist, and reconceptualists are theoretical frameworks that govern specific approaches to curriculum issues. Each of these frameworks can be characterized by the dominant and subordinate assumptions that govern the knowledge and values which underline their respective modes of inquiry.

Traditionalists

- Educational philosophy (Pernalism and Essentialism)
- General Philosophy (Idealism and Realism)
- Educational Psychology (Behaviorism)

History

The field of curriculum studies began in the early 1920's, and grew out of the necessity and need to define, organize and implement the public school curriculum. The early field of curriculum was dominated by administrative notions, and curriculum was viewed as the organization of time and activities to be managed according to sound business principles. The idea of "scientific management" as articulated by Frederick W. Taylor was applied to schooling. Cubberly articulated this concisely when he described schools as "factories in which the raw products (children) are shaped and moulded into products to meet the various demands of life". The important Traditionalists are Ralph Tyler and Hilda Taba.

The classical ideals of education, that is, the cultivation of intelligence and sensitivity, were no longer central. The goals of the curriculum had to be specified, making behavioural objectives and observable and measurable outcomes necessary. It has been suggested that it was after superintendent Newlon's work in curriculum revision, in the early 1920s in Denver, that the need for curriculum specialist became clear. Newlon, school administrator, asked teachers who demonstrated an interest in curriculum and its development to leave classroom teaching and enter an administrative office from which they would attend fulltime to matters curriculum. There were no departments of curriculum in colleges of education in the 1920s; Newlon and other administrators could go nowhere else but to the classroom for curriculum personnel. The programs of the Association for Supervision and Curriculum Development (ASCD) annual meetings indicate a considerable and growing presence of school personnel.

Philosophical Basis

Traditionalists are mentally disciplinarians, espousing the belief that if you exercise the mind like any muscle it will get stronger. They encourage rigorous mental involvement to strengthen the mind, and traditionalist theory is based on perinnialist and essentialist philosophies, outgrowths of realism and idealism. Perennialism is one of the earliest educational philosophies, where reality is a world of reason and God, truth is in reason and revelation, and goodness is in rationality. Schools exist to reveal God's will, and the instructional objective is to educate the rationale person and to cultivate the intellect. For essentialism, reality is the world of intellect, truth is in consistency of ideas, and goodness is in rationality. School's exist to sharpen the mind and intellectual processes. The instructional objective is to promote the intellectual growth of the individual. The major difference between essentialism and perennialism is that essentialism calls for core courses. Education is constant, absolute and universal, therefore the same curriculum should be for everybody.

- Theory, in the traditionalist point of view, is not essential to the improvement of practice. "Curriculum development is a practical enterprise not a theoretical study" (Tyler). For traditionalists, curriculum is defined as what will be taught in schools; the content; the subject matter.
- The work of most curriculists who are in this campaign continues to make use of the "conventional wisdom" of the field, summarized by the work of Ralph Tylor (Rational Model). Ralph Tyler, well-known for formalizing traditionalist ideology and very influential in the field, exemplify four phases that he put forth as fundamental to curriculum development: (a) The identification of educational objectives (b) The selection of learning experiences (c) The organization of learning experiences (d) The evaluation of the educational program.
- Traditionalists tend to be involved in structural theorizing that focuses on identifying key elements in the curriculum (Educational objectives, Learning experiences, Instruction practice, and Evaluation) and determining their relationships. Such theorizing centres on the decision and decision makers involved in curriculum planting. Those who focus on curriculum development and curriculum planning emphasize rationality and logic.
- As structural theorists, some traditionalists believe that educational practice is not an art but rather, extensively, a science, or at least a scientific approach. They assume that the key element occurring in the educational process can be identified, described and to some extent controlled. Frances Klein believes that these traditionalists, when considering curricula, believe in a scientific, technological and rational process. They presume that curricula can be created by taking a behaviouristic, reductionalistic process (step by step process). They also maintain that it is possible to create curricula prior to its employment within the classroom. Therefore, educational objectives, learning experiences, and instructional practices can be preplanned; moreover, teachers can be trained to present such curricula efficiently and effectively.
- Curriculum change is measured by comparing resulting behaviours with original objectives. Accepting the curriculum structure as it

is and working to improve it is compared to adjusting an automobile engine part in order to make it function more effectively.

- What makes this work one territory is its fundamental interest in working with school people, with revising the curricula of schools Relatively speaking, there exists a close relationship between traditional curricularists and school personnel. But this closeness has prevented them from creating new ways of thinking and talking about curriculum that could result in more productive educational programs.
- The reason for curriculum writing or curriculum work generally is captured in the phrase "service to practitioners". Traditional writing tends to be journalistic in order that it can be readily accessible to a readership seeking quick answers to pressing, practical problems. Traditionalist writing tends to give practical, useable advice to practitioners on current school concerns, curriculum writing tends to have school teachers in mind. In short, traditionalists' curriculum work is focused on the schools.
- Curriculum work tends to be field based. The first curricularists were former school teachers, and school service of some sort is overwhelmingly viewed as a prerequisite to entering the field. Traditionalists' allegiance is to school practitioners, and they have an explicit thematic focus on the current issues of schooling. Curricularists are former school people whose intellectual and sub cultural ties tend to be with people practitioners. Many traditionalists tend to be former school people, and they tend to remain loyal - intellectually and culturally - to their former colleagues. They tend to be less interested in basic research, in theory development, in related developments in allied fields than in a set of perceived realities of classrooms and school settings generally (They were practitioners not Theorist).
- Traditionalists have tended to be concerned about principles guiding curriculum development and implementation. The term theory has been employed to indicate that such principles are abstraction from actual experience of practitioners. In a social scientific sense of the term, or in the sense it is used in the humanities, traditionalists have not been theoretical. In their books they have focused on school people. Although some traditionalists would maintain that theoretical considerations and research findings may be employed with discretion (the ability to decide what is most suitable to be done).

- Traditionalists view curriculum as a plan, and stress those procedures required for creating such plan. They are concerned with the essential role of the key curriculum players, i.e. teachers' developers, and the bases for selecting, organizing and sequencing of curriculum content, some traditionalists define curriculum as "the content subject matter, or what is to be taught and learned." Buswell, for example, defines curriculum as "whatever content is used." Other traditionalists have described curriculum as a "written document and the "ground which pupils and teacher cover to reach the goal or objective of education." According to these traditionalists, curriculum is what students should be taught at schools, i.e. the content, which is identified with certain subject matters-the cumulative tradition of organized knowledge.
- Identifying curriculum as content assumes that: (a) There is no distinction between a subject and curriculum. (b) There is a clear distinction between instruction and curriculum. Whereas curriculum is the content (the what), and instruction is the process (the how), traditional educators have maintained that, if one knows a subject well, then one can teach it well.
- While traditionalists' orientation to curriculum emphasizes the role of organized subject matter there is among these traditionalists and school practitioners some consideration of new ways of organizing curricula. Some traditionalists such as John Dewey (progressivism), Ralph Taylor, Helda Taba and George Beauchamp integrated core curricula, science, technology, and society, and they exemplify this way of conceptualizing and theorizing about curriculum.
- Traditionalists agree that issues about teaching methods and "the hidden curriculum" are relevant to what children learn at schools, but believe that these issues are not questions about the curriculum (They separate between Curriculum and Instruction. curriculum is the content and the Instruction is the Process).

Points of Contention

- According to Beauchamp, traditionalists lack underlying and explicit structures, ideas and assumptions about learning and schooling, and greater ideological links to society at large.
- Early curricularists were so enmeshed in school activities and the queries of the teachers that they were not afforded the critical distance necessary to theorize about the purposes and impact of the curriculum (Pinar, 1978).

- Critics such as Pinar say traditionalists have a "technician's mentality", accepting the curriculum structure as it is and only working within it to improve it.
- Emphasis is on what information is taught to students, not how it is taught.
- Social and emotional needs, interests and experiences (background) of the students are not considered in curriculum planning.
- They view curriculum as a plan that consists of : Educational objectives, curriculum, instruction, learning experiences, and evaluation.
- Educational Objectives: it should be determined prior to the instruction, achievable, and measurable.
- Curriculum: Content, Subject matter
- Subject Matter: General Curriculum (1) Learning Experiences - Improve Students Skilled in different Subjects (2) Culture - Through generation.
- Instruction is putting the plan in action.
- The Subject matter is important than instruction: what is to be taught is more important than how to teach it, the teacher who is strong in his subject matter could teach it better.
- Evaluation: teacher is responsible about the evaluation, student is not involved, and it measures how much is the objectives are achieved.
- Psychological basis is essentialism and perinallism: Learning Experiences: 1) Building skills and 2) Knowledge (Culture heritage)

Applications:

- Traditionalists spend more time preparing teacher to be strong in their subject matters.
- Teachers have minimal involvement in the curriculum development process.
- Role of Teacher: Viewed as an authority and an expert; plans activities; supplies knowledge to students.
- Teaching strategies: Interpret, tell, drill; lecture, discussion. Socratic method.
- Homogeneous grouping.
- Content is predetermined by authorities outside of the school; therefore, it would be easier for governments, especially centralized ones, to control curriculum content.

- Emphasis is on what knowledge is to be taught to students at schools, not on how it is taught.
- Curriculum focus: Disciplinary subjects, literary analysis, doctrine, eternal truths. Essential skills and essential subjects (3 it's, science, history, foreign languages).
- Curriculum trends: "Back to the Basics", raising "national standards", competency testing, excellence in education.
- Students' needs and interests and their social experiences are not considered when planning curriculum.
- Role of student: Receive, memorize.

Conceptual-empiricists

- Educational philosophy (Progressivism)
- General Philosophy (Pragmatism)
- Educational Psychology (More Cognitivism, Behaviorism)

History

After World War II the country experienced a knowledge explosion. Technology developed during war, and then was applied to domestic life. The development of the Cold War and world ideological conflicts fostered the need for greater technology. The launch of the Russian satellite Sputnik in 1957 also launched the field of curriculum in a new direction. The National Defence Education Act set aside money for teacher training programs, science development, etc. Great efforts were made to update and upgrade the curriculum. The result was the development of a research-based, scientific approach to curriculum, allied with natural science. The important Conceptual Empricists are Joseph Schwab, George Beauchamp, and Decker Walker

Philosophical Basis

Conceptual-empiricism is based on experimentalism and progressivism, two closely related philosophies stemming from pragmatism. In experimentalism, reality is a world of experience, truth is what works, what is, and goodness is the public test. For progressivism, reality is what is experienced, truth is what presently functions, and what is perceived as good changes according to situational needs. Schools exist to discover and expand the society we live in, and the instructional objective is to promote democratic living.

- Conceptual-empiricists apply scientific methods to educational research. Curricularists who are in this campaign are often researchers and/or measurement oriented, and views their primary mission as engaging in research that will be theory producing. Results of research function to serve school practitioners in content and instruction, but traditionally, an exerted effort has not been made to make school practitioners a part of the research team itself.
- Conceptual empiricists' work can be so characterized by their employing of the two terms "conceptual" and "empirical" in the sense scientists typically employ them. This work is concerned with developing hypotheses to be tested and testing them in methodological ways of techniques and criteria of the main stream of social science. Moreover, this work is reported, ordinarily at the meetings of The American Educational Research Association (AERA).
- Conceptual empiricists' view is a social scientific one, which is dependent upon setting: hypotheses, collecting data, and interpretation. This group argues that scientific knowledge of human behavior, including the curriculum is possible through research. They claim that the research and the resulting theory are of practical value, because they enable school practitioners to articulate reasons for their actions, and this, in turn, increases the likelihood that they will realize the traditional goals of the school.
- Their primary identity is with the cognitive field. Such individuals view themselves as primarily psychologists, philosophers or sociologists with research interests in schools and education-related matters. People in this camp such as Bloom, Bruner and Posner are actively looking into application of cognitive science to curriculum and instructional research, as well as to cognition and learning to guide the arrangement of curriculum content and its delivery in the classroom.
- They focus on content even more than traditionalists because curriculum experts are specialists in the fields, such as physicists, chemicists, etc.
- Conceptual empiricists are involved in substantive theorizing which aims at highlighting and identifying an appropriate curriculum content. They analyze current situations and suggest alternatives to current patterns of content and experiences included

in most curricula. Moreover, they question: what teachers are teaching, why they have arranged the school content in the ways they have, and what influence they have on learners.

- Most conceptual empiricists emphasize content-based theories. A well known content-based theory is the structure of disciplines. This theory states that knowledge can be structured according to its key concepts, then these concepts can be organized in a manner that reveals major relationships among them. Therefore, They develop large curriculum packages based on the theory that each discipline has a structure, and the best way to learn a discipline is to learn and understand its structure. Conceptual empiricists believe that in a curriculum so organized, students could easily grasp the conceptual basis of knowledge resulting in a more detailed understanding (From whole to part).
- For conceptual-empiricists, teaching should focus on a discipline's structure and its proof process , that is, it's method of investigation. As the traditionalists, conceptual-empiricists use behavioural objectives, but they also develop extensive teacher's manuals to guide instruction.

Points of contention

- According to Tyler, a major weakness of conceptual-empiricists is their failure to work extensively with school teachers to understand the specific problems they were facing with the curricula or to consider their ideas for improvements.
- A curriculum designed with rigid instructional methodology (a.k.a. teacher-proof) is rejected by creative, intellectual teachers who feel insulted by the assumptions of the curricularists about their teaching ability and personal dedication to the field.
- When students fail to learn, the fault lies with the students themselves rather than with the manner by which the content was organized or with teaching methods.
- Pinar faults conceptual-empiricists in that they view education not as a discipline itself, but an area to be studied by the disciplines.
- Curricularists are trained in specific disciplines and often ignorant of the history of the field of curriculum. Many had no experience in classroom teaching.
- It has to have a theory for curriculum
- Every knowledge has its own structure.

- Every knowledge has basic concepts. There is a relation between these concepts. These relationships are governed by roles.
- Curriculum is not predetermined as in traditionalists but depends on scientific research for (learner, society, and knowledge)

Applications

- Extensive research can be done so that various disciplines can be organized and presented in ways that make it easily understood by the learners.
- Curriculum focus: based on student interests and experiences, involves application of human problems and affairs; organization of disciplines; knowledge that is worth knowing is based on empirical research
- Large curriculum packages are developed, because of the belief that every discipline has its own structure of concepts, relationships, and rules, and that the best way to learn the discipline is to learn the structure (Whole to part).
- The ultimate goal is to structure the content so those learners will learn better. The problem is, if students fail to learn, it becomes their fault, not the teacher's, the methods used or the content.
- Role of student: active participation, contributes
- Specialists from outside the field of education are consulted and play essential roles in developing school curricula.
- Role of teacher: Consultant, guide for problem solving and scientific inquiry
- Teaching strategies: Problem-solving, project method, focus on active and interesting learning; structure of discipline guides instruction.

Reconceptualists

- Educational philosophy (Reconstruction)
- General Philosophy (Existentialism)
- Educational Psychology (More Humanistic, Pragmatic)

History

Reconceptualism in a sense has two agendas. The first focuses on human concerns, emphasizing the psychological and social development of the human being. A basic premise is, the more the students understand themselves, the more they will understand the world. The second focus is on society, as the development of reconceptualism began in the late 60's and continued into the early 80's when free speech, personal rights and other social issues such as emancipation and freedom from power structures were the focus of society. The important Reconceptualists are William Pinar, Henry Giroux and Michael Apple.

In the seventies there was a great deal of controversy over the issue of whether or not the curriculum field is being revitalized through the development of a new movement in the field of curriculum studies. Pinar argues strongly that a new movement is indeed visible in the field. Some have termed it "reconceptualization" others "the new curriculum theory". The question what is this reconceptualization? The answer, to a considerable extent, the reconceptualization is a reaction to what the field has been and what it is seen to be at the present time.

A reconceptualist tends to see research as an inescapably political as well as intellectual act. As such, it works to suppress or to liberate not only those who conduct the research and those upon whom it is conducted but as well those outside the academic subculture. This political emphasis distinguishes the work of reconceptualists from the work of traditionalists and conceptual-empiricists. Curriculum development is political connected with a view of history and the contemporary social order. Reconceptualists have no organized group such as ASCD or AERA. Individuals at work, while sharing certain themes and motives, do not tend to share any common interpersonal affiliation.

Philosophical basis

Reconceptualism is based on existentialist and reconstructionist philosophies. Reconceptualists' principles are grounded in existentialism philosophy and humanistic psychology. Therefore, they tend to be trained in the humanities, and they developed in the late 60's and the beginning of 70's as a reaction to the conceptual empiricists who were so scientific, technological and behavioristic. In existentialism, reality is a world of existing, truth is personal choice, and goodness is freedom. Learning is highly personal and unique for each individual. Students need to learn how to process their experiences and get meaning from them, in order to control and improve their lives. Reconstructionists are concerned with the relationship between school and society. Their effort is on using schools as a mechanism to reconstruct society. Schools exist to aid children in knowing themselves and their place in society, and the instructional objective is to improve and reconstruct society. Education for change and social reform.

- Reconceptualists are focusing on a critique of the field, which they believe is too involved in practical issues, and is too technologically oriented. Curricculists who are in this campaign maintain the view that intellectual and scientific distance from the curriculum practice are required, and they actively critique and theorize existing programs. According to their view, theory does not drive practice, theorizing is done to support practice.
- While conceptual-empiricists make the curriculum so technologically focused, reconceptualist focus on emotional and social development (affective aspect). They believe that the more the students understand themselves, the more they will understand the world around them and the different aspects of their life.
- Pinar describes the work of reconceptualists as the development of an emancipatory discipline of curriculum. Curriculum research must emancipate the researchers themselves if the curriculum is expected to emancipate the students and teachers.
- Curricularists must be free themselves from assumptions in the field before they can develop curricula which can free students and teachers and improve education. An underlying assumption was that schools should not teach children what to learn, but they must teach them how so the students can choose what for themselves.
- James Macdonald coined the term "reconceptualist" when he said that empiricists were too concerned with logic and rational approaches, and that they needed to reconceptualize their approach to curriculum development. According to the reconceptualists' orientation, curriculum development should move from organizing content-based curricula (Traditional) and structuring disciplines (Conceptual empiricist) to focus on the development of the individual person. Therefore, social issues such as self freedom, collective freedom, civil rights, equality of life and others influence curriculum development, and liberation, which comes from within the person as described in existentialism philosophy, is a key concept in the reconceptualists' curriculum. They view research and theorizing as an inescapably political as well as intellectual activity.
- Learning is highly personal and unique to each individual. Students need to learn how to process their experiences, get meaning from the experience and therefore control their lives. Macdonald and

Pinar recommended a method of self-analysis by which learners can study their responses to life and therefore to educational situations. The recommended method for self-analysis includes: (a) Recalling and describing the past and then analyzing how it relates to the present. (b) Describing one's imagined future and determining its relation to the present. (c) Relating personal analysis of experiences to cultural and political contexts.

- Paulo Freire is a reconceptualist who influenced curricularists in his questioning of the educational power structure. He asks questions such as, Who controls the curriculum and the school? What are their goals? Who determines/controls the knowledge learned in schools? Who creates the criteria that will determine success? What options do we have for students? Are we addressing the needs of students?
- Reconceptualists are influenced by critical theory, based on Marxism and Neo-Marxism which contends that education should give less advantaged people the skills to look at their situations and take steps to change the system. According to these Marxism-Oriented theorists, people are poor or disadvantaged, because wealthy people control the system of society. Some reconceptualists draw a critical theory, which is based on Marxism and Neo-Marxism theory. According to this theory: (a) Education should give people the skills they need to look at the social and political situations of their society, analyze them, and take steps to change the system. (b) People need to be organized socially so that they will have the power to create new worlds and societies. (c) Students should learn to realize what structures in the system support their standards of living, and what structures in the system oppress them. They also should learn how to analyze the social and political values of their society, and takes steps to improve it so that no one is discriminated against. Reconceptualists, who adopt these principles, like Harold Rugg, George Counts and others has FBI files, because they considered radical for their era that they want to stop discrimination against poor people and working class.
- Capitalism enslaves people; students learn to value rewards and obtain meaningless certificates, and grades, to the point that they are more interested in the document than in intelligence. Students, for instance, are more interested in passing tests than in gaining knowledge.
- Reconceptualist believe that students should be actively involved in the learning process. The aim of the curriculum is to develop modes

of criticism and social practices which free "individuals and social groups from the subjective and objective conditions that bind them to the forces of exploitation and oppression". Reconceptualists as critical theorists wish to use theory to enable curriculum developers to create programs that will free students from this form of existence. They want to reorganize the values included in the curriculum, and they believe that research is a political as well as intellectual act. The main aim, according to them, is to make students fully aware of themselves, and of the fact that society must be changed to allow both self-freedom and collective freedom.

Applications:

- Reconceptualists' view can be applied in any situation where the educational system does not consider students' needs and interests, and does not respect their intellectual abilities.
- Curriculum trends: Equality of education; cultural pluralism; international education; futurism.
- This view puts all people of the society in charge of the educational process, and gives all individuals the right to educate themselves in ways they believe appropriate to them, and meet their needs and interests.
- It emphasizes the development of dialogue skills, critical thinking skills, problem solving skills, decision making skills and personal values clarification through an appropriate curriculum content to students' needs and interests.
- It influences instructional theory, i.e.; teachers are responsible and should determine how to teach curriculum content so that these skills are developed. They are involved in curriculum planning and development.
- Teaching strategies: Emphasize problem solving, critical thinking, and decision making skills; process oriented, less focus on outcomes; heterogenous grouping and integration of students by ability; teacher and students plan activities; students learn on their own, independent from teacher; teacher-student dialogue, student initiates much of the discussion and activities.
- Role of teacher: Questions, assists student in personal journey; arousing personal responses; an agent of change and reform; helps students become aware of problems confronting humankind.

- According to the reconceptualists, curriculum content is less dictated by government and more determined by local school districts.
- Curriculum focus: Child-centered; emphasizes subject matter of art, ethics, philosophy; skills and subjects needed to identify and ameliorate problems of society; learning is active and concerned with contemporary and future society; emphasis on social sciences and social research methods; examination of social, economic and political problems; focus on present and future trends as well as national and international issues.
- Students are involved in deciding what they want to learn, and teachers as well as parents are part of the educational process.
- Role of student: Active, determines own rule.

Curriculum Development

The Development Philosophy: Curriculum development philosophy is based on the following resources: (1) Educational psychology (2) Educational philosophies (3) Society (4) Specialists in different areas - politics, economics, education, etc.

The Curriculum Development Process: The process of curriculum development requires two basic tasks. **First:** Curriculum considerations, which include the educational objectives, content, and learning and teaching experiences. **Second:** Instructional considerations, which include teaching methods and approaches (instruction, teachers, books and schools).

The curriculum development process should be continuous and serve these two considerations to make the educational system achieve high levels of success in students. In the end of each period from the curriculum used there should be a comprehensive evaluation proccss for curriculum and instructional considerations. The evaluation result should be as feedback for each component of curriculum and instruction.

The process of curriculum development in order to be completed needs specialists from different fields: Viz. Educational psychology, Economics, Technology, Politics, Sociology.

Curriculum Considerations

The process of educational development has to study the educational objectives in detail, so that the educational system in each country can achieve these objectives for its students. These educational objectives are derived from the educational and learning philosophy in that country. Also, these objectives should serve the learners' needs and their interests and should be consistent with technological development in the world.

The next step is to choose the suitable educational content to serve the educational objectives. The process for choosing this content needs specialists from different fields. Specialists are necessary because the content to be covered is from different disciplines (religion, thinking, social issues, economics, culture, technology and politics).

It should be considered that these educational objectives and content which are suitable and serve in specific time and place may be will not be equally suitable at other times and places. Also, the educational objectives which serve the educational philosophy in one country at one time may be will not be suitable for other countries and other times.

This process will be continued after choosing the content to identify the educational experience for each discipline. The process for identifying experiences should consider the following: (a) Some experiences should have practical and observable application functions. (b) These experiences should help the students develop the level of intellectual thinking. (c) These experiences should be able to serve the educational objectives as identified above. (d) The learning and teaching experiences should be well sequenced, i.e., the students cannot start working with a new concept until they mastered the prerequisite concepts.

The educational development process should consider the evaluation procedures. Curriculum developers should identify the suitable evaluation procedures which reflect a high level of validity and reliability.

Instructional Considerations:

The second consideration in the educational development process serves the instructional process, which include:

- **Teaching methods and approaches (instruction and procedures):** The educational development process should deal with and analyze the present method of teaching used in the classroom. Also, the development process should provide the teachers through the educational supervisors the new methods of teaching to be applicable during their teaching.
- **Textbook and instructional tools:** The educational development process serves to produce new textbooks which include the content its scope and sequence. The typing should be clear, and pictures and tables should be included to clarify the concepts for

students. The educational development process makes use of the instructional tools, such as television (educational programs), video and slide projector. These tools will make the instructional process more easily understandable for teachers and students. A team of specialists should provide these instructional tools.

- **Teachers:** The educational development process should consider teachers. The teachers should be specialists from different areas in order to provide the students with the most accurate knowledge and information. Also, continuous professional development opportunities should be provided to the teachers in order to help them become aware of new methods of teaching and new instructional tools. Professional development should also include topics in behaviour management to help teachers deal with student behaviours in positive and productive ways. Also, educational development process should serve the studying of teachers' situations and their salaries. That is, the teacher who comes from a long distance to reach the school where he or she works should be as motivated and energetic as the teacher who lives nearby. The teacher who has a low salary, maybe will not be psychologically relaxed, and this will affect his performance in the classroom. Also, the educational development process should serve the teachers' health situation by including them in the free comprehensive health insurance and retirement benefits.
- **Schools:** The educational development process should include maintenance of school facilities. That is, school buildings should be designed in modern ways and located in ideal places in the community. The classrooms should include adequate heating and circulation systems. Also, the classrooms should include movable desks and chairs to facilitate various methods of teaching (i.e., cooperative learning). In addition, the schools should include new libraries which contain different books in different areas to provide the students different knowledge. Also, the schools should have extracurricular facilities, such as sports fields, basketball courts, and a swimming pool. These activities will help students stay physically fit, which will enhance their mental growth. Also, the schools should have clean and healthy restrooms.

Evaluation:

After serving the curriculum and instructional considerations in the curriculum development process, there should be a comprehensive evaluation process. The people responsible for this final step are the same as those who took part in the curriculum development process (specialists in different fields). The evaluation results provide these people feedback so that they can restructure their educational philosophy to redevelop one or more of the components.

References

Butchvarov, P. (1970), The Concept of Knowledge, Evanston, Illinois: North Western University Press.

Chomsky, N (1986). Knowledge of Language; Prager, New York.

Datta, D. M. (1972) Six Ways of Knowing Calcutta University Press, Calcutta.

Dewey, John. The Child and the Curriculum, University of Chicago Press: Chicago.

Fry, H., Ketteridge, S. and Marshall, S. (1999) A handbook for teaching and learning in Higher Education: enhancing academic practice, Kogan Page, London.

G.W. Ford and Lawrence Pungo, (1964); The Structure of Knowledge and the Curriculum Rand McNally and Company, Chicago.

https://www.mutah.edu.jo/userhomepages/drmajali/t1.html

Joseph Schwab, (1969). The Practical: A language for Curriculum. School Review, November.

Keddie, N. (1971): Classroom Knowledge, in. M.F.D Young.

Kelley, A. B. (1996). The Curricular Theory and Practice; Harper and Row, U. S.

Kumar Krishna (1997). What is Worth Teaching, Orient Longman, New Delhi.

Margaret, K.T. The open Classroom, Orient Longman: New Delhi, 1999.

Nirantar (1997) Developing a Curriculum for Rural Women, Nirantar, New Delhi.

P.H. Phenix, (1964) Realms of Meaning. Mc. Graw-Hill, New York.

Padma M. Sarangapani (2003) Constructing School Knowledge; An Ethnography of learning in an Indian Village, Sage Publication Inc, New Delhi.

Paul Hirst: Knowledge and Curriculum.

Prema Clarke (2001). Teaching & Learning: The Culture of Pedagogy, Sage Publication, New Delhi.

Taba, Hilda (1962). Curriculum Development; Theory and Practice; Har Court, Brace and Wald New York.

Tyler, R.W. (1949). Basic Principles of Curriculum and Instruction; Chicago: University of Chicago Press.

Chapter - 5

Curriculum Determinants and Considerations

Introduction

Ever since the term curriculum was added to educators' vocabularies, it has seemed to convey many things to many people. To some, curriculum has denoted a specific course, while to others it has meant the entire educational environment. Whereas perceptions of the term may vary, it must be recognized that curriculum encompasses more than a simple definition. Curriculum is a key element in the educational process; its scope is extremely broad, and it touches virtually everyone who is involved with teaching and learning. Several factors determine curriculum development in the any countries situation which include student demands, societal expectations, commerce and industry as future employers, politicians, government expectations, technological advancement, among others.

The Curriculum is at the heart of the education process: it sets out what is to be learned, and how and when it is to be taught. It underpins all other parts of the system: it guides the day to day experiences of the classroom, it forms the basis for teacher training programmes, the content of textbooks and other materials, it determines how learning is assessed through the examinations systems, how standards are developed and how performance is monitored through school inspection and supervision systems. The curriculum is a major determinant of what graduates from the education system bring to the **world of work**. An education system's capacity to effectively contribute to national social and economic development is therefore shaped by the curriculum: are the right skills, competencies, knowledge and attitudes being developed to drive national progress?

Why do we embark on curriculum reform? The curriculum is rarely static, it undergoes regular and almost constant change, matching new policies and demands with new descriptions of what is taught and how. Periodically, countries may embark on a major reform, where the curriculum is felt to be outdated and out of line with emerging economic and social needs. Typically this will come in response to a shift in economic and labour market policy that point in a new direction; moving to a knowledge economy and becoming more competitive globally in an increasing technological world for example. It may also result from evidence that learning outcomes are low (though this may not be the fault of the curriculum), a political decision (on national language policy for example), or a major societal change (e.g. the Arab spring, or reconciliation after conflict).

Effective delivery of the curriculum relies on other parts of the system: a well-structured and relevant curriculum itself is no guarantee of the desired learning outcomes. Teachers require the appropriate skills, combined with other resources to enable effective learning. Curriculum reform needs to also to include reform of teaching and learning materials, re-orienting and preparing teachers, and changes to how learning is assessed.

Social-political-cultural-geographical-economic Diversity As A Determinant Of Curriculum Making

Educational policies are subject to influence from politicians and political groups. This is because education can be used to further political ideologies. This, in turn, influences power structures in the society. Any changes in policies or political ideologies influence the education system. **Special Interest Groups** was raised by the respondents that organisations such as religious bodies, non-governmental organisations (**NGOs**), professional organisations and trade unions have an interest in education. They pursue policies with the aim of improving the quality of curriculum content and implementation based on their ideologies. *The Catholic Commission of Peace and Justice* resisted the introduction of sex education on the grounds of violation of religious rights. **Parents Teachers Associations** contribute substantially to curriculum improvemcnt through monitoring procedures and providing instructional resources. The schools are the training ground of teachers colleges.

Society has its own expectations about the aims and objectives that should be considered when designing the curriculum. It also has a perception of what the product of the school system should look like. It is therefore necessary for curriculum designers to take into account these societal considerations. If this does not happen, the curriculum becomes irrelevant. The knowledge, skills, values and attitudes imparted to learners are expected to prepare them to fit in society. The issue of increasing access to school education in India has resulted in the opening up of several programmes like the District Primary Education Programme (DPEP), Sarva Siksha Abhiyan (SSA) and Rashtriya Madhymic Siksha Abhiyan (RMSA) over and above the opening of many schools. Emphasis has been laid on guidance and counselling in Teacher Education curriculum as a way of preparing teachers to cope with diverse behavioural disorders which have resulted from social problems.

Parents are regarded as an important component of the education system and have an input in curriculum development. Society expects that curriculum addresses its philosophies and its expectations for the future. **The State** has a moral responsibility to define the content and purposes of education. The Ministry of Human Resource Development (MHRD) has the authority that is backed by formal acts of parliament to determine the direction and constituents of the education process. The University grants Commission (UGC) assures quality of all programmes and gives direction of the curriculum. The National Assessment and Accreditation Council (NAAC)is there for accreditation purposes of all programmes offered in Higher Educational Institutions.

Membership to various **international organisations** has influenced curriculum reform. Membership to the Commonwealth, United Nations and its specialized agencies like UNESCO, UNICEF, and UNFPA, has led to the introduction of programmes such as HIV/AIDS Education, Environmental Science Education, Culture of Peace, Reproductive Health Education and Population Education, into the curriculum. As such, a number of universities have introduced degrees in Peace, among others. Where donors have had interest in certain areas of the curriculum, they have managed to influence government to institute curriculum reforms.

Curriculum development should be a participatory process in which all key stakeholders are involved. These stakeholders form panels and academic boards which approve all curriculum development before it is implemented.

Curriculum development is done to meet the needs of the **global village**. With **globalization** there has been increasing pressure on higher education institutions in the region to move towards the use of new Information and Communication Technologies (ICTs) to widen access to their programmes.

Higher education systems for many countries have been undergoing fundamental reforms, especially in recent years, to respond to the trend of globalization and to meet the ever changing expectations of the respective communities in their development into knowledge-based societies. Globalization has provided a rationale for restructuring the Higher Education systems worldwide, mainly to meet the need for a workforce that is equipped with not only the traditional discipline knowledge and skills, but also a broad range of generic capabilities. The restructuring has in fact resulted in a shift that emphasizes the idea that equips the students with "operational competence" for the world of work, and a trend that favours the discourses about privatization, marketization, commodification, managerialism and performativity.

At the **policy decision stage**, a formal request is made for the development of a new curriculum, revision of the existing curriculum or adaptation of the existing curriculum to address the special needs to be effected. Input from stakeholders such as industries, trainers and educationists is needed so that the knowledge, skills, attitudes and values included are marketable and match of the needs of industries and society.

It was noted that institutions of higher learning change their curricula in order to meet **government expectations**. Government's policy directives are a contributory factor for curriculum construction. Some institutions of higher learning are private by nature and government directives are given so that there are no wide gaps in the curricula offered. The government uses the ideological state apparatus in the formulation of educational policies at everywhere. Political influences include regulations that stem from the legitimate role of state and national political institutions. States have the authority to set minimum essentials of the curriculum.

In the light of the above discussion, we can conclude that curriculum development should be based mainly on the trends of globalization. Products of higher education should fit well in society and without the requisite skills and knowledge needed by the market, they will not survive. It is also important to base the curricula on the needs and expectations of the students. Curriculum designers should keep in mind that gone are the days when institutions of higher learning come and take what we offer but to say we offer what you want to take.

Economic Factors

Formal education is possible where production exceeds consumption. This may be the result of tremendous industrial development or favourable natural circumstances. This will depend upon the fertility of the soil, abundant mineral deposits and proper climate conditions for work. Such conditions provide men with leisure to pursue education. Where there is a subsistence economy, it is a far cry to afford time for formal schooling. This is the reason why poorer and undeveloped countries have a minimum education for their children while industrially advanced countries keep nearly all their children at school and for a longer time. Education is the result of economic development. It is true in all its aspects. The quality of education is also decided by economic development of the society. A poor country cannot provide for all its citizens costly educational facilities. It is applicable in the case of a family also. The type of education is also determined by the economic condition. The education needed by an agrarian and an industrialized communities/ countries will be different.

Industry and commerce also a major determinant of the curriculum. It what industry and commerce want that must be taught. If a student graduates without the requirements of industry and commerce he or she becomes a misfit, and thus jobless. Institutions of higher education certainly follow the demands of commerce and industry, otherwise they produce large numbers of loafers of the streets.

Like parents, employers have also an input in curriculum development because they know the curriculum that is marketable in the **world of work**. The demands placed on education by the knowledge-based economy are best encapsulated by the educational theorist, Abby Riddell (1996): "Changing trade patterns influence the productive possibilities of the economy and thereby the demand for education, the uses put to education, and the demands made on education for tailoring the workforce to those demands.

The geography of any particular place is often natural, which means that it is undefined by man. Man in this respect ought to behave in accordance with the geography and nature in particular. In this regard the education system cum school system is influenced by the geography of the particular region. By and large the geography of a particular area dictates the type of building and equipment, means and methods of transporting children to school, school going age of pupils among others. However, there are three major geographical aspects that influence the educational system directly. These are, **climatic conditions**, **population distribution** and **land configuration**.

In regard to **climatic conditions** they influence the system of education in terms of, content of education depend on the continental climate, for example, training of doctors in the tropics is likely to emphasize more on tropical disease like malaria. Extreme low temperatures in Continental Europe, affects accessibility to school by young children. Temperatures also affect the time at which schools can reasonably begin in the morning and when they end. In Norway, for example, the sun does not rise during winter until ten o'clock in the morning and often temperatures fall to negative 20 degrees. Thus in the Scandinavian countries there are no infant schools or early childhood education departments in some schools because of extreme temperatures. Climatic conditions also influence the education system in relation to time of vacations. In North America and many countries in Europe take school vacations during cold winter and others during hot summer. In hot climatic conditions especially experienced in arid and semi-arid areas, learning often takes place during morning hours when it is cool. When it is hot in the afternoon very little learning takes place due to excessive heat.

In regard to **population distribution**, which is often as a result of geographical influence also affects the educational system. Generally worldwide, population is either concentrated in the urban centres, or scattered in the country side. For example Australia has two systems of education, that is, one for the urban areas and the other for rural areas. In the urban areas there are well-equipped schools with adequately qualified teachers and administrative personnel. While in the rural areas, schools are small with one teacher for ten up to forty students. This is because farms are far from the nearest schools and daily attendance is difficult. Therefore the central government is responsible for their administration and financing. The government also provides the means and organization of correspondence, tuition and travelling teachers. As such most students receive education through correspondence and occasional visits by the travelling education inspectors.

In regard to **land configuration**, this also influences the education system in terms of architectural structure of farm houses, school buildings, village location and also the whole way of life and thinking of people because of the rigours of the climate, in some cases, because of closeness of family ties, boarding schools for children are non-existence, except for the few who come from far and inaccessible places on daily basis. By and large land configuration determines settlement and location of schools.

Socio-political Aspirations, Including Ideologies And Educational Vision

Philosophy influences every aspect of education namely the aim, content, method and discipline. It is philosophy which determines whether the aim of education should be intellectual, spiritual, liberal, aesthetic, moral or vocational. For example, the Hindu philosophy in ancient India resulted in the evolution of the *Gurukula* system of education. The militant philosophy ancient Sparta gave rise to the regimental system of education. The Nazism of Germany gave rise to the Fanatic, anti-Jewish system of education. Philosophy influences the methodology too. Naturalistic philosophy emphasizes child-centred methods, idealism emphasis Socratic and lecture methods. Pragmatism emphasis the project method.

In the case of curriculum, naturalists start with present experiences and interests of children. Idealists stress the study of religion, culture ethics and literature. Pragmatists advocate the study of functional subjects which have utility value. Philosophy influences the discipline in education. Autocratic philosophy leads to repressionism, idealism leads to impressionism, naturalism leads to emancipation and modern pragmatism leads to free discipline. The teacher must possess a sound philosophy of life. He/she must be a lover of wisdom, a seeker of knowledge and a man/women of virtues/ values. Then only he/she can bring about desirable changes in his pupils.

Education reflects the **social pattern of society**. The tremendous explosion of science and technology has shaken the old leisurely outlook on life and has created intricate problems of social adjustment. A new emphasis has been placed on literacy. A growing interest is shown in re-organizing the curricula at all stages. The new forces in the social structure of the Indian society have provided a fresh incentive for educationists to pattern the educational system. Education will be different in different kinds of society since total way of life of a society influence education. Even the same society, education provided at different time spans will be different. Although it is said that education is one of the causes in social change, it could be seen that in most cases educational change trends to follow rather than initiate social changes. Educational institutions and other organizations are inter-related with the rest of the social structure. A.K.C. Ottaway stated, "Education is an activity which goes on in a society and its aims and methods depend on the nature of the society in which it takes place".

Culture and education are initially and integrally connected. Hence the cultural pattern of a country conditions its educational pattern. E.g. A society based on the spiritual pattern of culture emphasis the attainment of moral and eternal values-truth, goodness and beauty- of life through education. At the same time a society based on materialistic pattern emphasis the attainment of material values through education. Culture influences aims of education, curriculum, methodology, discipline, and text books.

Political ideologies go a long way in determining the aims and the system of education. Different political ideologies like totalitarian or fascist communist or socialist and democratic will call for different systems of education. Political philosophy of a nation has great influence on its education. Today we have different forms of political systems. They are totalitarianism, communism and democracy. A totalitarian state will assume complete control of the educational system. The rulers will prescribe curriculum, syllabi, text books. Education will be directed to secure mechanical discipline, duty and unquestioned obedience. There will be no room for community participation. E.g. Education in ancient Sparta. Communism conceives education as one of the principle instruments for economic advancement and social progress. State produce text books and they conduct training in order to attain the goal of socialism. Education will be a national concern. Individuals will have only limited freedom in educational sector. Education will be free at all levels.

In a India like democratic setup education under the control of society. The powers and resources age distributed between central and state governments. The state provide educational facilities. A kind of participatory approach and de-centralized planning is adopted here. Universal education is a matter of social necessity in a democratic society. Education aims at improvements in vocational and practical efficiency. Significant place is given to the total development of each individual. The schools indicate respect for the national flag and National Anthem. Exceptional children/ poor/disadvantaged are given special consideration. Education of ancient Athens up to an end this kind. The ruled nations had a different educational system than their rulers as they were being exploited by their rulers. The system of British education was implanted in this country from purely political motives.

History of a nation must influence the education of that country. History of a nation includes, its past politics, culture, social system, economy etc. Thus, influence of any of the above factors will influence education also. E.g. Still in India, we following British system of education. If a nations history was full of wars, the education in that nation will give much importance to training of troops and developing modern Ammunitions/ weapons. If a nation was under the rule of some other nation, its education will be influenced by the culture, politics and social system of that ruling nation. Definitely education in present will be influenced by history.

The **influence of religion** is very powerful as it penetrates the emotional depth of human nature. the *Brahmanic* system of education, the Buddhist education, medieval Islamic education were dominated by religion. In Europe, the protestant countries were wedded to the education of the masses and the catholic countries to the education of the classes.

Schools at large often and closely reflect the **social patterns** prevailing in a particular country. As such the education system is usually seen as a **social factor** which must reflect the ethos of the people that it serves. In this regard, it is the prime aim of education to ensure cultural continuity through fostering the growth and development of national characteristics that often act as stabilizing forces. In its simplest definition a culture of a society is the total way of life of the society. Every society consist of human beings and in whatever state they find themselves they always have some kind of educational system. This form of education of the society will always strive to perpetuate and protect its traditions and aspirations. As such a close study and analysis of each education system will always reveal the cultural concept and pattern of the community in question. Also the social patterns of the people in any particular community or country are reflected in its system of education.

It is important to realize that the culture of the people often changes at a slow pace. In each culture, there are certain values which are not affected by time and place, for example, faith in God, love for truth and non-violence and the ideal of universal motherhood and justice are the permanent values of many cultures of the world. However, radical reforms in a society may be slowed down or blocked at the level of implementation because of the cultural lag. In India the various projects for educational reform does indicate that there has been basic cultural changes in the life of a people from the colonial period into the post independence period. In many countries of the world today, changes have occurred in the attitude of the youngsters towards their elders, for example students do not show due respect to their teacher as students did some twenty five or thirty years ago. The teachers also now care more for the increments, in their salaries and other allowances then for teaching. In many meetings of teachers, there is more talk of groupism, backbiting and salaries, than of students' welfare. In some circles, guardians and parents also do not respect teachers as they did before. All these and others are a clear indication that the relations between parents and children, sisters and brothers, husband and wife, masters and servants and between many other units of society have undergone great changes. Thus, we have begun to discard many old mores and modes and are adopting more liberal attitudes. As such time and place have been changing many elements of culture and as a result it is being reflected in the education system in various ways.

Another view of cultural and social change is in the reshaping of the educational machinery to make for equality of educational opportunity for all. This has led to the widening of the school curriculum and increased emphasis on the importance of the right kind of technical educational for the new technological age. As a result, the old dichotomy between a liberal and a technical education is slowly broken down and the social distinctions which existed mainly because of that divide have become of no consequence and has been minimized with time. In this regard therefore, it is necessary to develop love for one's own culture through the education system because it strengthens nationalism. In order to make the country strong and prosperous, the spirit of nationalism must be nurtured. In each country there are various types of communities, classes, castes, and interests and due to the lack of national feelings many people ignore national interests. In many cases minorities are suspicious about the majority and in certain contexts this may be true of the majority as well. This makes it necessary to inculcate love for the country's culture and especially through the adoption of a national system of education.

Economic Necessities As A Determinants Of Curriculum Making

The type of education largely depends on the economic strength of any country. Also the economic factor determines the content and method of an education system. It is important to note that formal education is often possible where production exceeds consumption. In indigenous traditional education people were trained depending on the economic conditions and needs of the community. From an economic perspective, expenditure on education refers to the amount or percentage of national revenue spent on education by both individuals and the government. If the economic condition is poor, education becomes backward in many aspects while if the economy of a country is strong, then educational aims and the curriculum are given a special direction for making the country prosperous. For example, in the USA and Japan, education system is patterned so as to make the individual graduate, strong and capable enough to stand on his or her own feet after having received education. While in India, college and university graduate do not know where to go after completing their education and most of the students continue to stay on in the university as long as they can so that one can post pone for a few years the problem of the educated - unemployed.

Another economic influence on education is that, the poorer classes in communities tend to be content with minimum education for their children, and the richer classes are known to be able to keep their children longest at school because they can afford to meet the costs. In a subsistence economy, that is, one is which people are just able to make ends meet, educational systems tend to be informal occurring on the job. On the contrary, where there are enough grants in systems of education, minimum requirements are met and thus the quality of education is often high. For example, Britain, France, Japan and the USA among other strong economy countries, they provide enough grants that are allocated to their systems of education; actually they have enough funds to support all educational programmes in their education systems. Unlike the case of developing countries, where funds are very scarce, which affects even payment of teachers salaries, essential resource materials such as textbooks are not adequate and in some cases not even available. As such, this greatly affects the nature of the systems of education in terms of the content and methods in learning institutions and in essence the whole system of education.

In this regard, the growth of the capacities of individual citizens and national development is of great importance. In fact, the education system should be such that, it provides opportunities for the maximum development of each citizen. The aim here is to ensure that the wealth of the nation is not concentrated in the hands of a few capitalists who manage to attain some level of education. It is actually by developing individuals that the overall growth of the nation can be guaranteed. At the same time, there should be no-class distinction in the planning of education that should be permitted, because this results in neglect of the education of other more capable citizens. If this happens it often results in social disparities and in the long run weakens the nation. Proper planning of the education system also calls for the establishment of a proper national character, which if it lacks, then the necessary leadership and co-operation of the people will also be lacking. Lack of a proper national character, means that the national education system will not be able to realize its objectives. Consequently, with good leadership and people's cooperation, there is much that can be achieved even when adequate economic resources are wanting. Thus, there is evidence to show that there is a very close relationship between economic security and the national system of education of any country.

Technological Possibilities As A Determinants Of Curriculum Making

Technological changes cannot also be ignored in education. Technology and especially modern technology also influence the education system of the country. Historically, emphasis on industrial and technical education followed the industrial revolution. Technology affects the type of education as well as the means of instruction. With the emergence of computer, internet, this has revolutionalised the whole education system especially in the developed countries. Through information communication technology, home learning has been made possible. Universities are also adopting e-learning. Today the influence of technology in education cannot be ignored. Indeed the challenge is for the educational administrators and policy makers to see to it that the right infrastructure is in place in order to allow the use of information communication technology fully and be able to reap its maximum benefits in the education system especially in the developing world.

Curriculum development should accommodate technological advancements. These may be related to pedagogy, such as open learning where learners can tune in to the lesson and access information via satellite. They may be advances that are unrelated to pedagogy but which influence knowledge.

In recent years a synthesis of communication technologies has been occurring, serving to continually extend the capabilities of communication networks. The scale of this trend suggests that many of the central issues for education in the coming years will be driven by technological change. Indeed, the influence of these new technologies is such that they may well form an underlying mechanism for the future of education. From the perspective of curriculum development, these technologies create new challenges. Their impact is shifting educational focus from getting enough information, to the challenge of surviving amid so much information. A consequential change is that one of the core literacy's now required for social and vocational fitness is the ability to filter and decipher knowledge. This is a fundamental change. Technology is affecting education in revolutionary ways, and the momentum toward these changes is irreversible. What impact does this have on the social construction of curriculum?

Technological change is redefining not only how we communicate, but in turn, is redefining how we need to educate. The ready availability of information has lessened the necessity of rote learning, but raises new issues in terms of effective searching and the development of an ability to evaluate information. The development of analytical skills and higher order thinking is increasingly an important focus. The stakeholders and interest groups in this process are many and varied, with pressure for change and reform brought from teachers, schools and school councils, government authorities, industry and students themselves. All have differing perspectives on the best curriculum planning models to deal with this change.

The roots of change are in an increase in technological and networking capacity, but what are the ramifications for curriculum development, and interpretations necessary for the classroom? Many educators hold the view that computers and Internet connectivity are "tools" for learning and thus, believe an increased grade point average is often the only measure of value for technological resources. However, an important perspective for all educators, government administrators and school boards to consider is, that networking represents not just a new set of tools, but a new environment for learning and teaching. New communications technologies encourage new possibilities and develop new requirements. An outcomes based education policy must accept that the new communications technologies must impact upon core curriculum requirements and will influence diversity, context, assessment issues and practice. It is important to place our interpretation of current curriculum into as strong a future-proof context as possible and eventually, but not in the distant future, every student will need access to the information represented on the web in order to be competitive in their workplace.

While there are still liberal-humanist influences on our education system, a fundamental orientation of state secondary education is directed towards an economic-rationalist agenda of **vocationally orientated educational outcomes**, which in theory target industry needs. Brady refers to this as, "… human-capital theory" (Brady & Kennedy, 1999). Whether or not education based on this framework is a sound policy is in itself a topic for detailed analysis, but for the purpose of this dialogue we will not contest that vocational preparedness is a central preoccupation of the education system, and instead, focus on the way curriculum addresses this agenda. In what ways do the possibilities of technology influence curriculum designed and developed to address vocational outcomes? Traditionally, major decisions related to education course content arrive top down from administration. They are then implemented by teachers who, frequently, spend all but a small portion of their day confined to a room in which students are rewarded for working quietly and independently. In contrast, success in industry relies on collaboration and teamwork. The traditional education system is just beginning to transform into an environment that encourages collaboration as a focus in learning. Emerging technologies can catalyse this change and in fact encourage new systems of collaborative development. This is a fundamental transformation, in which the archetypical education system, in both theory and practice, now has the tools, not just the incentive, to facilitate a transition from a focus on providing information, to a focus on developing collaborative conceptual frameworks for educational activities. Educational practise should be located in a way that incorporates the demands of a vitally changing world, increasingly dominated by the technologies of electronic communication and collaborative networking.

Curriculum Models and Technological Resources

Curriculum developers must reflect on actual practice to understand appropriate curriculum development practice. There is a debate about the cost / value relationship of technology implementation in secondary education. While much technology may provide long-term advantages in educational budgeting, provided resources are allocated towards efficient collaboration, this is, however, dependent on a curriculum focus which identifies the need for collaboration and supports its' implementation.

A cost factor is obsolescence which is an important consideration in technologically related curriculum especially, due both to the cost factor of hardware, software and support. The power of change that technology supports means that the contexts applied to developing technological (and 'information') literacy become ever more important. Whatever choices are made, it is important to give serious consideration to the factor of rapid obsolescence, and design learning units that interpret curricula appropriately and are sensitive to the constantly changing nature of technology and consequent literacy demands. In response to this, educators can and should build courses that interpret curricula using tools and modalities that are as far as possible 'future proof', while still having sensitivity to current social context.

If this shift in curriculum focus is achieved, then technology can become a 'virtual' benefactor, providing the means to access greater resources than could otherwise be afforded, by virtue of the fact that resources so obtained can be broadly shared. A wide-band networked infrastructure with access to appropriate software tools allows students, classes, and teachers to access and produce online materials, do extensive collaborative work, and share instructional resources. The Internet, for example, provides online information and is a medium by which students and schools can communicate and collaborate, opening opportunities for broad consultation. In this way, Information Technology infrastructures can impact on conventional instruction processes by expanding learning resources beyond individual teacher and school materials, providing lower cost sourcing of information and expertise, and providing communication links for isolated students.

These advantages are only accessible however, if curriculum models facilitate their implementation, if the funding levels match the rhetoric, and if expenditure decisions are appropriate. Decisions which are not collaborative risk degeneration of the process of effective implementation of technological facilities and can cause overall degeneration in educational resources. Very few areas are more expensive than technological infrastructure. Assessment of current efforts in regards to collaborative decision making show mixed results across the world.

This is important consideration, as the cost of technology is frequently raised by advocates of barriers to incorporating technology into the educational environment. Blocks to the implementation of a strong technological infrastructure, associated with an appropriate curriculum, are largely psychosocial rather technical or directly economic. It is about what we choose to spend money on. The issue reflects the complications inherent in the social construction of curriculum, to which solutions can only be found through effective collaboration between community, educators and administrators.

The **resource sharing and collaborative communications** extensions provided by new technologies can only do so on a broad scale if the problem of **resource equity** be addressed. If not, the benefits will only be provided to a few and create more disparity. Resources required include not just hardware and software, but training so that educators can manage these new tasks, and IT support staff to operate and maintain the networks that are developed. The issue of inequitable distribution of these resources lead to **multiple forms of disadvantage**. It is due to awareness of the realities of disadvantage, that the principle of equality of distribution and access to technological resources becomes a central issue for educators. Teachers, who currently undertake roles of implementers of curriculum, of providers of civics and citizenship education, as progenitors for school review processes and in facilitating aims of continuous improvement, must now vitalise and actualise another aim, that of realising appropriate curriculum development relevant to the collaborative environment of electronically networked information and communication facilities, cooperatively in a shared environment.

It is important that teachers do not find that they are working towards integration of technology through the curriculum alone. It must involve input from all sectors of the community, and particularly those directly concerned with administration and decision making for educational budgetary allocations. It is important that there is no increase in the gulf between the **information rich** and **the information poor**, and to do this it is necessary to ensure that all educators, as far as possible, are working towards the incorporation of the tools of technology in a manner that facilitates equitable and broad distribution. Achieving this demands a broad consultative process and the elimination of short-term political agendas.

Rapid change is occurring, inequitably, with difference of opinion on how best to respond and what solutions to implement. But one thing that perhaps can be agreed to by all is that education does need to adapt to the changes at least as they are occurring. Current educational philosophies support processes which facilitate students development of willingness to experiment, comprehension of abstract concepts, advanced skills of problem solving, reasoning, awareness of social justice and ecological-sustainability issues, all within a framework of integration of technology in cross-curricular activities. The changes we witness in technology mean that these processes have become even more valuable. It is suggest that the most needed practical application for knowledge gained at school, in the industrial and technological 'real world', appears to be the ability to manifest higher-order skills within a context of thoughtful social awareness.

Cultural Orientations As A Determinant Of Curriculum Making

A strong cultural identity enables individuals to become independent and self-reliant people who function in their own environment. People who have little sense of their cultural identity or have been alienated from their culture can become dependent and lack skills for meaningful survival in their own environment. This predicament is particularly pronounced in societies that have suffered colonial domination in the past and that find themselves socializing their children with the cultural values and world view of the colonizing power which undermines their own cultural identity. It seems to be a lack of political will to make radical and effective changes to the curriculum.

Culture is a complex whole which includes knowledge, beliefs, arts, morals, customs and any other capabilities acquired by man as a member of the society. It is the sum total of a given society's way of life moulded and shaped by prevailing circumstances and environment. This implies that culture is not static but dynamic and it responds to external influences, which bring about changes and curriculum development in schools.

In every society, curriculum development in the schools is greatly influenced by the culture in which the school situates. It is a process and a flow from theory to practice and the feed of curriculum stands on the trench hold of becoming ordered. Curriculum was originally defined as a cost of study or training and a product. It consists essentially of disciplined study of command and mother tongue and the systematic study of grammar, identifying the curriculum as a finished product or static body of knowledge which caused curriculum planners great difficulties in the past. The definition of curriculum began to trench the growing distance between the planned curriculum and the experiences that were actually encountered. It is a sequence of potential experiences set up in the school for the purpose of discipline of children and youths in various activities. This set of experiences is referred to as the curriculum. In fact, education is seen as the transmission of culture from one generation to another. This definition refers to the general process known as enculturation.

Enculturation is the process of initiating the growing and inexperienced person into the way of life of his society. Enculturation is similar to socialization, but more embracing that it, as it influences curriculum in the school system. The school is a formalized and systematized institution, built in the society for the society. Therefore, the school is a specific, local and a dynamic institution in the society; and it is regarded as a knowledge factory in the society.

In fact, curriculum is generally considered to be all of the experiences that learners have under the auspices of the school. It is a plan for learning and it is concerned with result for the learner's continuous and wilful growth in personal-social competence. Hence, Oliver (1965) considers three components of what he calls "the educational programmes - another term for curriculum which consists of **programme of studies, programme of activities** and **guidance**. Whether at the primary or secondary school level, what is generally regarded as the curriculum is the syllabus, which contains a list of subjects taught in the school. The syllabus is primarily concerned with the exploration of culture. It was this emphasis of the syllabus on culture that made earlier curriculum workers believe that the school was built basically to "transmit the cultural heritage" which implies accumulated human experiences.

It therefore behoves the curriculum aspect to define what aspects of the cultural heritage to be taught in the context of a given society. Also programme of activities involves actual pupil activities on practical experiences which are wide ranging and would include group activities such as singing, theatre and cultural activities. It is important to note that in all cases, the programme of activities is an integral part of the curriculum, complementing the programme of studies. The activities are expected to mould the character of the pupils and assist in their personal development.

Relating to programme of guidance, it helps students to acquire the capacity for self directions, to become adjusted to their present situation and to plan their future in line with their interest, abilities and special needs. It's important as an integral part of the curriculum cannot be over stressed as is fully emphasized in the National Policy on Education. Although curriculum is seen as response to social forces and expectations for the schools in cultural context, the process of curriculum development has remained constant.

Thus, curriculum development is oriented towards providing school programs and is basically a plan of structuring the environment to coordinate in an orderly manner the element of time, space, materials, equipment, personnel and language. Since this discussion is mainly concerned with cultural basis of curriculum, it questions whether curriculum is in any way connected with culture. The definition, components and programmes of culture will provide answer to the question whether curriculum is in any way based on culture since education is seen as the transmission of culture from one generation to another which is a process of enculturation.

The term culture actually came into use during the middle ages. It derived from the Latin word for cultivation. Culture is the way of life of a social group and it includes actions, values and beliefs that can be communicated with necessary modifications from one generation to the succeeding one. Culture varies from one society to another and even within the same group of people depending on the period. This means that culture is not static but dynamic and it is expressed in terms of human behaviours, shared among a people and it is learnt rather than inherited. Therefore, the fundamental aspects of culture as it influences curriculum in the education system include belief, values, routines and customs. Therefore, culture or civilization, is that complex whole which includes knowledge, beliefs, art, morals, law, custom and any other capabilities and habits acquired by man as a member of society. The telling of this definition is that, culture is actually treated as a list of elements.

The elements of culture, whether materials or non-materials, can be taught and learnt only through interaction as members of a group. Culture is shared; that is, it is practiced by a whole group of people from generation to generation. Culture is maintained or modified through education by way of curriculum development. This is because where educational institutions discharge them duties well; they influence the total life of the society. This is the society's culture; and curriculum is a reflection of what people in the society feel believe and do. What people feel, believe and do is their culture.

Also, it is behaved that curriculum is an inevitable aspect of education. Therefore, there is no way in which culture can exist without some curriculum, particularly in formal setting in education.

Formal education demands the posing of some simple but fundamental questions such as "What? To whom? When? and How?". These are curriculum questions. In order to answer these questions, the curriculum planner must be "compelled to survey and interpret the nature of his own society, its basic stable values and the areas in which it is changing. He must then be very familiar with the culture of the society being served.

From the foregoing, it seems obvious that curriculum has (and must have) a firm basis on culture. Indeed, culture is the substance of education. Culture is to education what current is to electricity. Any society whose education (and so its curriculum) is not based on its culture is in danger of being estranged by the social institution on which it should depend for its survival. The social institution is the school. In discharging its duties, the school (including all categories of educational institutions) must pay special attention to the different classes of culture; and educators themselves must be familiar with how culture is classified. In effect, culture traits were understood as representing one of a series of stages of mental and moral progress culminating in the rational society of industrializing.

Franz Boas, an early 20th century anthropologist, was instrumental in this reversal of perspective and laid out the ground rules for the modern anthropological orientation of cultural relativism. These elements rest on four postulates, which directly confront the evolutionist position that:

- Cultural aspects of human behaviour are not biologically or conditioned but are acquired solely through learning
- Cultural conditioning of behaviour is ultimately accomplished through habituation and thus acts through unconscious process rather than rational deliberation, although secondary rationalizations are often offered to explain cultural values.
- All culture is equally developed according to their own proprieties and values; none is better, more advanced, or less primitive than any other.
- Cultural traits cannot be classified or interpreted according to universal categories appropriate to "human nature". They assume meaning only within the context of coherently interrelated elements internal to the particular culture under consideration.

Therefore, culture is composed of everything symbolic that we learn. All culture is learned, but not everything learned is culture. In fact, research has played a major role in establishing the relationship between culture and its effects upon human growth and development and of the effect of socio-economic and social-class influences upon children's learning. As a result, the anthropological meaning of the term "culture" embraces the way of life, the goals and the mores of people. The work scientists and educators in determining the relationship between culture and what a child will become has significant implications for the school. Each child must be considered in his particular social class and cultural environment. The motivation, growth, socialization of a child from the slums will differ radically from those of a child of the upper or middle class. In fact, a large number of children in our schools lack in their cultural environments, experiences upon which the school puts a premium: and motivation for school learning differs radically among children from different cultural environments. Also, the family life of children differs radically in different cultural environments.

Aspects of culture in Curriculum Development

The fundamental aspects of culture in curriculum development include beliefs, values, routines and customs. Every culture has some **beliefs** which are accepted as true. These beliefs are sometimes called superstitious beliefs because of lack of empirical knowledge or lack of scientific proof. These beliefs are valued and so are accepted by majority of people in the community. For instance, the Isoko people of Delta State, Nigeria, believe that when an owl perches on the roof of a house, it portrays death. In Kerala, we believe that when you itch your right palm, it shows you will receive a gift or money. These beliefs are accepted by majority of the people in these societies or communities but the basis of commitment on these beliefs varies from individual to individual. These are some beliefs, which are accepted by individuals irrespective of the general beliefs of the community. Such beliefs that are accepted by individuals are referred to as private beliefs as against the general beliefs which are regarded as declared beliefs held by a majority of the people in the community.

Values are those aspects of cultural practices, actions or objects that are valued in high esteem in the society. The values of a society are also those aspects of the culture that society wants to preserve because their traditionally valued and they want to pass it from generation to generation. The values of the society are the aspect of the culture, which is needed in the society. These aspects of the culture that are valued should be passed from generation to generation so as to maintain a particular valid aspect of the culture. For instance, every society expects adults to get married for procreation to keep the society moving. Values and judgments are not only important elements of culture but they are also relevant to modern society.

Routines and customs are also very important aspects of culture. The three concept are interrelated - recipes, routines and customs. Recipes are the ideas and the understanding about how things should be done as prescribed by the culture in question. For instance, different societies have different ways prescribed by their culture in performing naming, burial, marriage ceremonies and so on. The above mentioned ceremonies are performed differently by two societies are identical in terms of the culture of the people. Routines and customs refer to the actual doings and the regularities of those cultural actions or elements. Customs serve as recipes and routines to which people regularly resort for recurring purposes.

Cultural determinants of the content of curriculum

Education is regarded as one of the social institutions of the society. However, several writers have come up with different definitions of the term. Education is the process by which society deliberately transmit its cultural heritage through schools, colleges, universities and other institutions. This means that the content of the curriculum in schools must be loaded with cultural elements of the society. Consequently, knowledge, which is produced in the school system, should be firmly grounded in the culture of the given society. This means that no two societies can have identical educational system. Since educational system is supposed to be a reflection of the society's culture, needs and aspirations, the nature of the knowledge available in any given society should be sought in the nature of a society's institutions and culture. This is because knowledge is disseminated and acquired so that members of the society can improve themselves and operate the social institutions of the society. This implies that the culture of a given society reflects the types of knowledge produced in the society.

If European types of education are based on European philosophies of education which reflect different national philosophies about German, French, British, Russian or Spanish character, it should be obvious that Indians should secure their cultural identity by fashioning their own philosophies of education. The structure, content and methods of education differ from nation to nation in the advanced world because national educational policies are formulated in line with the philosophies, values and history of a people. It is essential that any kind of educational policy and planning which is a key to development or an eye opener to the learner's self awareness and that of his surroundings make culture its base. This means that areas of emphasis in stipulated curricula course outlines and contents must necessarily reflect or related to the learner's cultural heritage.

It was discovered that the major cause of the failure of colonial education was that it was not adapted to the socio-cultural milieu in which it operated. Colonial education never incorporated valued aspects of the culture as its base and this why colonial education has been regarded as inadequate for Indians.

Culture has been described as a way of life of a people. There is no culture that is static. Since education has been defined as cultural transmission, it also plays an important part in achieving cultural change. This is because a good education system should have conservative, transitive and innovative functions as society is not static but dynamic. Aspects of society's culture which are not found adequate for the survival and progress of society at any point in time could either be modified or changed through the process of education. Therefore, knowledge in every society is relative to time and place. It therefore means that any good educational system should imbibe the culture as presented of the people. There it is the culture of the society that should determine the knowledge in the school curriculum. Similarly, the knowledge that is produced and transmitted through the process of education is in fact the cultural elements of the given society.

Culture is made up of speech, material traits, arts, mythology, scientific knowledge, religious practices, family and social practices, real and personal property has a corresponding body of knowledge packaged in the components of the school curriculum. This is because there can be no culture without the knowledge of it by the member of the given society. This is why different sociologists believe that culture provides the basis for knowledge both in the society and in the school curriculum.

From the foregoing, one can see that it is the cultural elements that determine the content of education and curriculum development. Every child is born into a society with a culture. The young child is not yet regarded as a member of the society in a society until she has learnt her culture through the process of education.

The terms curriculum and curriculum development

The word curriculum has a Latin origin "currus" which means "course" and by the 19th century, the word curriculum had come to be used in reference to education. Since curriculum came to be used in relation to education, the only general view about it is that it is a programme of studies to be completed by learners and teachers. The term "curriculum" is an organized instruction. A desirable curriculum should include extra class activities and counselling services. These elements - organized instruction, extra-class activities and counselling services - are indispensable components of the modern curriculum concept. They are also interrelated. The educational programme or curriculum consists of three basic elements: (1) Programme of studies, (2) Programme of activities (3) Programme of guidance.

Two basic points are clear from the foregoing: the consensus by curriculum experts that new concepts of curriculum include more than formal school subjects and organized instruction. The nature and type of elements involved are also specified. Secondly, it is clear that none of the elements on its own can stand for or interpret the curriculum. Rather, each of them is important and has specific contribution to the whole gamut of the educational programme. It is these elements working in concert with their individual special contributions and functions that constitute the curriculum or educational programme.

On the other hand, curriculum development is the planning process of learning opportunities intended to bring about certain changes in pupils assessments of the extent to which these changes have taken place. It is sometime misconstrued with curriculum planning. Curriculum planning is one of those terms in education that are marked by impression and doubts. **Curriculum planning** involves making series of decisions and choices which are based on values and grounds to be covered to reach the goals of education. However, **curriculum development** is the term used to describe the creation of curriculum materials that are products of curriculum planning for use by the learner.

The development of syllabus for various subjects at all levels of education and suggestions about teaching methods, textbooks, and other instructional materials represent aspects of curriculum development. There are three categories of curriculum materials. viz.,

- Texts, made up of main textbooks, supplementary texts, reference texts, workbooks, and teachers' guide.
- Non-texts, made up of electronic aids (visual, audio and audiovisual)
- Semi-texts, consisting of charts, drawings, cards, maps, and photographs.

The national cultural traditions are a major determinant and influence on education systems in general, on national curricula, and on teachers' pedagogies in schools. There is a powerful argument that systems are the main determinant for differences between countries. What is often neglected is that national cultural traditions are the philosophical base on which the systems are built. These traditions depend on philosophical beliefs about education, but once in place they become part of the structure of the system and teachers have to work within them. These findings suggest that curricula and pedagogies need to be analysed and understood in terms of the larger cultural context, and that without such understanding changes cannot be predicted to bc successful.

National Priorities As A Determinant Of Curriculum Making

The Education Commission (1964-66), said that the development of values such as a scientific temper of mind, tolerance, respect for the culture or other national groups, etc., will enable us to adopt democracy, not only as a form of government, but also as a way of life. This clearly shows that in a democratic country like India the first and the foremost goal of education should be development of democratic values. Indian democracy is made by the people who profess different religions, speak different languages, belong to different races, castes, classes and communities, keeping in mind these and several other characteristics of Indian democracy following should be the most appropriate national priorities of curriculum making:

Development of Democratic Values in the People : These values apart from those given above include a spirit of large-hearted tolerance, of mutual give and take, of the appreciation of the ways in which people differ from one another. No education is worthwhile if an educated man does not translate these values in his behaviour and no democracy in that case can survive for long. Hence, education has to make deliberate and planned effort on development of these values in the people.

National Integration : It means harmonizing religions, language, caste, and class and community differences as they exist in India causing social tensions. It is essential that the people of India in spite of these differences live peacefully and cooperatively and utilize their varied talents for the enrichment of the national life as a whole. Education through various programmes and tailored curricula should make efforts to develop in the people such attitudes and values. It is difficult but possible. These changes include realizing the importance of knowledge and education, learning various social skills, developing scientific attitude, computer literacy considering science and technology important, and so on. The Education Commission (1964) said that, "The most important tool in the process of modernization is education based on science and technology." But, the Commission, further said "Modernization, if it is to a living force must derive its strength from the strength to spirit"

The **Secondary Education Commission** (1952-53), has formulated three social or national aims of education. These are: (1) Development of democratic citizenship, (2) Improvement of vocational efficiency, and (3) Development of leadership which means training pupils for discharging their duties efficiently. Ishwar Bhai Patel Committee (1977) also reiterated the importance of development of citizenship as a social or national goal of education. The Adiseshiah Committee Report (1978) formulated the following goals to be achieved through education:

- Removal of unemployment.
- Removal of destitution, i.e., poverty.
- Rural Development.
- Adult literacy.

All these foregoing aims are social or national objectives to be achieved through education. They are the tasks completion of which is imperative for strengthening the society. These aims have been discussed here with special reference to India. Hence, they may be considered national goals of education or educational aims of national development. Our schools should develop a strong tradition of striving to generate a sense of national unity and national consciousness, in the pupils. This can be achieved as suggested by the National Commission on Education (1964-66), by (i) making pupils understand and revaluate our cultural heritage and (ii) by the creation of a strong driving faith in the future towards which we aspire. The first may be promoted by well-organized teaching of the language and literature, philosophy, religion and history of India as well as by introducing the students to Indian architecture, sculpture, painting, music, dance and drams. Faith in future would involve an attempt to bring home to the students the principles of the Constitution, the great human values contained in preamble of the constitution.

Development of Physical Resources : It is through the modernization of agriculture and rapid industrialization should also be an important aim of education in a democracy like India. To achieve this purpose education should be linked with productivity, science should be made a basic component of education, work- experience should be considered important, vocational education should be expanded, scientific and technical education should be improved.

Development of Human Resources : It should be considered still more crucial an aim of education in Indian democracy. This aim implies changes in the knowledge, skills, interests, and values of the People as a whole. In a democracy the individual is an end in him and the primary purpose of education should be to provide him with the widest opportunity to develop his potentialities to the full, through social reorganization and emphasis on social perspectives. Cultivation of essential values in the people, development of dedicated and competent leadership and educated electorate are essential for strengthening democracy. Education, therefore, must develop such human resources needed for the defence of Indian democracy.

Development of Social, Moral and Spiritual Values : In a democratic country like India it is inevitable to inculcate social, moral and spiritual values in the people. Knowledge in the absence of essential values may be dangerous. The success of democracy, its strength and stability are contingent upon people's developed sense of social responsibility and a keener appreciation of moral and spiritual values hence, education must make efforts on developing these values in the people. Pundit Nehru in his Azad Memorial Lectures (1962) said "Material riches without toleration and compassion and wisdom may well turn to dust and ashes."

The provisions of Education in Indian Constitution : India is not merely a modern democratic state but a country which is traditionally inclined towards democracy. A democratic constitution was adopted after independence. In 1938, Jawahar Lal Nehru said, "The Indian Constitution seeks to establish a popular government in the country on the basis of democratic principles outlined earlier. For this every citizen must participate in the administration, through his right to vote and to be elected. Every individual is guaranteed and given equal status and opportunity, because no one is discriminated against on the basis of religion, race, caste, community, sex, or on any other grounds. The government is responsible to the people and its elected representatives."

In order to achieve this objective of democracy, education is as necessary in India as anywhere else, a truth which the Indian people have been quick to realize. In the words of F.W. Themes, "Education is no exotic in India. There has been no country where the love of learning had so early an origin or has exercised so lasting and powerful an influence. From the simple poet of the Vadic age to the Bengali philosopher of the present day there has been an uninterrupted succession of teachers and scholars." Not only did the Indian constitution accept the ideals of democracy, it considered education the prime responsibility of the state.

In Article 21 A of Indian Constitution guaranteeing free and compulsory education to all children up to the age of 14. Articles 29 and 30 of the constitution give rights to every individual in connection with education and cultural development. According constitution, every Indian national living in any part of India will have the right to maintain his own specific language, script and his culture. No person can be refused right of admission to any educational institution, established by the state, by reason of religion, race, caste, language or any other similar consideration. According to article 30, every minority community will have the right to establish and maintain educational institutions of its own choice, irrespective of whether the minority is a linguistic or religious one. The state will also not refuse aid to any saucy institution created by a religious or linguistic minority. Articles 45 and 46 determine the policy for education as part and parcel of the directive principles.

According to article 46, the stage will pay special attention to the educational and economic interests of all backward classes, especially the scheduled castes and scheduled tribes. It also entrusts the state with the duty of protecting such tribes from social injustice and exploitation of every kind. The Indian Constitution laid the foundation for a federal government in which the functions of the state government have some duties with respect to education. It has been realised that there must be coordination between the central and state authority on education for a balanced development of the country. The modern Indian state is a welfare state whose objective is the complete development of its people. This welfare can be achieved only through education. Little surprise therefore if all the leaders of the nation stress the importance of education as a first step to improving the future of the nation.

The democratic ideals which the existing educational policy is trying to achieve have been outlined most precisely in the **Secondary Education Commission**'s (1952) explanation of the objectives of education:

- **Development of Democratic Citizenship** : The success of democracy depends largely upon the people's awareness of their rights and duties and the extent to which people fulfil their responsibilities. Education aims at developing this ability in the people, because education teaches the man to think and distinguish between right and wrong. He can understand social, economic and political issues, and reflect on the possibility of solving such problems. S/he can decide upon the political party or the leadership which should be entrusted with the task of forming a government and undertaking administration. S/he does this after thinking on the problems facing the country and considering the ability of each group or leader to face such problems. S/he can express his ideas and suggestion through lectures, essays, articles, etc. S/he can organize new movements or constitute various kinds of committees to solve the problems facing the country. It is the duty of the state to insist upon a syllabus which can be expected to generate such democratic awareness among the children being educated.

- **Training in Skilful Living :** Democracy can be said to have succeeded only if it translate the democratic ideals to its society. And, for this, socialization of the individual through education is essential. It is desirable to develop such social qualities as collective feeling, cooperation, discipline, tolerance, sympathy, brotherhood, etc., in the individual. Education must also aim to create faith in social justice and the willingness to rebel against injustice. Education helps people in adjusting to each other, and the educated individual is generally tolerant and liberal. Although he may differ from other people in their opinions, he has the ability to adjust to such people because he can understand their attitudes. Hence, education is the only means of removing the obstacles in the path of democracy and also of achieving some adjustment between people who differ from each other in respect of language, race, caste, religion, sixe, etc.
- **Development Vocational Skill :** The Secondary Education Commission has pointed out that another aim of education is to develop some vocational skill in the learner. No nation can progress in the absence of economic progress. The first duty of the state is to provide a system and means of education which imparts some vocational and professional skills to the learner so that they can earn their livelihood at the same time as they contribute to the nation's economic growth. The country urgently needs skilled craftsmen, engineers, doctors, teachers and administrators. For this, specialized colleges are required. Every child should be given the right to choose a profession of his own liking, and he should be given the opportunity to acquire the highest training and education in this profession.

- **Development of Personality :** The success of a democratic society also depends upon whether mature men and women form the majority or minority in its population. Democracy can succeed only if most of its members have developed mature personalities, because a mature person has gone through physical, mental, social, ethical and spiritual development. Hence, education should aim at the development of all aspects of the learner's personality through various kinds of training. Keeping this in view, most schools and colleges now provide many kinds of extracurricular training, which supplements all that is taught as part of curriculum.
- **Developing Leadership :** The success of a democracy depends upon the capabilities of the leadership. The democratic government is a decentralized government, and for that reason it requires skilled leadership at many different levels of administration. The democratic government is run by the elected representatives of the people, who should be possessed of special qualities. Expert leadership is required for development and progress in every sphere-political, social, economic, artistic, scientific and cultural. Education should aim at evolving such leadership, because without doing this education cannot make any real contribution to democracy, for then it is leaving unfulfilled one of its important responsibilities. The element of leadership can be encouraged through many kinds of curricular and extracurricular activities in schools and colleges.

Apart from these objectives of education laid down specifically by the *Secondary Education Commission*, it is desirable to reflect upon some other objectives, which have significance in view of the fact that India is a democracy. In fact, the aims of education vary a little bit with the level of education-the primary, secondary and university education-a fact which has been recognized by the different education commissions established from time to time. The aim of education, at the primary level, is to develop the child's mind by presenting the fundamental elements in the various areas of knowledge, and also to give him an opportunity to develop all his abilities-physical, mental, moral, motor, creative imagination, etc. At this stage attention should be paid to physical development no less than mental development, but attention must also be paid to the burden such an education places on the child. The education imparted should not become a burden. At the secondary level, attention should be focused on discovering the interests and abilities of every adolescent, and then developing such abilities. Education should be concerned not merely with the general welfare of society but also with the self-realization and personal development of each individual.

System Of Governance And Power Relations As A Determinant Of Curriculum Making

The development of civic competence requires an understanding of the foundations of political thought, and the historical development of various structures of power, authority, and governance. It also requires knowledge of the evolving functions of these structures in contemporary Indian society, as well as in other parts of the world. Learning the basic ideals and values of a constitutional democracy is crucial to understanding our system of government. By examining the purposes and characteristics of various governance systems, learners develop an understanding of how different groups and nations attempt to resolve conflicts and seek to establish order and security.

In exploring this theme, students confront questions such as: What are the purposes and functions of government? Under what circumstances is the exercise of political power legitimate? What are the proper scope and limits of authority? How are individual rights protected and challenged within the context of majority rule? What conflicts exist among fundamental principles and values of constitutional democracy? What are the rights and responsibilities of citizens in a constitutional democracy? Through study of the dynamic relationships between individual rights and responsibilities, the needs of social groups, and concepts of a just society, learners become more effective problem-solvers and decision-makers when addressing the persistent issues and social problems encountered in public life. By applying concepts and methods of political science and law, students learn how people work to promote positive societal change.

In schools, this theme typically appears in units and courses dealing with government, politics, political science, civics, history, law, and other social sciences. Learners in the early grades explore their natural and developing sense of fairness and order as they experience relationships with others. They develop an increasingly comprehensive awareness of rights and responsibilities in specific contexts. During the middle school years, these rights and responsibilities are applied in more complex contexts with emphasis on new applications. Learners study the various systems that have been developed over the centuries to allocate and employ power and authority in the governing process. High school students develop their abilities to understand and apply abstract principles. At every level, learners should have opportunities to apply their knowledge and skills to participate in the workings of the various levels of power, authority, and governance.

The political philosophy which controls the government of a country often has its inevitable impact on education. The political factor dictates the kind of administration the system of education will have. They also underlie the features in education system and the functioning of the same. For example, the fundamental ideas of socialism as a political philosophy were about the exploitation of labour by capital and this resulted in class mass. As a political philosophy, socialism recognizes property as the basis of the economic structure of the state which results in the concentration of civil and legal power in the hands of the property owning class. Socialism advocates for the nationalization of the means of production; where owners of means of production do not work and workers who produce do not own anything. A change of such a social order can only be achieved with reform in education. This would be through a state mechanism with full control of education and the curriculum and this means that the citizens must be trained by the state, for the state and in state institutions. In such cases, the details of the curriculum are often decided by the state authorities and involve functional training of citizens. The curriculum may also involve scientific training for social utilization purposes.

Good examples of countries that have introduced a socialist system of education are Mexico, Bulgaria and Cuba. The common features of their education system include monopoly of the state control on education, secularism, physical and military training political indoctrination in and out of school and also more emphasis on science subjects. In these states, freedom of individuals and the idea of tolerance are not accepted. Unlike these countries, France has a centralized system of education based on its political philosophy. In France, everything to do with education is controlled by the central government. In the case of USA and Japan, their education systems are highly decentralized, and are often based on the democratic influence and the capitalistic political philosophy of these countries.

There is also a close relationship between the national character and the national system of education. For example, the national character of USA is democratic as such its education system is democratic in most of its aspects. Nationalism also as a political ideology influences the system of education in a country. Nationalism could be defined as a psychological feeling within a group which believes they have common outlook and traditions based on myth of common ancestry. These common ancestries include race, language, religion and territory and often strengthen the consciousness of nationality. The racial aspect which is often within the political ideology of a country may play a significant role in determining features in the education system. Race refers to a tribe, a nation or a group of nations. Modern population includes people of different racial origins. The British colonial policy was based on the principle of decentralization and on the building up of a commonwealth of nations each of which should be free to develop its own culture and national character. Hence there is a close relationship between national character and national system of education and the former has been universally accepted as an important basis of national system of education. Thus the political system of a country is closely related with its educational programme.

International Contexts As A Determinants Of Curriculum Making

This module considers curriculum in an international context. It provides an understanding of the relationship between curriculum, power and politics from the level of a educational institution to ministries and international agencies. It then covers practical aspects of curriculum design, in a range of educational settings from universities to commercial training and street work. Diverse innovative ways to produce and deliver curriculum are considered - including the arts, ICT and public media - and the emphasis is on flexible, fast modes of curriculum development in response to changing circumstances in a globalising world.

The widely cited, though highly contested, idea that "the world is flat" carries with it a call for education to provide a levelling effect across continents and cultures, as the theory goes, are expected to experience a school curriculum that shares certain common elements, goals, and purposes. Such a globalized view is not, however, without its complications. We need to address some of the issues that arise when the transmigration of educational ideas occurs, with a particular eye toward the ethical dilemmas that curriculum workers face in international contexts. In many cases there are the stories of "donors" and "hosts," of structured inequities of power and influence, of disparities in material resources, and, as expressed in one of the cases, the dynamics of the "colonizer" and the "colonized." A recurrent theme concerns the challenges faced by educators working internationally to reconcile their own ethical predispositions toward equity and cultural responsiveness with certain tacit assumptions about the appropriateness or value of curriculum practices brought from the "developed" world for teachers and students in the "developing" world.

While educationalists and politicians argue about what should be in the National Curriculum, globalisation may be making their concerns irrelevant. The curriculum has traditionally been grounded in national contexts. Denis Lawton's (1989) description of the curriculum as a 'selection from the culture of a society' captured the essence of its role in preparing future generations for their adult lives. But as Alistair Ross (2000) has pointed out more recently, the increasing plurality of society, and of students' cultural backgrounds, means that making such a selection is bound to be contentious. At the same time, the notion of the curriculum as a body of knowledge owned by adults for transmission to the next generation is increasingly challenged as children acquire knowledge from a growing variety of sources. And technological changes means that we can no longer predict what knowledge and skills today's five-year old will need as an adult of 25.

The curriculum is also challenged by **globalisation**. Alongside growing diversity, an increasing recognition that the future for our children will be characterised by interdependence with other countries and cultures, and challenged by the effects of events in other parts of the world. It will be influenced by the necessity to develop what Hayward (2002) describes as 'intercultural literacy', essential even for those with no intention of moving beyond their national boundaries as adults.

A growing number of Indian schools are responding to this changing environment by introducing an international element to the curriculum. Resources to support them have been provided for some time. The aim is the preparation of young people 'for life in a global society and work in a global economy'. In addition, more and more schools are opting to introduce specifically international programmes, under titles such as global education, global citizenship education or international education.

Given the growing number of Free Schools and Academies that are under no obligation to offer the National Curriculum, international programmes such as these may well become increasingly attractive across the world. Reasons for the growing interest in such programmes are complex. But they include a growing awareness of the effects of globalisation, and of educational responses to it. This suggests an increasing appreciation of the role that international programmes can play in preparing today's youth for an adulthood which is likely to be very different from that of today's curriculum developers. While policy-makers, teachers and school leaders debate the detail of what should and should not be included in the National Curriculum, perhaps they should also consider the rapidly-growing interest in new forms of education which have been developed in a broader context, and which are already challenging the very concept of a national curriculum.

The landscape of research on the internationalisation of the curriculum in higher education is complex and meanings and practices in the area are vague. What is meant by internationalisation of the higher education curriculum? There is a lack of clarity around the concept of internationalisation of the higher education curriculum and its boundaries and further research is needed with respect to meaning and process. In particular, there is a need to construct a broader perspective on the concept, which stretches beyond just curriculum content. Equally, thinking in the area must move away from a narrow focus on international students and provide international experiences to all university staff and students so that they will perform successfully (professionally, economically and socially) within diverse contexts.

The 21st century university faces numerous challenges at local, regional and global levels (mass migration, environmental and geographical issues, super-diversity of the student cohorts, as well as the knowledge paradigms, the information overload, and global interconnectedness). Problems and issues in the current socio-economic and geo-political aspects demand broader, multi-perspective understanding about the world, life and work. As the most visible and significant site of knowledge creation, the university has a social responsibility to equip the members of the society with necessary competencies, knowledge, understandings, and new skills so that they can constantly negotiate the changing nature of work, the labour force, information technologies and cultural identities of people.

Teaching–learning sites in the 21st century university are super-diverse and participants bring multiple perspectives, understandings and competencies to the classroom. Knowledge creation cannot be constrained within nationalities. Hence, the term 'international curriculum' should be replaced by the term 'multi-perspective curriculum'.

Putting the Multi-Perspective Curriculum into practice

- Continuously expose students and staff to multiple views of the world (create different socio-cultural/educational societies, promote interdisciplinary activities, harness experiences of all the students in teaching and learning, value alternative world views, use comparative approaches to teaching);
- Encourage reflexive learning and teaching (reflexive dialogue, keeping reflexive diaries, reflexive teaching/learning logs) so that

students can constantly and critically reshape their approaches and views about learning and teaching;

- Seek to create a culture that makes students and staff feel that the university is a democratic meeting place where the encounter of diversity (in terms of gender, maturity, culture, nationality) creates opportunities to develop new competencies, knowledge and understandings.
- Increase opportunities for collaborative learning (communities of practice, group work, workshops, seminars) which exploit the diversity within the student body.

In recent years, much discussion has centred on the **world-class workplace**. This is a place where employees are world-class performers and their collective performance results in products and services that rank among the best and most competitive in the world. Why does one international hotel chain continue to expand while another continues to lose customers? Why is the service provided worldwide by car dealerships for a certain brand of automobile consistently better than the service given - by other dealers? Benchmarking against world-class standards, focusing on total quality, and empowering self-directed work teams are several of the ways that businesses and industries can become world class. Likewise, curricula that prepare students to work in these businesses and industries must be sure what is taught includes world class-focused learning experiences. Before graduating, each student should know what makes the difference between world class and less than world class performance and be prepared to perform in an occupation or field at a world-class level. As more and more companies are faced with worldwide competition, persons who work for these companies must be ready to produce and provide service at this level.

Considerations In Curriculum Development At The School Level

Educational values held by academic faculties subtly but strongly influence curriculum design in education. Five major value orientations of curriculum development are, Curriculum as the Development of Cognitive processes, Curriculum as Technology, Curriculum as Self-Actualization, Curriculum as Social Reconstruction-Relevance, and Curriculum as Academic Rationalism. The suggestion is made that these underlying value-orientations influence the choice of curriculum design more than do "available resources." A second component of curriculum design, i.e., evaluation of student performance, also influences and is influenced by the direction and development of physical therapy curricula. A plea is made for expressive objectives and outcome objectives to be considered along with instructional or behavioural objectives to yield more comprehensive and creative appraisals of student growth.

As you design your ideal curriculum for the school, it is important to take into consideration the following three items:

1. WHAT You Teach: What national, state and local standards and benchmarks do you incorporate?
2. HOW You Teach: What educational approach or philosophy do you identify with?
3. WHY You Teach: What inspires you? What excites you? Why did you become an art educator?

The answers to these three questions can turn into a simple teaching philosophy that stands the test of time.

The curriculum development process systematically organizes what will be taught, who will be taught, and how it will be taught. Each component affects and interacts with other components. For example, what will be taught is affected by who is being taught (e.g., their stage of development in age, maturity, and education). Methods of how content is taught are affected by who is being taught, their characteristics, and the setting. In considering the above three essential components, the following are widely held to be essential considerations in education:

- issue/problem/need is identified (issue !what),
- characteristics and needs of learners (target audience ! who),
- changes intended for learners (intended outcomes/objectives !what the learners will be able to do),
- the important and relevant content ! (what),
- methods to accomplish intended outcomes ! (how),
- evaluation strategies for methods, content, and intended outcomes ! (What works?)

With the implementation of compulsory education, every school-age child is entitled school education. For the maladjusted children who cannot benefit from the ordinary school environment, a specially designed curriculum geared to their needs is a necessity towards the actualization of equal chances in education for all. Curriculum for these children may be modified along the following principles :

- **Development of a Balanced Curriculum:** The existing curriculum is academically-oriented with more emphasis on cognitive development and less consideration on pupils' individual needs, abilities, interests, potentials and developmental history. Apart from this, personal and social development, self-understanding and various levels of life skills training have never been explicitly included in the curriculum as a unique subject. A balanced weighting of subjects should be worked out according to the available resources to meet the interest and ability of individual pupils, and give them chances to gain success and pleasure in their school life.
- **Development of Multiple Intelligences:** It has been the practice in the field of education to differentiate children into ability groups through intelligence tests. However, these tests are biased towards assessing abilities in languages and mathematical or logical thinking. Pupils who are slow in developing these two aspects may risk having other potentials left untapped. Howard Gardner (1983), a psychologist of Harvard University, has suggested that human beings possess multiple intelligences. At least the following seven have been detected: linguistic, logical-mathematical, spatial, bodily-kinaesthetic, musical, inter-personal and intra-personal. Gardner's theory has great implications to education since the developmental milestones of each intelligence vary with individuals and every child has his or her unique intellectual profile. Curriculum integration is a good way to nurture children's multiple intelligences through integrated and daily life learning activities. In addition, children can also figure out their own ways to develop different intelligences.
- **Tailoring with Consideration of Curriculum Continuity and Internal Coherence:** Schools should appropriately adapt the mainstream curriculum by means of simplification, abridgement, reorganisation, extension and selection. Teachers should be given a free hand in this process. At the beginning of each term, schools should call cross-subject curriculum meeting to ensure continuity and coherence of the whole curriculum. The actual curriculum tailoring should then be systematically conducted as designed by the well-experienced personnel.
- **Incorporation of Communication and Interpersonal Skills Training:** Children can establish effective relationship with their immediate environment be it their families, schools or communities

only if their communication and interpersonal skills improve significantly. Therefore these skills should be included in the curriculum as a subject, and widely incorporated into other subjects and their school life whenever appropriate. In selection of teaching content and learning activities, teachers should provide children with opportunities to practise the skills of conveying ideas and expressing feelings, so as to promote interpersonal skills and co-operation. Apart from it, teachers can also observe and assess children's progress.

- **Relevance to Daily Living:** The vast majority of children incline to crave for immediate gratification and short term interest. Therefore, the content of their curriculum needs to be relevant in order to be meaningful.
- **Content Comparable to Their Developmental Stage and Attainment Level:** Standard teaching materials should be appropriate to students attainment level. The teachers have to re-write or revise the standard teaching materials according to the developmental stages and attainment levels of their pupils.
- **Integration of Theoretical Studies and Practical Work**: Owing to their short attention span, pupils cannot stand passive learning for long. This will easily lead to discipline and management problems. So blending the theoretical study with practical work and ensuring pupils' participation during the course can help to sustain their interest and sense of achievement. It in turn motivates their further learning.
- **Attention to Individual Differences:** Without depriving pupils of appropriate group interaction, rooms and flexibility in the curriculum design should be allowed in order to cater for their individual needs.
- **Realistic Review of Achievement through timely and continuous formative and summative assessment:** The traditional norm reference assessment can only increase students' sense of failure. Besides, these children are easily disturbed by their emotions and thus may affect their performance during the assessment. Therefore, continuous formative assessment at appropriate stages of learning can be more accurate in revealing the effectiveness of their learning. Besides, the assessment should be target-oriented and the means need to be diversified. Through this process, teachers can get feedback on the effectiveness of

their teaching and also pupils can be immediately informed of teachers' comment on their performance, thus reducing their anxiety and gradually establishing confidence in school work.

- **Multi-disciplinary approach in curriculum design and delivery:** Since enhancing personal and social development is important in achieving the aims of education for pupils, professionals concerned can render educational and counselling services. So, their participation in curriculum design and delivery should be encouraged.

Curriculum Content for Schools for Social Development

Schools with residential service can provide children with whole day care in education and daily living. There must be close co-operation among teaching, residential and other non-teaching staff to ensure a consistent and coherent continuum of services. Since secondary school children may pass or near the age limit of compulsory education by the time they complete junior secondary education, they have a choice of vocational training or direct employment besides furthering their formal studies. So the curriculum should be flexible enough to cater for the needs of pupils of different abilities and aptitudes. However, it does not mean that pupils who opt for employment are shut out from academic pursuit since the core curriculum has already provided them a good subject knowledge foundation upon which further study through adult education or other channels of open learning is feasible.

Design considerations in a learner centred curriculum

Learner centred education is a matter of emphasis and philosophy, rather than a choice amongst alternatives. It is based on notions of **constructivist learning** which imply that learning is situated in the real world, that there is active interaction between the learner and the content, and that meaning is constructed by the learner on the basis of previous learning. In a learner centred curriculum it is critical that:

- clear learning outcomes are communicated to students;
- students take responsibility for their own learning and become independent learners, while lecturers' facilitative role is emphasised;
- suitable print and/or electronic learning materials support learning;
- learning is integrated with assessment, which should be continuous and formative;

- the curriculum caters for diversity, i.e. it includes adult students, mature students and part-time students;
- alternative modes of delivery and student learning styles are accommodated;
- the proportion of learning time (individually and in groups) is increased and teaching time is decreased

Institutional considerations in Curriculum Design

In the design of a new academic programme structure in merged institutions, the institutional considerations could be categorised as institutional policy, structure, operation and administration. The institution's vision, mission and strategic goals need to drive decisions about its programme structure, and its enrolment planning and Programme and Qualification Mix (PQM) need to address its size and shape generally.

Academic planning (i.e. planning, designing, approval and resourcing of programmes, modules and qualifications) is crucial for determining the most appropriate academic programme structure for the particular institution. There needs to be a strong link between the institution's academic programme structure and its transformational goals. For example, if **inclusivity** and **opportunity** are the goals, then the structure should include programmes which will achieve such goals and promote the institution's comparative advantage in the region, taking into account regional collaboration and possible rationalisation of programmes. If the institution's mission statement emphasise entrepreneurship , then this should be a component of the programme structure. Curricula should be reorganised around identified growth areas for the institution. The programme structure needs to provide customised learning pathways which will accommodate student diversity, taking into account mature, part-time or non-traditional students. To accommodate these diverse student groups, the institution needs to consider alternative admission policies, flexible assessment methods and an extension of the academic calendar . Any changes to the academic programme structure of course inevitably put pressure on the academic administrative system and increase the need for staff development.

Another important consideration is whether the institution will be able to sustain the academic programmes by virtue of their ability to attract students, generate income and provide pathways for students to the job market, and at the same time ensure the academic coherence and integrity of the programmes. Power differences in merging partners play a determining role in restructuring curricula, as curriculum integration depends on perceived hierarchies of status and authority, and thus of micro political struggles over whose content matters. Once the broad conceptual considerations and more specific institutional considerations are understood by all stakeholders, attention can be given to possible programme models.

Forms Of Knowledge And Its Characterisation In Different School Subjects

What are the different kinds of knowledge? What are the different ways of conceiving or conceptualizing knowledge? These epistemological questions prefigure any discussion of subject matter. In this section we briefly examine several knowledge classification schemes which have been influential in curriculum discourse and practice.

The classification of human knowledge into fields of study has been a scholarly and educational endeavour since the emergence of literate culture in the fourth century, BC. This can be traced to **Aristotle**'s organization of the disciplines into three major groups: the **theoretical**, the **practical**, and the **productive**. Theoretical disciplines included mathematics, natural sciences, and metaphysics. Practical disciplines consisted of ethics, politics, and human conduct. The productive disciplines were the fine arts, the applied arts, and engineering. This parsing of knowledge into different fields was premised on the assumption, contra Platonic dialectics, that different domains of human inquiry yielded distinctive truths, affiliated ways of knowing, procedures of inquiry and representational codes. In the nineteenth century **Auguste Comte** proposed a positivist classification scheme that supplanted Aristotle's. His positive hierarchy prioritized mathematics as the natural logic governing all fields. This was followed, in order, by physics, chemistry, biology, and social sciences. The logical positivist organization of knowledge, Schwab (1964) observed, has become "the most tyrannical and unexamined curriculum principles" and continues to drive curriculum sequences in secondary schools across the West, Europe and Asia. It is the basis for the relative allocations of value to different school subjects in senior secondary examination, matriculation and certification systems in many states.

These categorical divisions were translated into three groups of disciplines in universities: natural sciences, social sciences, and humanities. Each field is affiliated with different hierarchical relationships of power within the academy. In this way, schools and universities structurally reproduce hierarchical knowledge/power relationships based on the categorical grids of logical positivism. The valorisation of scientific knowledge is being reinvented and reinterpreted in the corporatization of university funding, structure and power.

There are, of course, powerful contradictions here. At once, knowledge which Aristotle would have considered "practical" and "productive" realms tends to be reframed as if it were "theoretical" in bids for the legitimacy of applied fields (e.g., the melding of arts and digital technologies into "creative industries"). At the same time, the new political economies of "knowledge societies" have tended to devalue those theoretical elements of "pure science" that appear to lack practical translation into commodities and strategic economic advantage (e.g., the closure of pure physics departments). Nonetheless, the logical positivist hierarchical organization of knowledge, as we will show here, is deeply embedded in contemporary discourse on subject matter. In secondary schools, it constitutes a "cognitive architecture" that differentially values specific fields and capacities in the rewarding of stratified educational credentials and outcomes. There is, therefore, a need to look at alternative classifications of knowledge that relocate and revalue knowledge in the practical, informal, and experiential realms of human experience, a longstanding claim of feminists, indigenous educators and critical race theorists.

Gilbert Ryle (1949) distinguished between knowing that and knowing how. The former can be enabled by the kind of propositional, theoretical, or formal knowledge that derives from discipline, and the latter involves the use of practical knowledge embodied in human practice and actions. Similarly, Pcars (1971) made a tripartite distinction among (a) propositional knowledge, (b) knowledge of how to do things, and (c) knowledge by acquaintance. The first two categories parallel Ryle's, and the last category refers to what we learn from everyday experience with objects and events, including firsthand and commonsense knowledge.

In this regard, "knowing by acquaintance" tends to resemble experiential knowledge based on everyday problem-identification and solution described in the social interactionist models of Dewey (1916) and Mead (1932). Further, Michael Polányi (1966) used the term tacit knowledge to capture a special kind of knowing embedded in practice, arguing that we can occasionally know more than we can tell. In his early work on European attempts to "order" the world through discourse, Foucault (1972) distinguished between what discourses of practice and discourses on practice, between the classifications deployed in practice, and those that are used to name and frame these and other domains in more formal theoretical taxonomies.

Three conceptions of knowledge can be derived from the above disciplinary and epistemological classification schemes. First, there is a disciplinary conception of knowledge that construes human knowledge in terms of canonical academic knowledge contained in various intellectual disciplines. This is associated with what **Aristotle** characterized as **episteme**, formal knowledge for purposes of understanding and explaining the world. Testing the validity of knowledge is a primary concern of disciplinary inquiry. Knowledge is here conceived of as a corpus of facts, concepts, and ideas which has been formulated and verified through the logical and discursive procedures of discourse communities. Bourdieu (1990) refers to these as "systems of objectification", institutionally legitimated ways of rationalizing and ordering the world under study. These in turn yield distinctive "grids of specification" (Foucault, 1977): naming ordered in hierarchical rank, category and taxonomy that in effect populate and constitute worlds.

Second, there is a practical conception of knowledge that construes knowledge in terms of knowing what to do in practices and actions, with an emphasis on the application of knowledge to practical and socio-cultural problems. Narrowly conceived, knowing what to do in practice involves knowing a set of procedures that may require mastery of artefact and technology. This can range from an embodied activity, such as riding a bicycle, or a more explicitly cognate activity, such as reading a book or running software.

These constitute and require procedural knowledge. However, practical knowledge cannot be reduced to merely knowing a set of procedures or skills; it involves making choices and actions based upon deliberate decisions, the meta-cognitive strategies that feature in learning theories and the kinds of embodied knowledge that feature in sociological models of "habitus" (Bourdieu, 1990). Aristotle characterized this knowing as "phronesis", standing for practical wisdom centred upon the contingent world of action. In contrast to episteme, one is less concerned with testing the validity of knowledge than with evaluating the usefulness of knowledge in light of the results of everyday actions. In practical realms, knowledge is viewed as the means of facilitating the solving of socio-practical problems; it is valued in terms of guides or "scripts" for action, social experience and everyday practice. Reflexively, we could argue that all practices, no matter how apparently habituated and mundane, taken together constitute particular cultural "logics of practice", coherent systems of exchange and value (Bourdieu, 1990).

Third, there is an experiential conception of knowledge, focusing on the social and cognitive, dispositional and practical elements entailed in making sense of the phenomena of everyday life. Whereas the disciplinary conception emphasizes knowledge as a final product or consummation of human knowing which has been set apart from ordinary affairs of life, this conception locates knowledge in the realm of ordinary human experience. According to Dewey (1916), knowledge and ideas emerge only from situations in which the learners had to draw them out of experiences that had meaning and importance to them. In this sense, knowledge cannot be separated from the knower and affiliated forms of meaning, both theoretically and practically construed. In his early epistemological theory, Dewey attempted to describe the dialectical reciprocity and co-dependency expressed in subject/object, actor/environment relations. In later formulations, Dewey (1934) viewed both education and art as the products of organism/environment disequilibria, whereby the identification and solution of problems generated a movement from "inchoate" to "choate" experience. By this pragmatist account, knowledge is an ongoing construction of meaning by social actors in relationships of exchange with their bio-social environments. In its later symbolic interactionist version, it contingent upon the availability of linguistic and semiotic, interactional and social behavioural resources.

The above three alternative notions of knowledge—disciplinary, practical, and experiential—constitute analytically distinctive, though not practically separate, modes of human knowing. There are, of course, other ways of conceptualizing knowledge or ways of knowing. In the eighty-fourth yearbook of the National Society for the Study of Education, Learning and Teaching the Ways of Knowing, ways of knowing are conceptualized in terms of scientific, practical, interpersonal, and aesthetic modes. In Frankfurt School sociology, Marxian ideology theory is developed into a recognition that "knowledge" is never ideologically and socio-culturally neutral or disinterested and necessarily reflects historically located and performed "human interests". In feminist and postcolonial theory, knowledge formation is explained in terms of historically located and gendered "standpoint", as always the product of identifiable class, gender and racialized relationships of power.

Given that so much of western philosophy and social sciences has been devoted to the diversity, uses and consequences of knowledge formation - it would be theoretically naive for curriculum practice to institutionally embrace a singular approach to knowledge to the exclusion of others. Set in the context of contemporary secular educational systems based upon democratic principles, curriculum theory and practice begins from a pluralist premise about the diversity of knowledge, historical and epistemological framings of knowledge, weighing and debating the concrete educational consequences of each for different communities and cultures. Knowledge, discourse and curriculum have material educational effects and consequences, ranging from the forms of cognition and "discipline" and how these are realised in everyday life, to their actual exchange value in educational attainment, credentialing, work and civic life.

Validity claims aside, once operationalized in the institutional domains of education, bids to define knowledge mark out a concrete linkage between epistemology and identifiable particular cultural and social, political and economic standpoints. That is, all theories of knowledge and claims to know are historically and culturally situated: "How a society selects, classifies, distributes, transmits and evaluates the educational knowledge it considers to be public reflects both the distribution of power and the principles of social control". Accordingly, a socio-political approach construes knowledge as historical, material and discourse construction, reflecting interests, power, and ideologies that underlie relations between individuals and between groups. The sociology of knowledge focuses on how formations and classifications of knowledge are produced in historical and cultural, social and economic context, ideologies arising from political economic and state structures. In this regard, any formations of subject matter can be taken as acts of power, as bids for the reproduction of particular knowledge and the exclusion or marginalization of others with effects including, inter alia, the stratification of educationally produced capital: the educational construction of differing kinds of knowing, speaking and acting human subjects.

Curriculum perspectives on subject matter

What knowledge is of most worth? What kinds of knowledge should be included and excluded? These are normative questions that teachers, curriculum theorists and curriculum policymakers ask when engaged in curriculum making, especially at the institutional level. Their responses to these questions depend on their theoretical orientations and perspectives, and, indeed, their ideological and cultural investments in the educational enterprise. At the heart of these are different teleology's of schooling, culture and society. In this section, we briefly identify four historical curriculum orientations: **academic rationalism, social efficiency, humanism,** and

social reconstructionism. All have continued salience in ongoing curriculum policy debates over the purposes of schooling and curriculum content.

- **Academic rationalism**: This tradition underscores the importance of the transmission of disciplinary knowledge for the development of the intellectual capacity of students and for the maintenance or reproduction of culture. Academic disciplines or organized fields of study are viewed as the authoritative sources from which curriculum content is derived. At its core is a disciplinary conception of knowledge, and subject matter consists of a canonical body of disciplinary knowledge, technique, and ways of knowing. This subjects academic rationalism to the instability and paradigm wars within and between disciplinary fields. Since disciplines are necessarily in historical transition and flux, influenced not only by internal problems of science but as well by complex external social and economic forces, it is increasingly the case that school subjects become sites for contestation between contending disciplinary paradigms.
- **Social efficiency**: This orientation emphasizes the importance of preparing future citizens with the requisite skills, knowledge, and capital for economic and social productivity. The construction of the school curriculum, therefore, is largely driven by statements about the production of *human capital*. Even where it may entail traditional subject field knowledge, the functional and utilitarian value of knowledge becomes predominant in this orientation. Subject matter consists primarily of knowledge and skills justified by reference to occupation, profession and vocation. With the transition from industrial to post-industrial economies, there is on-going redefinition of which applied disciplines (e.g., engineering, accounting, and marketing, among others) are the primary sources from which subject matter is derived. In this model subject matter can entail taxonomies of skills, competences and practices that might have demonstrable transfer to social and economic contexts of work, consumption, leisure and everyday life.
- **Humanism**: Liberal humanist approaches to curriculum conceive of individual learners as the central factor in determining what constitutes the subject matter. A school is a place for fostering personal development, self-actualization, innovation and creativity, with disciplinarily knowledge relevant insofar as it mirrors a

process of universal ontogenetic development. Humanistic educators embrace an experiential notion of knowledge, viewing subject matter as a series of developmentally arrayed activities which can provide learners with "intrinsically rewarding experiences that contribute to personal liberation and development". The development of a humanistic curriculum requires drawing upon a wide range of resources of knowledge and experience which could contribute to the pursuit of individual freedom, expression of interest, forms of self-realization and individual emancipation.

- **Social reconstructionism**: This orientation stresses socio-cultural contexts over individual difference and needs in curriculum making, construing education as a means of social reform and reconstruction. The making of social reconstructionist curriculum is based upon an examination of social contexts, social issues and futures, with the purpose of helping individuals reconstruct their own analyses, standpoints, and actions. Like humanistic educators, social reconstructionists conceive of subject matter in terms of activity structures, with the purpose of providing students with meaningful learning experiences that might generate social agency. They emphasize alternative ways of knowing, and the need to bring to bear a wide array of sources of experience and knowledge on designing and planning those activities. Starting with a socio-political conception of the relationship of knowledge to human interests, school knowledge is seen to be differentially constructed around dominant ideologies and discourses, with stratified transmission for different social classes and cultural groups. In this way, here are strong linkages between how subject matter is classified and framed in the school curriculum and the patterns of social inequality and distribution of power in the wider society.

The template above defines subject matter variously: 1) as disciplinary knowledge; 2) as practical or instrumental knowledge and skills; 2) as learning activities; 3) as learning experience, and 4) as socio-cultural action. In addition, it shows that programmatic versions of cultural knowledge (in all of their contending forms), the learner, and the society are entailed in the constitution of subject matter. The task of curriculum theory is to problematicize and foreground different claims on the formations of subject matter, understand their epistemological bases, their teleological assumptions about the purpose of schooling and education, to identify whose and which versions of knowledge, practice and experience are entailed, and to understand the educational and intellectual, social and cultural bases and consequences of these particular selections.

The above curriculum orientations are rather useful for understanding what counts as subject matter at the institutional level. They are concerned with the normative, ideological bases for the selection and formulation of knowledge for the school curriculum. However, they tell us little about how different kinds of knowledge are selected and transformed into curricula-as-programs (i.e., school subjects) to be used by teachers in schools. What constitutes the subject matter at the programmatic level needs to be analyzed by looking at stated curriculum theories and doctrines concerning the construction of school subjects—which remain central building blocks of the curriculum.

In what follows, we turn to four instances which take on the challenge of defining and conceptualizing subject matter at the programmatic level: John Dewey's logical-psychological distinction, the Tyler Rationale, the disciplinary doctrine, and Science for All. Each of these cases exemplifies a distinctive way of thinking about how to construct a school subject, and each in turn frame the current curriculum policy choices in different terms.

Relevance And Specificity Of Educational Objectives For Concerned Level

Learning can be defined as change in a student's capacity for performance as a result of experience. The intended changes should be specified in instructional objectives. Viewed in this context, an objective can be defined as a clear and unambiguous description of your instructional intent. An objective is not a statement of what you plan to put into the lesson (content) but instead a statement of what your students should get out of the lesson. A learning objective is a statement that describes what the learner will be able to do upon completion of the learning experience. Learning objectives help to:

- focus the overall purpose of the learning experience
- determine where the particular learning experience best fits within the larger curriculum
- select the appropriate learning experience
- select the appropriate method of assessment

Therefore, learning objectives are fundamental to creating effective learning experiences. The idea is simple but revolutionary: learning objectives put the focus on the student and learning rather than the teacher and teaching methods. If information architecture is a fairly new field, then the practice of teaching information architecture is even newer. Often instructors are experienced information architects who have little to no teacher training, and they must teach students with a wide range of experience and learning goals. Learning objectives are one tool that can make courses easier for teachers and more rewarding for students. The learning objectives are the equivalent of a project's goals. They are statements that describe what the student should be able to do after participating in the learning activity. A learning activity can be anything from a course or workshop to an article.

The easiest way to illustrate the benefits of learning objectives is to see them in action. Let's begin with some learning objectives for this unit. As a result of reading this unit you should be able to:

- Define learning objectives
- Describe at least three ways learning objectives can help you and your students
- Create learning objectives for your course that convey intended learning outcomes
- Select criteria to assess your objectives both before and after teaching

Many are interchangeably define the *objective*, *goal* and *aim*. Although the noun forms of the three words aim, objective and goal are often used synonymously, professionals in organised education define the words aim and objective more narrowly and consider them to be distinct from each other. Aims are concerned with purpose whereas objectives are concerned with achievement.

Usually an educational objective relates to gaining an ability, a skill, some knowledge, a new attitude etc. rather than having merely completed a given task. Since the achievement of objectives usually takes place during the course and the aims look forward into the student's career and life beyond the course one can expect the aims of a course to be relatively more long term than the objectives of that same course.

The **course aims** are the raison of the course. In the context of an organised unit of education, such as a course module or course programme, an aim is a (relatively) long-term goal. Sometimes an aim sets a goal for the teacher to achieve in relation to the learners, sometimes course aims explicitly list long-term goals for the learner and at other times there is a joint goal for the teacher and learner to achieve together. While the aim may be phrased as a goal for the teacher within the scope of the course it can also imply goals for the learner beyond the duration of the course. In a statement of an aim the third person singular form of the verb with the subject course, programme or module is often used as an impersonal way of referring to the teaching staff and their goals. Similarly the learner is often referred to in the third person singular even when he or she is the intended reader.

A **Course objective** is a (relatively) shorter term goal which successful learners will achieve within the scope of the course itself. Objectives are often worded in course documentation in a way that explains to learners what they should try to achieve as they learn. Some educational organisations design objectives which carefully match the SMART criteria borrowed from the business world. Because education is the most important thing you need to learn. Learning objectives should be S.M.A.R.T., that is:

- **S** – *Specific* – says exactly what the learner will be able to do
- **M** – *Measurable* – can be observed by the end of the training session
- **A** – *Attainable* for the participants within scheduled time and specified conditions
- **R** – *Relevant* to the needs of the participant and the organization
- **T** – *Time-framed* - achievable by the end of the training session

Learning outcomes: Since both aim and objective are in common language synonymous with goal they are both suggestive of a form of goal-oriented education. For this reason some educational organisations use the term learning outcome since this term is inclusive of education in which learners strive to achieve goals but extends further to include other forms of education. For example, in Learning through play children are not made aware of specific goals but planned, beneficial outcomes result from the activity nevertheless. Therefore the term learning outcome is replacing objective in some educational organisations. In some organisations the term learning outcome is used in the part of a course description where aims are normally found. One can equate aims to intended learning outcomes and objectives to measured learning outcomes. A third category of learning outcome is the unintended learning outcome which would include beneficial outcomes that were neither planned nor sought but are simply observed.

General Objective and Specific Objective

General objective: Statement, in more or less precise terms, of the trend of the learning activity. The statement, which defines the outcome of the learning activity, represents a particular point in the general orientation of a curriculum. (The general objective is the first level of specification of the aim from which it derives.)

Examples:

- To make the student of information science capable of identifying the needs of the users of a particular documentation system.
- To make the student of librarianship and information science capable of choosing and of applying the most appropriate means of making decision-makers aware of the importance of information in economic development.

Specific objective: Statement which describes the trend of the learning activity. It is formulated in terms of observable behaviour. (It is an interpretation of the general objective from which it derives.)

Examples:

- The student must be capable of giving printed documents their principal and secondary classification numbers using the LC (Library of Congress) and Dewey classification tables.
- The student must be able to identify different types of documentary information networks.

We shall give here the **characteristics of a specific objective** and explain them in order to distinguish clearly between an objective which is specific and another which is not. The first three characteristics are necessary if the objective is to be described as specific. Characteristics of the specific objective are:

- It is always expressed in terms of the student.
- It is unequivocal, in other words it is precise and supports only one interpretation.
- It describes an observable behaviour on the part of the subject.
- It specifies, where appropriate, the special conditions in which this behaviour is manifested and the criteria which will make it possible to judge whether the objective has been attained.

The requirement that an **objective is expressed in terms of the student** if it is to be designated as specific means that emphasis is placed on the student's learning rather than on the teaching given by the teacher. It is not enough for the teacher to have provided the teaching; it is also necessary for his students to have learnt. This requirement, in conjunction with the writing of specific objectives, should encourage thinking about the link between teaching and learning. The teacher should try to specify his objectives by concentrating not on what he teaches but on the changes he wishes to bring about in his students.

The specific objective **must be unequivocal**; in other words it must be precise and have only one interpretation. Nebulous expressions can be loosely interpreted. The objective must express clearly what the student must do. It is only on that condition that the objective will fulfil its role: to provide for clear communication between the teacher and the students and among the teachers themselves; to help the teacher to choose appropriate learning and evaluation activities. An objective such as 'the student will display curiosity' is open to interpretation. The same would be true of the following objective: 'the student will be capable of using the ERIC thesaurus'. In order to make these objectives unequivocal, it is necessary to consider what the student will do to demonstrate that he is displaying curiosity or that he is capable of using the ERIC thesaurus.

Certain terms may seem unequivocal and it is only by using them that one realizes that they need to be specified more precisely in order for the objective to be unequivocal. For example, the objective: 'to be capable of distinguishing between an aim and a general objective' may seem to be unequivocal. However, this objective may mean 'to give the definition of an aim and of a general objective', 'to give the characteristics which distinguish an aim from a general objective' or, for example, 'to identify a given statement as being an aim or a general objective'.

General terms such as to know, to realize, to understand, to familiarize oneself with, to become aware of, to appreciate, and so forth, lend themselves to differing interpretations. What is expected of a person who knows, realizes or understands must be specified if one is to infer that person knows, realizes or understands. Terms as vague as this are an indication rather of aims or of general objectives.

In order to clarify the general objective, one derives from it a series of specific objectives One chooses from among various possibilities the objectives which, given the context, seem to be the most relevant to the attainment of the general objective from which they derive. For example, the general objective 'to understand the meaning of technical terms' may give rise to the following objectives: 'to define a term in one's own words', 'to identify the meaning of a term when it is used in a context', 'to distinguish between terms which are similar in meaning'. Users must, therefore, reach an understanding on the terminology used and thus make the objective unequivocal.

The specific objective describes observable behaviour: The objective must describe an ability which the subject must have acquired at the end of the learning process. It is a question of specifying an observable ability and not a category of modes of behaviour such as those suggested by the words 'to understand' and 'to realize'. One must be able to grasp the reality of this ability by means of a concrete and observable action. Thus, an objective such as 'to see the value of such an experiment' is not specific. A distinction must be made here between the process and the outcome, between the means and what one wishes to attain. For example, 'to discover such-and-such a principle of classification' is not an objective but a one-off learning process; 'to read such-and-such a text' is not an objective but an activity, a task to be accomplished.

A distinction must also be made between the objectives in a list of contents, such as one finds in certain course outlines. An objective comprises at least three parts: a subject (the student), a verb of action (the observable behaviour which is expected) and a complement (the content). Thus, in the specific objective 'the student must be able to list different types of documentary information network', the subject is the student, the verb 'to list' refers to observable behaviour and the content is linked to the types of documentary information network. This content might be the subject of several other objectives: for example, 'the student will be capable of comparing various types of documentary information network' or 'the student will be capable of choosing the appropriate type of documentary network for a given requirement'. There can, therefore, be no confusion between objectives and lists of contents. The verb and the complement must be precise if the objective is to be specific.

It is all too often believed that where a very limited content is indicated within an objective, that is enough to make it specific. This is a mistake; the verb must be sufficiently precise to indicate an observable behaviour. To indicate, in an objective, that the student must know a very precise rule of indexing is not sufficient to make it a specific objective. It is necessary to specify what one means by knowledge of that rule: is it a question merely of stating the rule, as the cognitive level of knowledge might encourage us to believe? Or is it rather the ability to apply the rule which certain teachers encapsulate in the term 'knowledge'?

The specific objective states the special conditions in which the behaviour is manifested: This characteristic means that the objective must, where appropriate, mention the conditions in which the behaviour must be manifested and the criteria that will be used to determine whether the objective has been attained or not. The special conditions relating to the display of the behaviour are all those conditions which may make the difficulty of the objective variable and which make it possible to imagine a concrete situation in which the behaviour must be manifested. Although it is not necessary for all objectives to mention such special conditions, certain objectives demand that they should be mentioned. For example, the objective: 'the student will be capable of typing at a speed of 90 words a minute' could not be sufficiently precise to be specific if the time requirements in relation to the behaviour were not indicated. The same would apply for the objective: 'the student will be capable of drawing up automated search strategies appropriate to three given questions using only the descriptors of the ERIC thesaurus', if the conditions relating to the types of instruments used were not mentioned.

In conclusion, let us illustrate this fourth characteristic (in other words the **one indicating the special conditions in which the behaviour is manifested**). For example; "The student will be capable of calculating the mean and standard deviation of a series of data connected with librarianship, using statistical processing software".

Socio-cultural Context Of Students – Multicultural, Multilingual Aspects

It is an axiom of our times that our world is rapidly changing. With change comes not only a different view of the world, but also changes in language to name that *new world*. Old words take on new meanings and new words enter the vocabulary, resulting in another way of "seeing." It was not too long ago that as a nation we moved from an Agrarian Society concerned with conformity, through an Industrial Society concerned with nationalism and uniformity, to our present Information Society concerned with diversity within a global context, on our way to the Global Society of the 21st century with a planetary worldview. Such cultural and political upheavals have given rise to knowledgeable players in the game of social change, while leaving most people as confused bystanders, desperately hanging on to a past which in part is dysfunctional to the present and in many ways irrelevant to the future.

The needs of the 21st century demand a citizenry that is culturally sensitive and internationally focused, with an orientation toward the future rather than the past. Multiculturalism, as the new paradigm for education for the 21st century, is a political ping-pong term greatly misused and highly misunderstood. Since for many it is also a value-ladened concept, it has come under fire from diverse segments of the population, who due to their social position view the world differently. The fact that where you stand determines what you see is a reality in most situations, and it is especially true for the concept of multiculturalism.

What Makes a School Multicultural?

So how does this Total Quality Diversity Model work out in "real life"? The answer to this question lies in examining what makes a school or organization multicultural. Many schools and organizations regard themselves as "multicultural" simply on the basis of the ethnic diversity present in their midst. But is this what makes an organization multicultural? And if not, what does and what are the implications for effective schools in the 21st century?

The mere presence of an ethnically and racially diverse student population, due to legal, moral or social imperatives, does not make a school multicultural. This is merely being concerned with affirmative action. This was the main accomplishment of the 1960s and 70s, giving people access to the system. In the 1980s the concern was with "valuing differences." In the 1990s the push is for "managing diversity." But in the 21st century the focus of schools and corporations needs to be on "living diversity".

Many schools and organizations, however, have begun to go back on affirmative action, instead of going on to living diversity. What this means is that the number of ethnically diverse students sitting in the classrooms does not make a school multicultural. All that this may simply represent is that students have gained access to the school they have gotten through the front door. But if all a school does is to give access, then students may leave just as quickly out the back door.

Neither is it merely a concern for understanding, respecting, valuing and celebrating the differences among the various groups represented in the school. Valuing diversity is important, as it may engender an awareness of and a sensitivity to differences, but it does not necessarily translate into structural changes.

What makes a school multicultural is whether or not its "Five Ps":

- Perspectives
- Policies
- Programs
- Personnel
- Practices

Implement the following Four Imperatives:

(a) Reflect the heterogeneity of the school - the dynamic of Affirmative Action;

(b) Are sensitive to the needs of the various groups comprising the student population - the dynamic of Valuing Differences;

(c) Incorporate their contributions to the overall mission of the school - the dynamic of Managing Diversity;

(d) Create a cultural and social ambiance that is inclusive and empowers all groups in the school - the dynamic of Living Diversity.

These four imperatives form the basis of multicultural education. This is an approach to education and curriculum construction that acknowledges and respects the contributions which the various racial/ethnic groups have made to society, and incorporates these contributions in an overall program of instruction which meets the needs of an ever-changing society and is sensitive to the personal and social development of all persons concerned.

In other words, at the heart of what makes a school multicultural lies managing diversity - the proper management of the diversity in a school for the empowerment of all groups, which includes changing mindsets as well as the underlying culture of a school, especially if this culture is what is impeding change, in order for the school to begin living diversity so as to more effectively accomplish its mission. This is what makes a school multicultural. The point behind this is that unity in diversity needs to be the basic premise of all that is done in education.

This is where the five "Ps" come into play, because the rapid changes taking place in society are forcing schools to move away from a lethargic business-as-usual, reactive mindset, to a proactive one that anticipates and implements change.

Perspectives refers to the vision without which education as well as schools perish. What is "vision"? Vision is the bifocal ability to see what lies ahead (farsightedness), as well as the various impediments in the present (nearsightedness), and how to avoid them in order to arrive at the future. It must be bifocal, for focus on the future at the expense of the present, or vice versa, will result in loss and in a detour in the mission of the school.

Of these five Ps, the most important one is the last one, "practices." A school may have the best perspectives, policies, programs, and personnel, but these are only cosmetic until practiced. And it only takes a small number of personnel who in their practice refuse to go along with a program or fail to implement policy, for an otherwise well designed plan to be sabotaged. As the saying; "we can destroy with our feet what we build with our hands."

These five "Ps" have to alter present school structures and cultures, especially if these are exclusive and do not benefit everyone in the school. Why? The individual in his personal conduct is always compelled in so far as he does not resort to breaking up the existing social structure to fall short of his own nobler motives. This is why structural change a new paradigm of inclusion is necessary.

What is at issue in multiculturalism is not just sensitivity to other cultures and racial/ethnic groups that are marginal to the dominant culture, nor a transference of power, but an entire paradigm shift - a different mindset - which gives rise to a whole new way of seeing the world, as inclusive; and brings a change in institutional and societal structures, so as to create an environment (local, national and global) which is inclusive of all groups, is safe for differences and where everyone benefits. The basic measure of how well we are managing diversity is this: "If when all is said and done, you look around and notice that everyone looks like you, you have done it wrong!"

Multi-Lingual aspects

Language use in education depends on the linguistic situation of a country. Co-existence of many languages has been the essence of Indian heritage. Language uniformity is considered necessary for the economic development. Language is significant, not only as a medium of instruction but also as a determinant of societal access. An inclusive society is the foundation of a knowledge society. Today, a command over the English is a most important determinant of higher education and employment. English has been part of our education system for more than a century. Yet, English is beyond the reach of most of our young people. This makes for highly unequal access. There are many debates regarding the medium of instruction in India since independence. The *Three Language Formula* was first devised by the Central Advisory Board of Education in 1956 and formalized by the Education Commission (1964-66). The Constitution of India adopted many provisions about languages. It was claimed that, there should be one language which will be known throughout the length and breadth of the country and that Hindi which is prescribed as the official language at the Centre should be studied compulsorily. But still Hindi is not a communication device for many southern Indian states due to several reasons. As a result of historical causes, English has come to be the one language that is widely known among the educated classes of the country. Much of the national unity in political and other spheres of activity has been brought about through the study of English. This paper presents the social, educational, legal perspective of linguistic issues in India.

In India there are five distinct groups, of languages which have to be taken into consideration. That is;

i. the mother-tongue;
ii. the regional language when it is not the mother-tongue;
iii. the official language of the Centre, more commonly called the Federal Language;
iv. the classical languages-Sanskrit, Arabic, Persian, Latin, etc.; and
v. English which has come to be recognised as an international language.

In those areas where the mother-tongue and the regional language are the same, the number of languages to be taken into consideration will be limited to four and in those areas where the regional language, the mother-tongue and the language of the Union are the same; the number of languages to be taken into consideration will be limited to three. So far as the Federal language or the official language of the Centre is concerned we feel that the areas in the different parts of the country may be divided into three regional groups:

i. regions where Hindi is the mother- tongue, and therefore, is the regional language as well as the language of the Centre;
ii. regions where although it is not the mother-tongue, Hindi is spoken by a large number of people of the region;
iii. regions where Hindi is neither the mother tongue nor the regional language nor spoken or understood by the vast majority of the people. These are generally spoken of as non-Hindi speaking areas.

Languages and the Indian Constitution

The Constitution of India lays down that the official language of the Union shall be Hindi and that for a period of 15 years from the commencement of the Constitution, English language shall continue to be used for all the official purposes of the Union. Under Article 345 of the Constitution it is stated that "the Legislature of a State may by law adopt any one or more of the languages in use in the State or Hindi as the language or languages to be used for all or any of the official purposes of the State; provided that until the legislature of the State otherwise provides by law, the English language shall continue to be used for those official purposes within the State for which it was being used immediately before the commencement of this Constitution".

It also lays down that "the language for the time being authorised for use in the Union for official purposes shall be the official language for communication between one State and another State and between a State and the Union; provided that if two or more States agree that the Hindi language should be the official language for communication between such States, that language may be used for such communication. The President may, if he is satisfied that a substantial proportion of the population of a State desire for use of any language spoken by them to be recognised by that State, direct that such language shall also be officially recognised throughout that State or any part thereof for such purpose as he may specify". Under the special directives, it is stated that "it shall be the duty of the Union to promote the spread of the Hindi language to develop it so that it may serve as a medium of expression for all the elements of the composite culture of India and to secure its enrichment by assimilating without interfering with its genius the forms, style and expressions used in Hindustani and in the other languages of India specified in the eighth schedule, and by drawing whenever necessary or desirable, for its vocabulary primarily on Sanskrit and secondarily on other languages."

Regarding primary education in mother tongue, Article 350 (A) states that; "It shall be the endeavour of every State and of every local authority within the State to provide adequate facilities for instruction in the mother-tongue at the primary stage of education to children belonging to linguistic minority groups; and the President may issue such directions to any State as he considers necessary or proper for securing the provision of such facilities".

Above we seen the provisions of the Constitution, as time and again we found that witnesses had diverse views on what was envisaged in the Constitution and the manner in which education should be developed. From a careful study of the provisions in the Constitution it may be inferred that two objectives were kept in view. Firstly, that Hindi will eventually be used by the Union Government in all official correspondence with the States, and for communication between one State and another, or between a State and the Union. Secondly, Hindi should be developed so that it may serve as a medium of expression for all the elements of the composite culture of India.

Secondary Education Commission (1952-03) on Study of Languages

The Secondary Education Commission (Muthaliar Commission) was greatly impressed with the amount of interest evinced in all States in the study of language at the school stage. In view of the development of regional languages in the different parts of the country and the languages spoken in such areas, it may not be practicable or desirable to attempt to lay down a uniform policy for the whole country. On the contrary some witnesses were strongly of the opinion that there should be some uniformity in regard to the study of the languages and that there was need for a definite policy to be laid down on an all-India basis. It was claimed by some that there should be one language which will be known throughout the length and breadth of the country and that Hindi which is prescribed as the official language at the Centre should be studied compulsorily.

The Position of Linguistic Minorities

The Central Advisory Board of Education considered in 1949 the case of pupils belonging to certain minority groups, whose mother- tongue was different from the regional language, and passed the following resolution: "That the medium of instruction in the Junior Basic (Lower Primary) stage must be the mother-tongue of the child and that where the mother- tongue was different from the Regional or State language, arrangements must be made for instruction in the mother tongue. This Regional or State language where it is different from the mother-tongue should be introduced not earlier than Class 3, not later than the end of the Junior Basic stage. In order to facilitate the switch-over to the Regional language as medium of instruction in the Secondary stage children should be given the option of answering questions in their mother-tongue for the first two years after the Junior Basic stage."

"If, however, the number of pupils speaking a language other than the Regional or State languages is sufficient to justify a separate school in any area, the medium of instruction in such a school may be the language of the pupils. Such arrangements would, in particular, be necessary in metropolitan cities or places were large population speaking different languages live or areas with a floating population of different languages. Suitable provision should be made by the provincial authorities for the recognition of such schools imparting education through a medium other than the Regional or State language."

Muthaliar Commission has received a communication from the Chairman of the Inter- State Board for Anglo-Indian Education, inviting the attention of the Commission to certain special guarantees that have been given in Article 337 of the Constitution and also to the Fundamental Rights, guaranteed under Article 30 of the Constitution. Article 30 states: "All minorities whether based on religion or language, shall have: the right to establish and administer educational institutions of their choice." "The State shall not, in granting aid to educational institutions, discriminate against any educational institution on the ground that it is under the management of a minority, whether based on religion or language." These provisions being obligatory, we have no doubt that the governments at the Centre and the States will adopt necessary steps to see to the fulfilment of such obligations as are laid upon them by the Constitution.

Muthaliar Commission has given in brief the present position in regard to study of languages in the different States. In most of the schools in the States, the present position is that either the mother-tongue or the regional language has been adopted as the medium of instruction. Where minorities exist provision is made to give instruction in the mother- tongue, if the minimum number of pupils is available.

The Education Policy of 1968 had examined the question of the development of languages in great detail. The policy observes that, Good translations of foreign books into Indian languages will be supported. Besides the promotion of the link language, programmes will also be launched to increase substantially the translation of books from one language to another and to publish multi-lingual dictionaries and glossaries. The young will be encouraged to undertake the re-discovery of India, each in his own image and perception.

National Knowledge Commission (NKC) - 2005-2008 observed that, the time has come for us to teach our people - ordinary people- English as a language in schools. NKC recommendations broadly deal with the modalities of introducing English in schools from Class I, teacher training, language pedagogy and resource support for language teaching and learning. The NKC has emphasized the importance of an inclusive society as the foundation for a knowledge society. NKC has also recognized the significance of language, not only as a medium of instruction or a means of communication but also as a determinant of access. An understanding and command of over the English language is a most important determinant of access to higher education, employment possibilities and social opportunities. School-leavers who are not adequately trained in English as a language are always at a handicap in the world of higher education. More often than not, teaching is in English. Even if it is not, in most subjects, books and journals are available only in English. And those who do not know English well enough find it exceedingly difficult to compete for a place in our premier educational institutions. This disadvantage is accentuated further in the *world of work*, not only in professional occupations but also in white-collar occupations overall.

The middle income or lower-income households spend a large proportion of their modest income on sending their children to relatively expensive English medium schools. Such educational opportunities for children are a priority that is almost at par with health care for the family. But there are a very large number of people who simply do not have the resources for such investment. The outcome is exclusion. It is believe that inclusion is possible through public provision.

There is an irony in the situation. English has been part of our education system for more than a century. Yet English is beyond the reach of most of Indian young people, which make for highly unequal access. The time has come for us to teach our people, ordinary people, English as a language in schools especially at the State run schools. Early action in this sphere would help us build an inclusive society and transform India into a knowledge society. In just 12 years of schooling, it would provide the country's school-leavers with far more equal access to higher education and, three to five years thereafter, much more equal access to employment opportunities.

The NKC recommends that the teaching of English as a language should be introduced, along with the first language (either the mother-tongue or the regional language) of the child, starting from Class I in school. This phase of language learning should focus on using both languages to create meaningful learning experiences for the child without disproportionate emphasis on grammar and rules. Many states and Union Territories already introduced English as a compulsory subject at different stages in primary school, by Class V at the latest. However, the implementation is slow and the quality of English language teaching is simply not good enough. The support systems, such as the number of teachers or materials for teaching, are neither adequate nor appropriate. NKC is recommending a fundamental change that seeks to introduce, nationwide, the teaching of English as a language from Class I onwards. This is not meant to be a stand-alone, add-on subject, but is meant to be integrated into the school curriculum.

Language learning cannot be separated from, and must be integrated with, content learning. Therefore, English should also be used to teach some non-language, content subjects, starting from Class III in school. The choice of subjects for this purpose can be left to schools depending on the proficiency of teachers and availability of materials. This would, in effect, create multi-medium schools. It would also help reduce the divide between English medium schools and regional language-medium schools. The pedagogy of language learning as well as teaching should be suitably contextualized, to lend meaning to real situations and daily lives. Yashpal Commitee report (*Learning Without Burden* - 1992-93) also expressed same views on English language education at school level. Moreover, assessment should be based on proficiency rather than achievement or rote learning.

In order to meet the requirement for a large pool of English language teachers, graduates with high proficiency in English and good communication skills should be inducted without formal teacher training qualifications. They could be selected through an appropriate procedure developed by the National Testing Service and then given a short–term orientation. The nearly four million school teachers all over India, regardless of their subject expertise, especially teachers at the primary level, should be trained to improve their proficiency in English through vacation training programmes or other short-term courses. Most teacher training programmes are not based on a real assessment of needs of teachers. Thus, the entire teacher education system caters to pre-service and in-service training that exists today, including training for language teaching, needs to be thoroughly reviewed, recognizing the centrality of language in the curriculum. A multiplicity of English textbooks should be made available to address the diversity of English language environments in the country. However, to ensure that certain standards are maintained, benchmarks may be laid down for the content of textbooks at each stage. Since language learning takes place not only through direct instruction but also through assimilation from the environment, the classroom needs to be equipped with appropriate supplementary audio-visual and print material. Language learning opportunities should also be created outside the classroom through specific bi-lingual radio and TV channels, which could be introduced for formal and informal teaching and learning of English. State governments would need to be equal partners in the implementation of this idea.

What is the Purpose of Language Study? The question has often been raised as to the number of languages that can be learnt by pupils in the schools and at what stages the study of these languages should be commenced. While considering this problem, take into account the purpose which is to be served by the study of languages. There should be a clear' perspective of the purpose of study of each of these languages. It is ordinarily accepted that the mother-tongue is the most suitable language as a medium of instruction for the child beginning its study. If the same advance had taken place in regional languages as has taken place in many foreign languages, mother-tongue or regional language would have been the medium of instruction at all stages of the educational ladder. As the regional language is likely to be the language used by the majority in the region it is desirable to acquire knowledge of this language. Further, Hindi need to be promote as a link language among all peoples of the country. English language education will reduce the gap between different social classes and it also help to build of an inclusive and just Indian society. English occupies a special place in the domain of education. We are gradually moving towards an indigenous standardized Indian English.

Learner Characteristics

With today's classrooms full of digital natives, teachers are considering how to incorporate technology and new methodology into their classrooms. Our students have changed radically. Today's students are no longer the people our educational system was designed to teach. Today's students have not just changed from those of the past, nor simply changed as has happened between generations previously. Things have changed so fundamentally that there is absolutely no going back.

Today's students represent the first generation who grow up with this new technology. They have spent their entire lives surrounded by Technology and using computers, videogames, digital music players, video cams, cell phones, and all the other toys and tools of the digital age. Are the digital immigrant teachers prepared to teach a student with such profile? As an digital immigrant teacher what is there for me to do? How can a digital immigrant teacher up dated and put up with all these constant changes? These are some of the most common questions teachers ask themselves when reflecting about their performance along with the use of technology in the classroom.

What should we call these "new" students of today? The most useful designation it is found for them is Digital Natives. Our students today are all "native speakers" of the digital language of computers, video games and the Internet. Those of us who were not born into the digital world but have, at some later point in our lives, become fascinated by and adopted many or most aspects of the new technology are, and always will be compared to them, Digital Immigrants. As digital immigrants we find rather difficult to read e-books, we feel the need to print out almost any important document, sometimes we even phone a colleague to check if he received the e-mail.

But this is not just a joke. It's very serious, because the single biggest problem facing education today is that our Digital Immigrant instructors, who speak an outdated language (that of the pre-digital age), are struggling to teach a population that speaks an entirely new language. Digital immigrants have lots of wrong assumptions because they did not practice any of these skills during their formative years. The majority of university professors and elder teachers were educated without the personal computer, smart phone and/ or tablet. The majority of current students regularly use these devices in school and university. Does this gap make a difference to learning?

We have seen lots of lists that identify the characteristics of good teachers. They are great reminders of what we should aspire to be as teachers. We have not seen many corresponding lists that identify the characteristics of good learners. The characteristics of learners are enlisted below.

- **Good learners are curious** – They wonder about all sorts of things, often about things way beyond their areas of expertise. They love the discovery part of learning. Finding out about something they didn't know satisfies them for the moment, but their curiosity is addictive.
- **Good learners pursue understanding diligently** – A few things may come easily to learners but most knowledge arrives after effort, and good learners are willing to put in the time. They search out information—sometimes aspiring to find out everything that is known about something. They read, analyze, and evaluate the information they've found. They talk with others, read more, study more, and carry around what they don't understand; thinking about it before they go to sleep, at the gym, on the way to work, and sometimes when they should be listening to others. Good learners are persistent. They don't give up easily.
- **Good learners recognize that a lot of learning is not fun** – That does not change how much they love learning. When understanding finally comes, when they get it, when all the pieces fit together, that is one special thrill. But the journey to understanding generally is not all that exciting. Some learning tasks require boring repetition; others a mind-numbing attention to detail; still others periods of intense mental focus. Backs hurt, bottoms get tired, the clutter on the desk expands, the coffee tastes stale—no, most learning is not fun.

- **Failure frightens good learners, but they know it's beneficial** – It is a part of learning that offers special opportunities that are not there when success comes quickly and without failure. In the presence of repeated failure and seeming futility, good learners carry on, confident that they all figure it out.
- **Good learners make knowledge their own** – This is about making the new knowledge fit with what the learner already knows, not making it mean whatever the learner wants. Good learners change their knowledge structures in order to accommodate what they are learning. They use the new knowledge to tear down what's poorly constructed, to finish what's only partially built, and to create new additions. In the process, they build a bigger and better knowledge structure. It's not enough to just take in new knowledge. It has to make sense, to connect in meaningful ways with what the learner already knows.
- **Good learners never run out of questions** – There's always more to know. Good learners are never satisfied with how much they know about anything. They are pulled around by questions—the ones they still can't answer, or can only answer part way, or the ones without very good answers. Those questions follow them around like day follows night with the answer bringing daylight but the next question revealing the darkness.
- **Good learners share what they've learned** – Knowledge is inert. Unless it's passed on, knowledge is lost. Good learners are teachers committed to sharing with others what they've learned. They write about it, and talk about it. Good learners can explain what they know in ways that make sense to others. They aren't trapped by specialized language. They can translate, paraphrase, and find examples that make what they know meaningful to other learners. They are connected to the knowledge passed on to them and committed to leaving what they've learned with others.

Good teachers model this kind of learning for their students, which makes us believe that "good learner" belongs on those lists of good teacher characteristics. Now it's your turn. What would you add to the list of characteristics of good learners?

Teachers' Experiences And Concerns

Teacher is primarily a subject expert but basically a human being who has to be physically healthy, intellectually alert, socially sensitive, emotionally balanced, morally upright and spiritually oriented. Any prospective teacher needs to verify with in oneself whether he has developed adequately in all these necessary dimensions. One has to be enthusiastic while doing with the subjects and students, loyal to the profession, face the challenges as opportunities for personal growth to be an inquirer and investigator in the new areas, help the needy, reform the problematic and narrow minded student, achieve the goals laid and maintain harmonious relations for the prevalence of peace. Prospective teachers can know where one is having lapses in all these necessary functions. If the Prospective teachers care for self assessment and self awareness of their current strengths a weaknesses, if they ensure their strengths and are cautions about their limitations, surely they will develop an integrated and balanced personality which builds strong convictions to modify their behaviour and change is their pattern of thinking and feeling. Thus they may be supported to be excellent us their personal professional lives. Here some top teaching concerns are enlisted.

- **Exhibiting command of the material** – It is about those questions new teachers are afraid they cannot answer and what that does to their credibility. At what point do we start realizing that what we do not know enables us to join students in the learning adventure?
- **Balancing authority and rapport** – "I don't want to be some Patton-like instructor that rules with an iron fist," writes one teacher trainee, but he also doesn't want to get emails that greet him with "Yo" and call him "dude." How do we balance being caring and empathetic with upholding standards? We can strike the balance with one student or in a course, but it tips easily, often unexpectedly.
- **Dealing with communication anxiety** – Teaching involves public speaking, and that makes most people very nervous. After teaching for some years, we learn to control the anxiety. But does it ever go away? How do you feel on the first day of class?
- **Engaging students** – The concern here: how to teach and not bore students. Perhaps this should be of greater concern to some faculty who either do not know or don't care that they're boring students. The challenge is getting and keeping students interested in subject matter they pretty much expect to be boring. We acquire strategies. Some of them work, some of the time. It is another of those ongoing quests.
- **Managing students' perceptions** – New teachers often look like students. It is a concern that passes all too quickly.

- **Juggling roles** – Interesting that right from the start, these new teachers were not so much concerned about transitioning between roles but about finding time for all of them. It is another balance issue — finding time for all the responsibilities of an academic position and for life beyond work. If you care about teaching and want to do it well, it demands a lot of time. But how do we know when it is consuming too much time?
- **Resolving grade complexities** – The mixture of concerns here started with making the judgment calls grading requires. It also included having high but reachable standards, being challenged about grading policies, and dealing with irate students who are firmly convinced they have been graded unfairly. Again, we acquire strategies along the way. Some of them work, some of the time. We get caught in the grades-matter conundrum. As long as they do, we have to be concerned, but being concerned inflates their importance still further.
- **Being memorable** – These new teachers aspired to be remembered by their students, not just for course content but because the course had value beyond the content. Most of us begin teaching careers with high aspirations. Most of us discover that we infrequently end up changing students' lives. Should we abandon attempts to be memorable for something more realistic?
- **Negotiating flexibility** – It is about when to enforce a course policy and when the student deserves a pass. It is also about when to change an assignment that is not working, or when to adjust the calendar to tackle some major confusion in a class. Now it is about cell phone policies—to take a stand, cave in, or find something in the middle. Is being appropriately flexible a skill that can be mastered?
- **Overcoming cultural differences** – It was last on the list of concerns for these students, but at least it is on the list. It is a concern if you are from a different culture and a concern if you are teaching students who do not belong to the majority group. It can be as straightforward as coming from the country and teaching urban students, or as confounding as cultural norms about gender and race. It is an ongoing concern and deserves a place higher on the list.

Critical Issues: Environmental Concerns, Gender Differences, Inclusiveness, Value Concerns And Issues, Social Sensitivity

Environmental Concerns

Today more than ever, society needs high-quality **environmental education** programs that succeed in moving values and changing behaviours in the direction of sustainability and environmental conservation. Effective, relevant evaluation offers a very powerful way to improve these education programs and enables them to succeed in accomplishing more of their objectives and goals. Since the mid-1980s, thousands of sustainability initiatives have emerged across the globe. These have been a response to international calls for improved quality of life, ecological protection, social justice and economic equity. Despite this increased activity, many experts have pointed out that progress has been modest and there appears to be little evidence of positive achievement. People have recognised the need to focus, coordinate and direct energies in sustainability towards specific goals. This has resulted in the development of an increasing number of regional and national sustainability strategies. However, the profile of education and learning for sustainability has remained low within national sustainability frameworks. The outcomes of the **Johannesburg Summit** and the establishment of a **Decade of Education for Sustainable Development** affirm the need to integrate sustainable development into education systems at all levels in order for education to be a key agent for change. The Decade aims to promote education as the basis for sustainable human society and to strengthen international cooperation towards the development of innovative policies, programmes and practices of education for sustainable development.

Up until the second half of the twentieth century, our planet seemed to be immense, limitless and the effects of human activities were locally segmented. There are strong and objective reasons to think that we are living amidst a crucial historical transition. Besides, the changes affecting us cannot be reduced to a specific zone of the globe, but are spread everywhere. The situation is so worrying that at the Conference of the United Nations for Environment and Development, held in Rio de Janeiro in 1992, a course of action was asked for from the educational system to make citizens aware of the problems and prepare them for well-founded decision-making. What is happening a decade after the Rio Conference? We continue to find an almost complete absence of works on the state of the world. We still educate the young for the most part as if there were no planetary emergency. In the same vein, several authors lament the scarce attention given to planning for the future by our educational systems. Most of the works on environmental education are focused exclusively on local problems without paying attention to the global situation. Environmental and development problems are not solely caused by physical and biological factors, but an understanding of the parts played by aesthetic, social, economic, political, historical and cultural elements is required.

Thus, it is propose that students should be stimulated to explore "alternative futures" and to participate in actions which may favour these alternatives. We educators of every field should contribute to enable citizen participation in the search for solutions. But there is a serious difficulty in fulfilling this task, because our perceptions of the world situation are, generally, as fragmented and superficial as those of most citizens, including the majority of national and international leaders in the fields of politics, business or science. For this reason, teacher preparation should be the "priority of priorities".

The National Policy of Education (NPE 1986) states: "There is a paramount need to create a consciousness of the environment. It must permeate all ages and all sections of society, beginning with the child. Environmental consciousness should inform teaching in schools and colleges. This aspect will be integrated in the entire educational process."

Gender Differences

Think of the activities that take place in an average household during the course of a day. Food is cooked; cleaning is done – sweeping, mopping, and dusting. Groceries and other household items are purchased. Clothes are washed, dried, ironed. Sometimes household repairs are carried out. Garbage is discarded. Also, the people who live in the house need to be looked after. Sometimes they may have special needs – for example babies need constant supervision.

These are some of the things that are required to be done to keep homes functioning. These activities take a lot of time, and many are to be done on a daily basis. The people who do them expend a lot of energy and may be exhausted when they are finished. Most of the time, women perform these tasks. Put together, these tasks are called housework. Given this name, it may be surprising to learn that housework is not considered to be work in economic or social terms. It is seen as a set of tasks that is naturally performed by the women of a household. It is not, for example, calculated as part of the country's Gross Domestic Product (the sum of all goods and services produced in a country in a given period). This is in spite of the fact that if the women of the house are unable or unwilling to do these tasks, other people will do them – but only if they are paid to do so.

Housework is not the only area in which women's work is not recognised as work. We would generally see women rushing about the city, obviously very busy. But according to the prevalent statistics, only a tiny fraction of women are in the workforce. The question that is to be raised, then, is 'why is the economic contribution of so many women seen as being trivial?'

These examples reflect certain changes in viewpoint that are very significant from the point of view of gender studies. They reflect a change in perspective – a change in the way things is looked at. Gender studies is a field of study that looks at the world from the perspective of gender. This means that while studying something – the distribution of resources within a household, a social unit like a caste group, a bill placed before Parliament, a development project, the classification of different species – are done in a manner that takes into account the fact that different genders exist in the world. These genders are differently placed within social reality such that various processes impact them differently.

Thus gender studies recognises that gender has to be taken seriously. It is also a field that recognises that often, within academic disciplines and also other spheres of society, the perspective that has been applied has been that of the most powerful people in society, and that this is often at the expense of less powerful people. Gender studies then exists as an important means of correcting such imbalances.

Women's Studies, Gender and Women's Studies or Gender Studies it poses challenges to traditional knowledge and works towards change. Established knowledge have been produced by groups from which women were absent or marginalized. This new and an adjusted lens need to access and intend strategies to construct social, power relations and intellectual change. It particularly focuses on alternative ideologies, intersecting meanings of gender, race and class, and ranges over disciplines, nations, times and cultures.

The critical evaluation of change in society is an important aspect of women's studies. And we must not forget that feminism itself has a cultural context, intellectual context and it represents dimensions of contemporary thought and consciousness. It is relativistic and sceptical of overall gender issues especially investigates the lives of the powerless and the ignorant. Gender and Women's Studies curriculum underpins second wave of **feminism** (1960's to 1980's) in the West.

Feminism is a philosophy that holds with this ideal of equality. It is the belief that although they are different, men and women are equal. Feminism recognizes that women have been oppressed and repressed in certain societies throughout history. It also carries with it the commitment to change the attitudes and behaviours of those who do not see men and women - all people, really - as equals. This equality should be manifested in economic, political, and social equality for both sexes.

This Feminist wave of change reached our part of the world a decade later. It not only appraise established practices but it visions and develops new enabling and empowering practices. The discipline acts as catalysts for promoting and strengthening gender streamlining through teaching, research, action, fieldwork and extension. It intends to develop a theoretical framework for analysis of the various dimensions of women's status in the development process.

Therefore, Women's Studies contribution to knowledge in various fields, understanding the women's marginalization in the society and theorizing perspectives give an insight to dimensions of empowerment. The most pragmatic utilization of the subject could be creation of alternative concepts and distinctive way of looking at the world and basis of enquiry. It establishes methodologies and theoretical paradigms to contextualize women and gender as a variable into a wider intellectual framework of social sciences. The discipline has also provided alternative spaces to academia of social sciences who examine their subjects with a feminist appraisal.

The **second wave** of gender studies emerged in the middle to late 1960s, courses explaining and developing feminist theory began to be taught on college campuses. By 1970, the phrase "Women's Studies" was applied to them. By 1980, over twenty thousand courses were being taught in that "discipline." Today there are programs at all levels of study - undergraduate minor, undergraduate major, master's degree, doctorate. It even has its own association, the National Women's Studies Association, and journal.

The third wave of Gender Studies emerged in the mid 1990's. The third wave Led by **Gen Xers**, daughters of 2nd wave. They questioned what 2nd wave had not yet done and took feminism more international, more multicultural, and more gender open. They focus on gender as performed allowing more freedom on gender continuity spectrum.

The established disciplines of social sciences distinguish themselves by obliterating gender concerns from their research agenda. The paradigms based on women and gender as a central variable can transform the existing academic disciplines in a fundamental way by introducing multi-disciplinary, inter-disciplinary and trans-disciplinary scheme of studies.

For last few decades the headway of involving women in the development processes and recent emphasis of gender mainstreaming is an agenda of every public or private sector institution. Therefore, the importance and demand of Women and Gender Studies has augmented. Therefore, the discipline can play a role of catalyst to take forward the agendas of international organisations in true character by sensitizing the masses about gender issues and also the planners, implementers, civil society, NGOs etc. Besides bridging these gaps the understanding of indigenous gender perspectives is also very important for effective implementation of these schemas.

Inclusiveness

All are born equal with some limitations and with the help of inclusion be able to actively participate as equal citizens in all aspects of society and community life. Inclusive Education denotes that all children irrespective of their strengths and weaknesses will be part of the mainstream education. The feeling of belongingness among all community members and other functionaries is developed through inclusive education. A dominant problem in the disability field is the lack of access to education for both children and adults with disabilities. As education is a fundamental right for all, enshrined in the Universal Declaration of Human Rights, and protected through various international conventions, this is a very serious problem. In a majority of countries, there is a dramatic difference in the educational opportunities provided for disabled children and those provided for non-disabled children. It will simply not be possible to realize the goal of Education for All if we do not achieve a complete change in the situation.

Children in special schools were seen as geographically and socially segregated from their peers, and the initial movement to vocationally integrate these students in mainstream schools shifted to one where the whole school was encouraged to become more adaptable and inclusive in its day-to-day educational practices for all students. Pedagogy in particular was highlighted as the key to meeting all students' educational needs by making the curriculum flexible, and so more accessible. By recognizing that teaching methods which can make curriculum accessible to children with disabilities can also make learning accessible to all students, a teacher or school principal is well on the way to improving the overall quality of their school. In this way, inclusive education is not a disability-only issue, but an educational quality issue.

In developing contexts with large numbers of out-of-school children, inclusive education tends to be more broadly concerned with school access and education deprivations for marginalised groups such as girls, ethnic minorities, poor families and disabled children, who have never attended or dropped out of school. It seems that there is currently an expanding discourse on inclusive education developing amongst some academics and teaching professionals in India. This discourse is attempting to shift perceptions of disability from the medical model to the social model. However, there are many conceptual difficulties with the terms of integration and inclusion in India, which are often used interchangeably. Further, varying definitions of disability and subjective interpretations of what 'type' of child a teacher is willing to include in their classroom add to the confusion. The concept of inclusive education in the mainstream as opposed to specialist segregated provision of schooling.

India is one of the few countries worlds over where the education of children with special needs doesn't fall within the purview of human resource development ministry. It is under ministry of social justice and empowerment, the prime focus of which is rehabilitation, not education. In fact, till today it does not have education as part of its agenda and the issue of education of children with disabilities remains imperceptible, hidden from the public domain, a private problem for families and NGOs to deal with. The segregation of children with challenging needs is morally unjustifiable and a violation of human rights. Therefore, inclusive schools have to address the needs of all children in every community and the central and state governments have to train their teachers to manage inclusive classrooms. Any child may experience a special need during the course of educational years. Some children feel 'left-outs' and never enter school or enter only for a few years and, as repeaters, become 'drop-outs' or, more correctly 'pushed-outs', without their needs having been met. These children are a vivid illustration of the failure of schools to teach rather than the pupils' failure to learn. A school system emphasising Education for All should ensure the right of all children to a meaningful education based on individual needs and abilities.

Value Concerns And Social Sensitivity

It is widely agreed that the primary function of education of concerned with values. Education transmits cultural and social values to the children. Along with that education helps children to cultivate values. In this book we will look in detail on the values associated with education. We will look at the social values and the moral values. These values include love, sharing, honesty, patriotism, loyalty, truthfulness and so forth. These values help the members of any given society to live in a peaceful way. It also helps the existing resources to be distributed equitably and fairly. This brings about progress, growth and development in a society and country. In any country there are vices within the society that are against the moral values. These vices include corruption, armed robbery, stealing, raping, cultism, examination malpractices, rioting, assassination, touting and so forth. **Social sensitivity** is the personal ability to perceive, understand, and respect the feelings and viewpoints of others.

Values can be defined as "temptation, form-fitting objectives, principles that guide people's lives, and have varying significance". Values are the essence of our personality, and affect us to make decisions, trust people, and arrange our time and energy in our social life. *Values education* is the process by which people transmit values to others. It can be an activity that can take place in any organization during which people are assisted by others, who may be older, in a position of authority or are more experienced, to make explicit those values underlying their own behaviour, to assess the effectiveness of these values and associated behaviour for their own and others' long term well-being and to reflect on and acquire other values and behaviour which they recognize as being more effective for long term well-being of self and others.

Values education can take place at home, as well as in schools, colleges, universities, jails and voluntary youth organizations. There are two main approaches to values education, some see it as inculcating or transmitting a set of values which often come from societal or religious rules or cultural ethics while others see it as a type of Socratic dialogue where people are gradually brought to their own realization of what is good behaviour for themselves and their community.

Some researchers use the concept values education as an umbrella of concepts that includes moral education and citizenship education. Themes that values education can address to varying degrees are character, moral development, Religious Education, Spiritual development, citizenship education, personal development, social development and cultural development.

There is a further distinction between explicit values education and implicit values education where: *explicit values education* is associated with those different pedagogies, methods or programmes that teachers or educators use in order to create learning experiences for students when it comes to value questions.

Another definition of value education is "*learning about self and wisdom of life*" in a self exploratory, systematic and scientific way through formal education. And let us know, the most important Human Values are *wisdom, integrity, trust, beauty, faith, respect, love, honesty, caring and co-operation.*

- **Wisdom:** Wisdom is something that is the most important human value in many ways; under-appreciated in its importance, in its value in our lives and in its true meaning. Wisdom is also very often confused with words like knowledge or intelligence but the word wisdom is defined as the quality of having experience and good judgment and the resulting soundness of that action or decision. Wisdom is so vitally important and yet we often confuse it with other words or disregard a wise opinion because we are too vain or egotistical, to be truly wise is to understand the way the world works.
- **Integrity:** Society once saw integrity as valuable as trust but now we think of integrity as, more common than not, a weakness. The quality of being honest and having strong moral principles can be seen as a non-willingness to change or to adapt to a new way of thinking, and to an extent that is correct, but that's not thinking of integrity in the true sense of the word; moral uprightness. The state of being whole and undivided, not just in your physical decisions but spiritually as well, being metaphysically undivided is the true nature of integrity. As a human value it is imperative that we stand spiritually undivided and hold true to our integrity, the importance of which is often forgotten.
- **Trust:** Trust can be interpreted many ways, but ultimately it comes down to reliability and truth. Without trust the world simply would not function, we create documents, money and bulletproof glass because we have lost faith in trust, which is why it is now one of the most important human values someone can have. Learn to trust and be trusted, it's no easy task, but the importance is beyond measure, In a world without trust no one can survive.
- **Beauty:** Beauty is something that has really been tainted by our society. The way we think about something that is beautiful is judged on a purely physical response, but the true meaning of

beauty is being in balance and harmony with nature. Many would argue that beauty is not a human value and, although beauty is a subjective experience, when you analyze what a subject of beauty is, it becomes anything that resonates with personal meaning, not just emotion. The importance of this Human Value is clear when you think about the things that bring meaning into your life such as family and friends, these things become beautiful in a greater sense. Finding things that have personal meaning in your life and allowing them to fill you with emotion is one of the most important values.

- **Faith:** Faith and the way we perceive it today has, in a sense, been hijacked by religion. That is not to say Faith cannot represent religion, it absolutely can, but it means so much more than what religion uses it for. It is complete trust or confidence in someone or something, not only living with invisible means of support but knowing that there is an ocean, because there is a river. Certain things in life require a bit of faith because the world isn't black and white; sometimes you need a little bit of unknown to accomplish things you never thought you could.
- **Respect:** Many feel that respect should be given as opposed to earned, but no matter who you are Respect needs to be earned just as trust and honesty need to be as well. Respect is a feeling of deep admiration for someone or something elicited by their abilities, qualities, or achievements. The rub to this is that when you want to be treated with respect, you will treat others with respect; it's one of those rare instances that in obtaining this feeling you will better the way the world views you.
- **Love:** Love seems like something that we do know the importance of, but in fact it is misunderstood and forgotten about daily. Not in the sense one would think, but rather it loses its importance in the over use of the word. In its over-use, the word love has depreciated in value, not in the feeling but in the word, just as saying a word repeatedly you eventually forget it's meaning, the words love has become a little too common. The trick is to remember the feeling behind the word and not lose faith in the fact that it is over-used.
- **Honesty:** Honesty feels like something you don't come by often these days, but in the realm of human values, it is extremely important. The idea of staying true to oneself can often feel

intimidating and impossible, but what most people fail to realize is that it is not the act of simply telling the truth that makes someone honest rather the *quality* of person who is being honest. An honest person is often straight, upright, sincere and fair and being an honest person brings more reward to the soul than the damage a lie could do.

- **Caring:** Often seen as displaying kindness and concern for others, the true importance of this value comes from the work or practice of looking after those unable to care for them-selves. Caring for others both physically and spiritually is a vitally important value to have; people will always rely on someone else for help at one point or another, but we often fail to realize how much of a difference caring for another person can make.
- **Co-operation:** It is the process of working together to the same end, but many view co-operation as a luxury and not an important human value. It is undeniably one of the most vital assets one can have when working through a problem. Having the opinions and voice of another person will not only draw out a discussion of the topic, but also lead you to a well-rounded solution. Co-operation has been under-appreciated for years in its importance and should be held in high regard.

Make social sensitivity part of curriculum

With more reports of crimes against women, a group of schools from across the India are preparing a draft proposal to include 'Education on Social Sensitivity' in the school curriculum from kindergarten to Class 12. The schools will submit the proposal to the human resources and development (HRD) ministry, various state governments and education boards across the country. The new subject will teach students to be sensitive towards and respect women, senior citizens, weaker sections of society and the environment. The draft will contain the best practices to teach social sensitivity to students through various activities incorporated in the school curriculum, and will recommend making the subject mandatory for all students.

The schools met for a two-day conference on the proposal in Mumbai recently. "It is an abstract subject and cannot be taught through textbooks, unlike value education. Teachers will need to inspire students to bring about an attitude change," said Rekha Vijayakar, director, Guru Harkrishan High School, Santacruz. "Generally, such subjects are introduced only in secondary section, but a lot of students drop out after primary school, and so they never get the chance to learn about it," she said. "Toddlers can be taught compassion through activities that encourage them to look after a plant or a pet animal. Older students can be asked to adopt a neighbourhood or a road, giving them the responsibility to keep it clean," Vijayakar added. (hindustantimes, March 28, 2013)

Conclusion

The unit analyzed the determinants that facilitate or hamper curriculum change. These determinants are directly related to the purposes of education. The purposes can be cultural transmission, environmental adaptation, and total personality development. Transmission leads to adaptation and adaptation to personality fulfilment. Conversely, the cause of adaptation is enhanced by personality fulfilment and it later enhances the cause of transmission. However, the objective of total personality fulfilment is debatable. The values that a culture live by help in establishing a curriculum. Education's future course will be decided by the decision that the culture renders on the current value debate. Humanism for all versus humanism for some and the cognitive man versus the mentally-healthy man are the two emotion-arousing issues which are included in the debate. In the past, the Curriculum Development course was not considered necessary for beginning teachers. It was assumed that they would use the curriculum provided by schools, which would be primarily taught through textbooks. In recent years, however, teachers have been seen as curriculum decision-makers who need to understand both the 'how' and the 'why' of curriculum design. If teachers understand how a curriculum has been developed, they are likely to be more prepared to make it educationally fruitful for their students. Moreover, if adaptations are necessary, they will reflect an understanding of the overall goals, purposes, and design principles inherent in the curriculum they are teaching. In many cases, teachers may find themselves creating unique curricula to meet the context-specific needs of their students and the communities in which they are situated.

Model Questions

1. Identify factors that shape and influence education systems of the world. Explain how any of these factors have shaped the education system of your country.
2. What student characteristics are most important to take into account when planning instruction? How realistic is it to expect a teacher to plan instruction that takes into account the important needs of all the students?
3. Which subject areas are the most difficult to plan for? Why?
4. What would be the characteristics of a class that would be easy to plan for?

What would be the characteristics of a difficult-to-plan-for group?

5. What differentiates a well-stated expectation or learning outcome from one that is poorly stated?
6. What are the most common exceptionalities that students have? How might they influence planning, instruction, and assessment?
7. A teacher's skill at instructional planning has been linked to his or her students' academic success. Explain why this is the case? What other teacher characteristics may be correlated with student achievement?

References

Dannels, D. P. (2015). Teacher communication concerns revisited: Calling into question the gnawing pull towards equilibrium. *Communication Education*, 64 (1), 83-106.

The implications of changes in technology on the construction of curriculum. retrieved on 27-03-2016 from http://www.ozedweb.com/info paper_technology_and_curriculum.htm

Factors influencing national systems of education. retrieved on 27-03-2016 from http://camponotes.blogspot.in/2013/01/factors-influencing-national-syastems.html

Primrose, K. & Alexander, C. R. (2013) Curriculum development and implementation: factors contributing towards curriculum development in Zimbabwe higher education system. *European Social Sciences Research Journal*, 1(1), 55-65.

Thamarasseri, Ismail. (2007). *Education in the Emerging Indian Society.* New Delhi: Kanishka Publishers.

Nakpodia, E. D. (2009). Culture and curriculum development in Nigerian schools. *African Journal of History and Culture* (AJHC) Vol. 2 (1), pp. 001-009, January, 2010 retrieved from http://academicjournals.org/article/article1381853278_Nakpodia.pdf

http://epathshala.nic.in/wp-content/doc/NCF/Pdf/aims_of_education.pdf

Kumar, S. *What is the National Objectives of Education in India?*. retrieved from http://www.publishyourarticles.net/knowledge-hub/education/what-is-the-national-objectives-of-education-in-india/5207/

National Curriculum Standards for Social Studies: Chapter 2—The Themes of Social Studies. retrieved on 03-04-2016 from http://www.socialstudies.org/standards/strands.

Mason, Terrence C., Ed.; Helfenbein, Robert J., Ed. (2012). *Ethics and International Curriculum Work: The Challenges of Culture and Context.* IAP - Information Age Publishing, Inc. retrieved on 20-04-2016 from http://eric.ed.gov/?id=ED535560.

Balsley, J. *Important Considerations For Developing Your Curriculum.* retrieved on 20-04-2016 from https://www.theartofed.com/2015/06/30/3-important-considerations-for-developing-your-curriculum/

Erasmus, A. *Design considerations in the development of a new academic programme structure.* retrieved on 20-04-2016 from http://www.che.ac.za/sites/default/files/publications/d000132_Erasmus_Design_academic_structure.pdf

Overview of the curriculum development process. retrieved on 20-04-2016 from http://www.fao.org/docrep/009/ah650e/ah650e03.htm

Deng, Z. & Luke, A. *Subject Matter: Defining and Theorizing School Subjects.* retrieved on 20-04-2016 from https://www.researchgate.net

Thamarasseri, Ismail. (2014). *Issues and Challenges of Indian Education.* Agra: Shri Vinod Pustak Mandir.

Weimer, M. *Seven Characteristics of Good Learners.* retrieved on 20-04-2016 from https://globaldigitalcitizen.org/seven-characteristics-good-learners.

Welikala, T. (May 2011). *Rethinking International Higher Education Curriculum: Mapping the research landscape.,* A position paper commissioned and published by Universitas 21, leading globalnetwork of research universities for the 21st century.

Pednekar, P. (Mar 28, 2013). '*Make social sensitivity part of curriculum*'. retrieved on 20-04-2016 from http://www.hindustantimes.com/india/make-social-sensitivity-part-of-curriculum/story-KsnD3TbcOSSXDTdOpODFhO.html

Hayden, M. (16 April 2013). *Internationalising the curriculum in a national context.* retrieved on 20-04-2016 from https://cerp.aqa.org.uk/perspectives/internationalising-curriculum-national-context

Curriculum Development (December 2014) DEVCO B4 Education discussion paper. retrieved on 27-03-2016 from https://capacity4dev.ec.europa.eu/system/files/file/04/03/2015_-_1152/final_curriculum_development_2014_12.pdf

Curriculum Design. retrieved on 20-04-2016 from https://cd.edb.gov.hk/la_03/chi/curr_guides/Maladjusted/ema-3.htm

General objective and specific objective. retrieved on 20-04-2016 from http://www.unesco.org/webworld/ramp/html/r8810e/r8810e07.htm

Rosado, C. *What Makes a School Multicultural?.* retrieved on 20-04-2016 from http://www.edchange.org/multicultural/papers/caleb/multicultural.html

Chapter - 6

Curriculum Development at School Level

Introduction

"Every Journey Begins With The First Step."

Curriculum is a written plan which drives instruction. It delineates the skills and concepts taught and evaluated to enhance student achievement. Composed of a content area philosophy, strands with definitions, program goals, aligned scope and sequence, learner outcomes, and assessment tools, it is intentionally designed to meet district, state, and national standards. In this unit, we will describe briefly how it is developed.

The development of an effective curriculum is a multi-step, ongoing and cyclical process. The process progresses from evaluating the existing program, to designing an improved program, to implementing a new program and back to evaluating the revised program.

Conflicting views about the advantages and disadvantages of centralists and School-Based Curriculum Development (SBCD) practice have been intensified by differences in defining the component elements of the complex term 'school-based curriculum development'. The expression 'school-based' in the term school-based curriculum development is also interpreted in various ways. Connelly (1972) avoided the expression and substituted 'user-developer'. While these two expressions often have the same meaning and may refer to the same person, i.e. the classroom teacher, this is by no means always the case. A 'user-developer' is not necessarily school-based, and 'school-based' is not necessarily the same as 'user-developer'. The expression 'user-developer' may refer to a team of teachers from various schools working under the guidance of an external curriculum consultant to adapt a set of commercially disseminated instructional materials to the needs of their students. Participation in such a team may take place within the framework of a university-maintained in-service training programme, to which teachers may register on their own initiative and on an individual basis.

By using instructional materials developed by the team, a teacher participating in the in-service programme becomes a user-developer, but the programme used by the teacher is not school-based. It was not initiated by the school and it may well be that it was not adopted by other teachers teaching the same subject in parallel classes. If, on the other hand, a school adopts a programme produced or revised by a team of its own teachers, then the programme is school-based, but those teachers who did not participate in its development are not user-developers. One may also ask who participates in the development of school-based programmes? All the teachers teaching a particular subject? Some of the teachers only? If in a certain school, within the framework imposed by an external authority or by the school authorities, the teachers enjoy a relatively high level of autonomy in determining what to teach and what kind of instructional materials to use, does such a situation represent school-based curriculum development?

As indicated by Sabar (1989): "...school-based curriculum development ought not to be, and indeed cannot be, reduced to teacher-based curriculum development, important as teachers' roles are at every stage. It should be participatory, that is decisions should be shared with all those involved in the educational experience." (p.202) Sabar lists several potentially legitimate partners in school-based curriculum development: parents, if possible learners themselves, other institutions and agencies in the society.

Frequently, in educational practice, representatives of the local authorities or of the local educational authorities participate in curriculum decisions. A variety of interest groups such as religious denominations, labour unions, universities and other institutions of higher education, as well as industrial and commercial chambers, claim a say in the school curriculum. Quite often, local authorities prescribe the school programme for all schools in the geographic area of their jurisdiction. Certainly, such arrangements do not represent instances of school-based curriculum development. In the curriculum literature, devolution of power in matters of the curriculum and school-based curriculum development are treated quite often under one heading, while in practice these are two different phenomena. Devolution is a precondition of school-based curriculum development: it may precipitate school-based curriculum development, but it does not in itself constitute a sufficient condition. Without full awareness of the differences between the concepts of devolution, user-developer, and school-based curriculum development statements made about curriculum development may remain void of exact meaning.

The broadest definition of SBCD implies not only full autonomy for the school to decide what to teach, but also a commitment on its behalf to prepare instructional materials for the courses offered, with a minimal reliance on available textbooks. The narrowest definition of SBCD would stipulate that the central educational authorities delegate some freedom to, or bestow some autonomy upon the local or the school authorities in determining a certain part of the school programme. In practice, we never encounter a full realization of the broadest definition of SBCD .

There are no schools which the meaning of school-based curriculum development operate according to the principles represented by this broadest definition. On the other hand, employing the narrowest definition, one may say that all schools incorporate some elements of SBCD approach in their routine activities. The subsequent sections describe SBCD activities which have a substantial impact on life in the school. wiz;

- Meaningful communication about SBCD is possible only if the terms of the discourse are precisely defined. Consequently, deliberation about curriculum should start with defining the terms used.
- Contradictory statements and recommendations about SBCD may reflect differences in definitions of terms and, therefore, when used in decision-making context, they must be analyzed with regard to meanings originally attributed to them.
- Precise definition of terms may lead towards identification of areas of consensus which, in turn, may create a favourable climate for negotiating.

Understanding Different Approaches To Curriculum Development

There are many approaches to curriculum development. They differ by the various perspectives. Curriculum developers construct regarding the key curricular elements - curriculum, teachers, students and the context. Some curriculum developers focus on students and their learning goals where others focus on the effect of the teacher's action upon learning. Still others focus on the context of learning and the degree to which individuals are viewed autonomously or as the objects upon which the work of curriculum is acted. In this section we will focus on various significant and contrasting approaches to curriculum development.

Subject-centred Approaches To Curriculum Development

Subject centred curriculum is the oldest and the most widely accepted form of curriculum organization. The earliest example of this sort of organization is the seven liberal arts in the schools of ancient Greece and Rome and in the monastery and Cathedrals of the middle ages in the Medieval Era.

The seven liberal arts consisted of two divisions:

- *Trivium*: Its lower division consisting of: i. Grammar ii. Rhetoric iii. Dialectic (logic)
- *Quadrivium* consists of Arithmetic, Geometry, Astronomy and Music.

These subjects were broad. The seven liberal arts do not conform precisely to modern subjects having the same titles: In the modern period the *Trivium* was further divided to include literature and history and the *quadrivium* to include algebra, trigonometry, geography, botany, zoology, physics and chemistry. In this manner subjects went on being added one after the other so much so that in 1930 there were over 300 distinct subjects of instruction. Despite all this the seven liberal arts are still the nucleus of the subject curriculum. In subject curriculum each subject is taught as a separate unit. In this pattern of curriculum organization a student may take four or five different subjects each taught by a different teacher and at a separate period of the school day.

Any relationship which may exist between two or more subjects is left un-noticed by a teacher who always try to think about his own courses. The vast increase in content of all areas of life has introduced the necessity of specialization in an educational programme. Thus we find it necessary to train teachers relatively in small areas of human knowledge but they remain ignorant in other areas. The subject curriculum has also led to the acceptance of subject matter as the main goal to be achieved in education. This has caused great emphasis to be given to such tasks as definition, classification and memorization. Application, analysis and problem solving have been largely neglected.

Throughout the 20th century, most curriculum specialists relied on three or four data sources for making curriculum decisions: the child, the society, learning processes, and subject matter. Although alternative curriculum development approaches or models have been advanced that relied on the first three sources, the subject areas have dominated school curriculum since the beginning of formal education. Subject-centered curriculum remains the most common type of curriculum organization in most states and in most schools today. In subject-centered curricula, the subject matter itself serves as the organizing structure for what is studied and how it is studied. In its purest form, the curriculum for each subject-area is designed by subject-matter experts and is intended to.

Curriculum design is about how a person envision what a curriculum should be. There are several standard models of curriculum design. One of the most prominent is the subject-centred design. The subject-centred designer divides the curriculum into nice and neat subjects such as maths, science, history, literature, etc. This structuring of the disciplines is for practical reasons. It organizes the curriculum into basic concepts that are combined based on what they have in common. The essential knowledge of each area is gathered together to be taught to students.

Where the division of the curriculum stops depends on its purpose. Any expert in education knows that subjects overlap and the division is often arbitrary. In addition, every subject can be further divide into smaller parts. For example, English can be broken down into writing, reading, speech, grammar, and more. A major criticism of this design is the lack of integration or horizontal articulation. The learning is compartmentalized and the students often never see the connections across subjects. In addition, the subject-centred design does not take into account the needs and interest of the students. The textbook is made by experts in the field who already know what knowledge and even experiences a child requires. Despite this, the subject design is by far the most popular approach. It is easy to do and practical. It is appropriateness needs to be left to the educator who is trying to help their students.

In this system, the main focus is on curriculum development, with subject specialists developing "high standards" for student uniformity — what our society believes all students should know and be able to do at grade-level check points. Teachers are told what and how to teach.

Characteristics of subject-centred approaches to curriculum development

The main goal and purpose is to standardize students, to make them alike with a "core curriculum." A large amount of meaningless testing is imposed on teachers to inflict on students. Teachers have big classes that restrict teachers from getting to know each child well enough to form a close relationship. Parents are usually not involved, except to help their child with the teacher-assigned homework. Teachers spend much time imparting the state curriculum. They focus on what students don't know and can't do. Students are required to do teacher-assigned homework. Students are not encouraged to ask questions. Learning, merely to pass tests, is shallow and temporary. Following are the characteristics of Subject Centred Curriculum

- *Learning subject matter is an end in itself*: Listening to lectures, studying the textbooks and studying for examination are all practices that show the influence of the subject centred curriculum approach. The subject teacher considers it of great importance to cover the prescribed textbook. Since a specific amount of subject matter is to be learnt in a set time. If subject matter has been learnt, the teacher and students feel satisfaction.
- *There is a predetermined uniform standard of knowledge*: Those who follow the subject centred approach strongly advocate minimum standards. They advocate set standard for a class to be achieved by all students in order to qualify the examination. In other words a time limit is placed on achievements and if the pupil fails, the course must be repeated. The teacher attempts to bring the pupil up to the set standard. Thus failures are required to repeat a grade or they are dropped out from their institutions.
- *Practice in skills is emphasized:* Drill in specific skills is one of the typical characteristics of the subject curriculum. Drill session, remedial work, review work, coaching classes are often devoted to such type of drill. This drill is given in equal amounts to all pupils in the group.
- *Emphasis is placed upon acquiring information for future use:* The subject matter selected for a course, is considered to be of value in adult living rather than child's immediate needs. Thus adult problems are given more weight than problems of children in youth.
- *Progress is measured by how much of the subject a pupil has learnt:* As the subject matter is an important thing to be learnt, learning is measured by how well the subject matter has been mastered. Frequent tests are given to check the extent of achievement by the students.
- *Each subject is distinct entity (unit) with a logical organization of its own:* Emphasis is placed on the acquisition of skills, facts and information in different logically organized subjects. The members of the staff, teaching different subjects do not plan courses together and they do not discuss common problems.

- *Subject matter is selected by adults previous to the teaching, learning situations:* As the subject matter is taught in logically organized discipline, therefore, the content of the course is selected before it is taught. For this purpose they receive help from subject matter, specialists, supervisors, administrators and textbook writers.

Environmentalist Approaches (Incorporating Local Concerns) To Curriculum Development

"If the world is saved, it will be saved by people with changed minds, people with a new vision. It will not be by people with old minds and new programmes. It will not be saved by people with old vision but a new programme" – Daniel Quinn

India greatly realizes that moving towards sustainability lies in its strategy of unprecedented mobilization of people's mind, ideas, institutions and resources to come up with a socially just and environmentally sustainable blueprint for survival (MOEF Report, 2002). Education has been recognized to play a central role in this odyssey. Recognizing the centrality of education in environmental protection and conservation, India's National Policy on Education (1986) states "There is a paramount need to create a consciousness of the environment. It must permeate all ages and all sections of the society beginning with the child. Environmental consciousness should inform teaching in schools and colleges. This aspect will be integrated in the entire educational process"

Subsequent to this policy statement, several efforts have been made to reorient and reorganize school education and get Environmental Education (EE) more formally established. School textbooks, by and large, in all subjects and at all levels, have been revised for their contents and methodology from an environmental perspective (greening of textbooks). It is, however, recognized that salutatory effects of these curricular revisions will not be sustained unless it is coupled with appropriate changes in teacher education curricula (pre-service and in-service). Realizing the significance of introducing EE in teacher education, the National Council of Teacher Education has made an attempt to develop a curriculum framework in Environmental Education for the four levels of teacher preparation, viz., Early Childhood Care and Education (ECCE), Elementary teacher training, Secondary and Senior Secondary and Vocational education.

One of the major concerns of this millennium is taking good care of the environment which nurtures all of us. We have now been living in a situation where environmental degradation is occurring at an unprecedented pace. Hence the immediate need of the day is bringing about an awareness of the environment and its problems at all levels. Sincere efforts are needed to re-establish our links with the environment. We must protect the environment from 'ourselves'. It is our own life style, greed, selfishness and lack of awareness that is the starting point of all the problems related to the environment. The great scientist Albert Einstein has said "you cannot solve a problem with the same mind-set which created it at the first place". It is only when we truly begin to see ourselves as an indivisible part of the environment, and then there would be a fundamental shift in our mind set towards its conservation.

Teachers play a significant role in the society because of their influence on the children with whom they interact. An important challenge before us at present is to infuse in to the learning process, a spirit of question. In this process, environment becomes a medium for engaging young minds in the excitement of first-hand observation of nature and understanding the patterns and processes in the natural and social worlds. In this context, it has necessitated a relook in to the curriculum of teacher education, so as to "prepare the young minds to appreciate the importance of environment in a holistic manner, not only for human survival but also for all life forms on Earth".

Recognising the central role of education in environmental protection and preservation, the National Policy on Education (NPE) states that "There is a paramount need to create a consciousness of the Environment. It must permeate all ages and all sections of society, beginning with the child. Environmental consciousness should inform teaching in schools and colleges. This aspect will be integrated in the entire educational process" (NPE, 1986). The NPE, 1986 and the subsequent educational policies have positioned environmental awareness and education firmly in school education. The latest National Curriculum Framework (NCF) 2005 recognizes the critical role of the environment as the context in children's learning by emphasizing that "Learning takes place through interactions with the environment around, nature, things and people, both through actions and through language. The physical activity of moving, exploring and doing things, on one's own, with one's peers or in the company of adults, and using language—to read, to express or ask, to listen and to interact—are the key processes through with learning occurs. The context in which learning takes place is thus of direct cognitive significance for meaningful learning" (NCF 2005).

Agenda 21, the action plan of the United Nations on sustainable development, states "Education, including formal education, public awareness and training should be recognized as a process by which human beings and societies can reach their fullest potential. Education is critical for promoting sustainable development and improving the capacity of the people to address environment and development issues. It is widely accepted that Education is the most effective means that society possesses for tomorrow. Education is humanity's best hope and most effective means in the quest to achieve Sustainable Development (UNESCO, 1997).

Realizing Education as a potential instrument of social change, the National Policy on Education, 1986 made Environmental Education a part of the general education at all levels, in particular at the school level. The significance and urgency of creating environmental awareness in school children has also been upheld by the Supreme Court through its directive to the Central and State educational authorities to make EE compulsory at the school and collegiate levels. (Honourable Supreme Court Directive - 2003).

However, what has been well realized is that it is the teacher who is the key to the successful implementation of Environment Education in the classroom as he/she would ultimately be analyzing, interpreting and implementing it. If teachers (pre-service and in-service) do not possess the necessary knowledge, understanding, skills or commitment to environmentalize and transact the curriculum, it is very unlikely that they will be able to produce environmentally literate students. Given this central role of teachers, Teacher Education both at the pre-service and in-service levels becomes vital. Hence, UNESCO describes teacher preparation in Environmental Education as the "Priority of Priorities".

Endorsing the significance of intensive teacher preparation, the National Document brought out by the National Council of Educational Research and Training (NCERT), 2004 states "If Education has to be an effective tool of change in the general attitude towards the treatment of the environment, teacher education will have to respond to this need effectively at all levels. The content and processes of teacher education will have to equip teachers with a proper understanding of and love for the nature around and the skill of inculcating these among their students. This may result not only in a healthier society, both physically and mentally, but also the much needed replenishment and sustenance of natural resources notwithstanding all the material and industrial development" (NCERT, 2004).

The education system in India had incorporated certain aspects of environment in school curricula as early as 1930. The Kothari commission

(1964-66) also suggested that basic education had to offer Environmental Education and relate it to the life needs and aspirations of the people and the nation. At the primary stage, the report recommended that "the aims of teaching science in the primary schools should be to develop proper understanding of the main facts, concepts, principles and processes in physical and biological environment" Environmental education at primary, secondary, higher secondary levels was treated in a different way. Environmental education is an essential part of every pupil's learning. It helps to encourage awareness of the environment, leading to informed concern for active participation in resolving environmental problems. It was introduced without any delay from class –1 as Environmental Studies (EVS), as a subject so that right from their childhood, the right attitudes towards environment will be nurtured in the young minds.

It is important that we capture this enthusiasm and that no opportunity is lost to develop knowledge, understanding and concern for the environment through school education. The curricular, cross-curricular attempt of environmental education also should be a joy for the learner. A curricular framework of environmental education (EE):-

- It envisages the place of EE in the school curriculum.
- Place of EE vis-à-vis other subjects of study.
- Mode and strategy of inclusion of chapters at different levels.
- EE in terms of time and allocation of marks.
- Development of syllabi and instructional material for dissemination at different levels of school education.

Aims and Objectives of environmental education

The objectives of environmental education is to increase public awareness about environmental issues, explore possible solutions, and to lay the foundations for a fully informed and active participation of individual in the protection of environment and the prudent and rational use of natural resources. The resolutions provide the following guiding principles for environmental education:

- The environment as a common heritage of mankind.
- The common duty of maintaining, protecting & improving the quality of environment, as a contribution to the protection of human health and safeguarding the ecological balance;
- The need for a prudent and rational utilisation of resources;

- The way in which each individual can, by his own behavior and action, contribute to the protection of environment;
- The long-term aims of environmental education are to improve management of environment and provide satisfactory solutions to environmental issues.
- Provide opportunities to acquire the knowledge, values, attitudes, commitment and skills needed to protect and improve the environment.
- Encourage pupils to examine and interpret the environment from a variety of perspectives-physical, geographical, biological, sociological, economic, political, technological, historical, aesthetic and ethical.
- Arouse pupil's awareness and curiosity about the environment and encourage active participation in resolving environmental problems.
- Environmental education is closely linked to the other cross circular themes of other subject areas.

Environmental education has an ability to solve the societal needs, the needs of a community problem and their solutions and workforce for tackling cooperative minds. We need the school children to share and develop the motivation from school about various environmental issues, which are the challenges of today and prepare them for the future.

Environmental education must become a vehicle for engaging young minds in the excitement of first hand observation of the nature and understanding the patterns and processes in the natural and social worlds in order to take care of the habitat and its surroundings which becomes a major part of EE in both primary and upper primary stages of school education. In the secondary and senior secondary stages also some of the major issues such as environmental protection, management and conservation are to be dealt in more detail.

Primary stage: EE is imparted as EVS, which forms a common component of syllabus, prescribed by the States and CBSE. The textbooks for environmental studies which are prepared by N.C.E.R.T has taken cross curricular approach to teaching environmental concepts through language, mathematics about the environment. In classes I and II there is no separate EVS book. For classes III and IV, EVS textbooks are available. EE has been further reinforced under the Art of Healthy and Productive Living (AHPL) for which a single teacher's handbook has been developed for classes I to V. The contents and concepts covered in these books are as follows:

- Familiarisation with one's own body;
- Awareness about immediate surroundings;
- Need for food, water, air, shelter, clothing and recreation;
- Importance of trees and plants;
- Familiarisation with local birds, animals and other objects;
- Interdependence of living and non-living things;
- Importance of cleanliness and sanitation;
- Importance of celebration of festivals and national days;
- Awareness of sunlight, rain and wind;
- Caring for pet animals;
- Awareness about air, water, soil and noise pollution;
- Need for the protection of environment;
- Knowledge about the source of energy;
- Importance of the conservation of water resources and forests and
- Indigenous and traditional knowledge about the protection of environment.

The textbooks lay emphasis on raising awareness levels and sensitising children about environmental concerns. Emphasis has also been laid on the need to organise learning in local specific contexts, which will provide more meaningful experiences to children. Aspects of indigenous knowledge have also been introduced. There are references and suggestions for conducting activities in and outside the classroom. The NCERT textbooks for environmental studies generally take a comprehensive view of the natural, physical, social and cultural environment. It is evident that the textbooks represent relevant ideas commensurate with the age and developmental level of children so as to provide them the necessary understanding about their immediate environment. However, there is a scope for inclusion of more activities to enable children to translate awareness into effective behavioural action.

Upper Primary stage: The contents of textbooks present an extension and elaboration of the concepts introduced at the primary stage. The textbooks in Rajasthan and Madhya Pradesh (Classes VI-VIII) and in Karnataka (Classes V-VII) contain environmental concepts by and large in the textbooks of science and social science. The textbooks of Karnataka for class V in the subjects of science, social science and language have environmental ideas infused with these subjects. The State of Orissa, deals with the environmental concepts and concerns in its textbooks for science and geography. These are also included in a single textbook of history and civics. The NCERT textbooks of 'Science' and 'Social Science' have incorporated such concepts in the textbooks. The major concepts dealt with in these textbooks are:

- Adaptation of living beings in environment;
- Natural resources;
- Water cycle;
- Food chain;
- Importance of plants and trees in keeping the environment clean;
- Classification of plants;
- Role of plants and animals in environmental balance and soil conservation;
- Ecosystems;
- Necessity of clean air for healthy living;
- Animals and their characteristics;
- Effects of environmental pollution and the consequences of air pollution-(i) Greenhouse effect, (ii) Ozone layer depletion and, (iii) increase in carbon dioxide;
- Role of microorganisms in the environment;
- Dependence of the community on the environment;
- Basic knowledge about the Earth and its atmosphere;
- Physical features of the country;
- Population and environment;
- Care and protection of livestock;
- Necessity of wildlife protection;
- Impact of deforestation;
- Impact of industrialisation on environment; and
- Role of civic society in protection of the environment, personal and public property including monuments.

While most of the areas of EE have generally been covered, there is a need for the inclusion of more individual and group activities and project work in order to promote both the effective and cognitive domains of learning. Co-scholastic activities including organisation of plays, cultural programs, debates, mock parliament, discussions and community activities may help further in achieving the objective.

Secondary stage : The concepts of EE have been provided in the textbooks of science and social sciences in the states of Rajasthan and Madhya Pradesh. In Orissa, there are textbooks, namely science part-I (physical science), Science part-II (biological sciences) and geography. The environmental concepts both are at concrete and abstract levels. The concepts covered are:

- Biosphere;
- Greenhouse effect;
- Ozone layer depletion;
- Use of fertilisers and pesticides;
- Wildlife protection;
- Soil chemistry;
- Management of domestic and industrial waste;
- Pollution of noise, air, water ad soil and control measures;
- Ecosystem;
- Management of non-degradable substances;
- Edible and ornamental plants;
- Sewage disposal and cleaning of rivers;
- Nuclear energy;
- Radiation hazards;
- Gas leak;
- Wind power;
- Bio-energy; and
- Environmental laws and acts.
- Environmental concepts also extend to subject areas like languages and social sciences, which reinforce learning and internalization of all such concepts.

Higher Secondary stage : This is the stage of diversification. Students opt for either the academic stream or the vocational stream. The treatment of concepts becomes deeper and more discipline oriented since the content caters to the demands of the concerned subject, as an independent discipline a comprehensive view about EE is not available in the textbooks. Majority of the concepts are found in the textbooks of biology, chemistry and geography, which are optional subjects. Students opting for any one of these subjects would accordingly benefit in different aspects of EE. The coverage of EE concepts in the textbooks of various subjects includes:

- Environment and sustainable development;

- Atmospheric pollution- global warming,
- Greenhouse effect,
- Acid rain,
- Ozone layer depletion;
- Water pollution- international standards of drinking water,
- Importance of dissolved oxygen in water,
- Bio-chemical oxygen demand,
- Chemical oxygen demand,
- Land pollution,
- Pesticides,
- Ecology.

In short, Environmental approach to curriculum development is a process that aims at the development of environmentally literate citizens who can compete in global economy, who have the skills and knowledge and inclinations to make well informed choices concerning the environment, and who exercise the rights and responsibilities of the members of a community. Environmental knowledge contributes to an understanding and appreciation of the society, technology and productivity and conservation of natural and cultural resources of their own environment.

In all the four familiar areas of the school curriculum, i.e. language, mathematics, science and social sciences, significant changes are needed with a view to making education more relevant to the present day and future needs, and in order to alleviate the stress with which children are coping today. This NCF 2005 recommends the softening of subject boundaries so that children can get a taste of integrated knowledge and the joy of understanding. In addition, plurality of textbooks and other material, which could incorporate local knowledge and traditional skills, and a stimulating school environment that responds to the child's home and community environment, are also suggested. In language, a renewed attempt to implement the three-language formula is suggested, along with an emphasis on the recognition of children's mother tongues, including tribal languages, as the best medium of education. The multilingual character of Indian society should be seen as a resource to promote multilingual proficiency in every child, which includes proficiency in English. This is possible only if learning builds on a sound language pedagogy in the mother tongue. Reading and writing, listening and speech, contribute to the child's progress in all curricular areas and must be the basis for curriculum planning. Emphasis on reading throughout the primary classes is necessary to give every child a solid foundation for school learning.

Behaviourist Approaches To Curriculum Development

Behaviourist approach is anchored on the behaviourist principles, behavioural approach to curriculum is usually based on a blueprint. In the blueprint, goals and objectives are specified, contents and activities are also arranged to match with the learning objectives. The learning outcomes are evaluated in terms of goals and objectives set at the beginning. Behavioural approach which was started with the idea of Frederick Taylor is aimed to achieved efficiency. In the factory for example, the worker will be paid according to his output produced with in a specific period of time. In education, behavioural approach begins with educational plans that start with the setting of goals or objectives. These are considered as important ingredients in curriculum implementation as evaluating the learning outcomes as a change of behaviour. The change in behaviour indicates the measure of the accomplishments.

Although there are many instances where older ideas need to be exchanged by newer ones, that's not necessarily always the case. In the concepts of curriculum, the behavioural approach is without a doubt the oldest of the curriculum approaches. Its principles are based on the theories of Frederick W. Taylor, a mechanical engineer. "Logical and prescriptive, it relies on technical and scientific principles and includes paradigms, models, and step-by-step strategies for formulating curriculum" (Orstein, 2009). Its objectives and purposes are definitive and established. The entire framework is in essence a blueprint or a well organized plan to further the aims of the stakeholders. It uses scientific observation and evaluation in order to maximize all areas of emphasis to perfect learning outcomes. J. Franklin Bobbitt was innovator in the behavioural curriculum realm. While he is credited with many learning models, it was one of his students, Ralph W. Tyler who assumed the torch. Tyler's insights eventually lead to legislation and was the precursor to the Elementary and Secondary Education Act of 1965.

While a lot of Taylor's postulates are based on industrial models, the conclusions are clear. Criticism from opponents of Taylor's methods have described his system as "machine theory." Taylor was on the right path to learning; productivity can be meticulously staged in a controlled environment and manipulated to expand the results or outcomes. The Behavioural approach to curriculum is really the default when curriculum are in transition or in a state of failure. It is the last result when it should not be. If this approach is initiated properly and the variables regulated and recorded, it can be as effective as any other. The Cognitive model is a derivative in some of the assertions of the behavioural theory.

A person's approach to curriculum is really just their philosophy or beliefs about how curriculum should be created. There are many different approaches to curriculum and the same approach could have multiple names. Among the most prominent approaches are the behavioural approach and the academic approach. The behavioural approach is focused on, as you can guess, behaviour. This approach is grounded in scientific principles. Everything the students do must be observable as this is the evidence that the student has achieved the goals and objectives, which are also based on observable behaviours. All activities lead to students being able to do whatever the goals and objective specify. Even today, most curriculums are behavioural focus as this is very easy to assess.

The **academic approach** is a more focused on the structure on knowledge and organization of subject matter into subjects. The training and development of the mind is what is most important. Observable actions are not as significant in this approach. When people adopt this approach they believe in training the mind like a muscle. A strong muscle can be used in many different ways just as a strong mind can be used in many different occupations in life.

Behaviourist focus on training people to develop skills while academics focus on training the mind to think. In reality, these two approaches complement one another and help to make well-rounded individuals. Focusing on one over the other is not the wisest way to develop students.

Behaviourists assume that the only things that are real (or at least worth studying) are the things we can see and observe. We cannot see the mind or the unconscious, but we can see how people act, react and behave. From behaviour we may be able to make inferences about the minds and the brain, but they are not the primary focus of the investigation. What people do, not what they think or feel, is the object of the study? Likewise the behaviourist does not look to the mind or the brain to understand the causes of abnormal behaviour. He assumes that the behaviour represents certain learned habits, and he attempts to determine how they are learned. Example: Your objective is to change learners' individual attitudes: your goal/aim that at the end of your target certain time, students should be punctual, well discipline and academically competitive. But upon evaluation your objective was not realized, so therefore if there's no change, no accomplishment. So as a teacher you have to look for another technique/strategies in order to achieve your aim. Therefore behavioural approach is the end view focuses on the need for behavioural objectives to serve as guides to instruction and to determine whether its desires ends are realized.

Competency-based Approaches To Curriculum Development

Competencies should include more than facts. Competencies represent the integration and application of learned facts, skills and affective qualities needed to serve the society, the community and the profession.

"Competencies is the habitual and judicious use of communication, knowledge, technical skills, reasoning, emotions, values, and reflections in daily practice for the benefit of the individual and community being served." (Epstein and Hundert, JAMA, Jan. 9, 2001)

What drives the Competency based curriculum system? (1) Competency outcomes drive curriculum objectives, (2) Curriculum does NOT drive outcomes and (3) Fundamental shift from teacher centred to learner-centred orientation.

The concept of competency is a pillar of curriculum development and a driving force behind the process of change. It is defined as "the development of complex capacities that enable students to think and act in various fields of activity [...]. It consists of achieving knowledge in action, the result of a sound knowledge base that can be put into practice and used to explain what is happening" (Braslavsky, C.).

Competence can be used as an organising principle of curriculum. In a competency-based curriculum, exit profiles specify the classes of situations that learners must be able to handle competently by the end of their education. Depending on the type of education, these classes of situations are identified either on the basis of real-life or work-related situations or on the internal logic of the discipline in question. Competence as an organising principle of the curriculum is a way to bring real life back into the classroom (Jonnaert, P. et al, Prospects, UNESCO, 2007). It is thus a move away from the idea that curriculum is mainly implemented by having students reproduce theoretical knowledge and memorise facts (the conventional knowledge-based approach).

The essential competencies that citizens must possess to ensure national, regional and global development are acquired through education, and expressly through the curriculum. Even as this notion is accepted implicitly in educational contexts, there is a lack of explicit global recognition from the development community concerning the importance of the curriculum, what form it should take, and how best to leverage its value for development.

Competency-based learning or Competency-Based Education and Training is an approach to teaching and learning more often used in learning concrete skills than abstract learning. It differs from other non-related approaches in that the unit of learning is extremely fine grained. Rather than a course or a module every individual skill/learning outcome, known as a competency, is one single unit. Learners work on one competency at a time, which is likely a small component of a larger learning goal. The student is evaluated on the individual competency, and only once they have mastered it do they move on to others. After that, higher or more complex competencies are learned to a degree of mastery and isolated from other topics. Another common component of Competency-based learning is the ability to skip learning modules entirely if the learner can demonstrate they already have mastery. That can be done either through prior learning assessment or formative testing.

For example, people learning to drive might first have to demonstrate their mastery of "rules of the road", safety, defensive driving, parallel parking etc. Then they may focus on two independent competencies: "using the clutch, brake with right foot" and "shifting up and down through the gears". Once the learners have demonstrated they are comfortable with those two skills the next, overarching skill might be "finding first: from full stop to a slow roll" followed by "sudden stops", "shifting up" and "down shifting". Because this is kinetic learning the instructor likely would demonstrate the individual skill a few times then the student would perform guided practice followed by independent practice until they can demonstrate their mastery.

Competency-based learning is learner-focused and works naturally with independent study and with the instructor in the role of facilitator. Learners often find different individual skills more difficult than others. This learning method allows a student to learn those individual skills they find challenging at their own pace, practising and refining as much as they like. Then, they can move rapidly through other skills to which they are more adept.

While most other learning methods use summative testing, competency-based learning requires mastery of every individual learning outcome, making it very well suited to learning credentials in which safety is an issue. With summative testing a student who has 80% in an evaluation may have an 80% mastery of all learning outcomes or may have no mastery what-so-ever of 20% of the learning outcomes. Further, this student may be permitted to move on to higher learning and still be missing some abilities that are crucial to that higher learning. For example, a student who knows most traffic laws and has mostly mastered controlling a vehicle could be treated equally to a student who has a very high mastery of vehicle control but no understanding of traffic laws, but only one of those students should be permitted to drive.

What it means to have mastered a competency depends on the learning domain (subject matter). In subject matter that could affect safety, it would be usual to expect complete learning that can be repeated every time. In abstract learning, such as algebra, the learner may only have to demonstrate that they identify an appropriate formula, for example, 4 of 5 times since when using that skill in the next competency, resolving a formula, will usually allow opportunity the learner to discover and correct their mistakes.

It is important to understand that this learning methodology is common in many kinetic and/or skills-based learning, but is also sometime applied to abstract and/or academic learning for students who find themselves out-of-step with their grade, course or program of study. Increasingly educational institutions are evaluating ways to include competency-based learning methodologies in many different types of programs in order to make learning success a constant while student pace can vary.

Competency-based learning is an educational technique that can be applied in many fields and learning environments. It is an area of pedagogical research and is not adequately understood in one, single learning domain.

Competency based learning empowers learners to focus on mastery of valuable skills and knowledge and learn at their own pace. This seems like a straightforward statement, but what does it mean in practice? Why do stakeholders in our educational ecosystems care about changing their practices to incorporate competency based learning? Part of the impetus comes from learner-centric shifts in education driven by social and economic pressures. There is also a growing realization that educational practices need to change to effectively focus on learning. And there are also potential benefits fundamental to the long-term success of our educational institutions. The practical benefits of competency based education are:

- Efficient and potentially lower-cost degree/credential options for students
- Greater understanding of learning outcomes throughout the academic institution
- Courses, learning resources, and assessments aligned to well-defined goals
- Motivated and engaged students
- Increased student retention and completion rates, particularly when prior learning can be applied to degree progress
- Learners' improved ability to recognize, manage, and continuously build upon their own competencies and evidence of learning

- Employers' improved ability to understand graduates' competencies and learning achievements
- Outcomes-based frameworks for continuous improvement at course, program, and institutional levels

How do we achieve these benefits? Competency based education approaches are already diverse and are continuing to evolve through the work of initiatives defining effective models. Different approaches share the common characteristics of being learner-centric, outcomes-based, and differentiated. These characteristics help us understand competency based education in practice.

The competency based education practices do not need to be dramatic or disruptive. Many effective approaches incorporate competency based learning processes into existing course and curriculum structures. In fact, one of the reasons why there are so many different approaches is because educational institutions adapt competency based learning to achieve their own goals. Competency based learning does not happen in a vacuum. Nor does it need to be viewed as something outside or counter to our educational traditions and values.

Competency based learning can be valuable for all of the stakeholders in our learning communities: learners have more opportunities to take ownership of their learning and expand their lifelong learning pathways; faculty grow professionally as they articulate the learning outcomes in their areas of expertise and embed them in rich learning experiences; academic leaders provide engaging curricula that advance knowledge and produce graduates who can demonstrate what they have learned; and institutional leaders focus on new ways of identifying barriers to success and achieving improved outcomes. The key characteristics of learner-centric, outcomes-based, and differentiated help us visualize what competency based learning means to these stakeholders.

Key characteristic: Learner-centric : First and foremost, competency based learning focuses on the learner as an individual. It provides opportunities for each individual to develop skills at their own pace, collaborate with others, collect evidence of learning, and become successful lifelong learners. Competency based learning empowers learners to:

- Understand the competencies they need to master to achieve their goals
- Progress through learning processes without time constraints

- Explore diverse learning opportunities
- Collaborate in learning activities with communities of peers and mentors
- Create learning artefacts that represent their competencies
- Reflect on their own learning achievements
- See what they have mastered, what they still need to accomplish, and where to improve
- Develop an online academic identity, including the ability to manage competencies and portable evidence of learning from multiple sources

Key characteristic: Outcomes-based : Competency based learning starts with well-defined learning outcomes. The structure for competency based learning comes from creating, managing, and aligning sets of competencies to learning resources, assessments, and rubrics, with analytics to track performance. Focusing on outcomes empowers faculty and academic leaders to:

- Develop robust sets of learning outcomes and competencies
- Reorient curricular design to start with learning outcomes rather than starting with time/term structures
- Build high-quality sharable resources, assessments, and rubrics designed to support learning outcomes
- Foster authentic assessment that includes demonstrated mastery of competencies
- Effectively identify risk in students' progress toward learning achievements and provide appropriate interventions
- Support transparent analysis of learning outcomes at every level of the institution
- Achieve short-term and long-term academic performance improvements focused on outcomes rather than inputs

Key characteristic: Differentiated : Differentiation refers to competency based learning practices that recognize and adjust to meet the needs of individual learners. Differentiation is multi-faceted and applies to learner support, communications, and interventions, as well as learning processes.

- **Prescriptive/Diagnostic:** providing different learning materials or assessments to learners based on what they've already mastered.
- **Affiliation**: learners receive different materials or delivery based on their relationship to the curriculum or program in cohorts or groups.

- **Adaptive**: content that is designed with learning alternatives and branching closely tied to the learner's specific interactions with the content.
- **Choice**: learners select from among different learning resources and pathways based on their own choices and preferences.
- **Personalized messages and notifications**: relevant, timely communications tailored to learners' individual activities and needs.
- **Appropriate interventions**: feedback, guidance, activities, or tasks designed to help individuals progress along their learning paths.

Most of these practices are already familiar and valued. This gives us many opportunities to be "now-ists" and foster bottom-up innovations that weave in more of the benefits of competency based learning while building on the investments we have already made in well-designed learning opportunities.

Benefits to innovating competency based learning within existing workflows:

- Leverage existing investments and valuable resources
- Lower barriers to entry and time to implementation
- Avoid costly retrofitting of deeply embedded processes
- Encounter fewer regulatory and accreditation complications
- Achieve faculty buy-in and engagement by focusing on learning outcomes rather than on disruption
- Meet existing faculty, student, and employer expectations because courses and credits are well understood
- Continue to transfer courses and credit hours for students moving among institutions
- Add new paths to employment rather than disrupting existing paths

We can take a variety of approaches to focus on learning and curricular outcomes throughout our learning ecosystems.

'Minimum Levels Of Learning' (Mll)

In line with the commitment of India to provide elementary education to all children, educational facilities have got tremendously expanded during the post-independence period. This is particularly true of facilities at the primary education stage. The number of primary schools in the country has increased from 2.2 lakhs in 1950-51 to nearly 6.32 lakhs. In addition, there are at present nearly 3 lakh non-formal education centres providing primary level education to out-of-school children in the age-group 9 to 14. This expansion has definitely helped in making primary level education more easily accessible to a larger section of the population. In fact, according to the All-India Educational Survey conducted by the NCERT in 1986, nearly 95 per cent of the population are served by a primary school within a walking distance of 1 km. However, the large-scale expansion has resulted in the creation of educational facilities with widely varying quality in terms of institutional infrastructure, teaching-learning processes as well as the quality of students passing out of these institutions. The quality variations become more pronounced in certain states, between schools of rural and urban areas, between schools managed by government and non-government bodies, and so on. Recognizing the urgent need for rectifying this anomalous situation with respect to quality, the National Policy on Education 1986 calls for paying immediate attention to (i) improving the unattractive school environment, the unsatisfactory condition of buildings and inadequacy of instructional material; and (ii) laying down minimum levels of learning that all children completing different stages of education should achieve. Keeping this policy directive in view, the Report of the Working Group on Early Childhood and Elementary Education Set up for Formulation of Eighth Five Year Plan states: The targets need to be spelt out not only in terms of participation, but also in terms of quality and outcomes. During the Eighth Plan, it should be our aim to bring about a substantial improvement in quality of education through improved infrastructure, improved teacher education, and substantial improvement in quality and quantity of learning materials. In terms of outcomes it shall have to be ensured that minimum levels of learning are laid down with reference to the conclusion of primary and upper primary stages and an appropriate evaluation system created to ensure achievement at least of the prescribed levels of learning. In fact, significant efforts towards specification of Minimum Levels of Learning (MLLs) had already been made at the NCERT during 1978 in connection with the UNICEF-assisted projects on 'Primary Education Curriculum Renewal' and 'Developmental Activities in Community Education and Participation'. As part of these projects, a 'Minimum Learning Continuum' was drawn indicating the learning outcomes expected to be achieved by all children completing Classes II, III, IV and V. The Primary Education Curriculum Renewal Project was evaluated in 1984 using a set of achievement tests developed for all the primary classes based on the competencies specified in the Minimum Learning Continuum. Utilizing the empirical evidences collected through this evaluation study and following the National Policy on Education 1986, the NCERT prepared another document entitled, 'Minimum Levels of Learning at the Primary Stage'.

In the context of these exercises and the specifications made by the Eighth Plan Working Group, the Department of Education, Ministry of Human Resource Development organized a seminar in December 1989 on the theme, 'Basic Learning Needs and Levels of Attainment'. Various issues related to basic learning needs of the children at the primary stage, the need for specifying minimum levels of learning and creation of appropriate mechanisms for assessment of learner attainment were discussed during the seminar. On the issue of laying down minimum levels of learning the seminar recommended for initiating concrete efforts at the national level.

Against this background, the Department of Education, Ministry of Human Resource Development, Government of India set up a committee on MLL dated 5 January 1990. The terms of reference of the committee were:

- Draw up minimum levels of learning for Classes III and V.
- Recommend a procedure for comprehensive learner evaluation and assessment.
- Look into the non-cognitive areas of learning and suggest concrete ways in which teaching in these areas can be improved. The committee was further informed that the terms of reference related to both formal and non-formal systems of education.

The committee was chaired by Dr. R.H. Dave, Director (Retd.), UNESCO Institute for Education, Germany.

Specification of MLL: A Curriculum Issue

Every curriculum, as it attempts to modify the cognitive as well as non-cognitive domains of development of the learner, lays down specific educational objectives and the corresponding learning outcomes expected on the part of the learners. Usually, these are defined with reference to targets of educational achievement under ideal conditions of learning, enabling the learning to fully realize their inherent potential and engage in socially useful life. However, the criticism levelled against the existing set of curricular prescriptions and the corresponding learning outcomes is that they are only designed to prepare students for secondary and university education. Consequently, there is an overload of content of facts and information that would have very little relevance to the life or needs of a majority of students.

Also, it is often pointed out that the outcomes of learning expected do not seem to be based on the maturity level of the learner especially during the initial years of elementary education. This ambitiousness in the primary level syllabus is now increasingly recognized as counter-productive to excellence in learning and dangerous to the concerns of equity. The syllabus load often compels the teacher to ignore altogether certain basic principles of the teaching-learning process. The need to complete the syllabus seems to take precedence over the need to progress according to the pace of learning of the whole class and teachers find themselves forced to ignore the strugglers, forego attempts at remedial teaching or considerations for experimentation, exploration, observation or activity-based learning. The conventional textbook and lecture method of teaching, being the quickest way to complete the syllabus, becomes the best option available, forcing upon the students a joyless rote memorization, an overemphasis upon textbooks and in many cases, a reliance on help from outside the school. The disadvantage this builds into the system for the already deprived needs no special elaboration-for those who have no support for learning at home or outside the school, no proper textbooks and learning aids, and who consequently have a complete dependence on schools for mastering their syllabus, it leaves little scope but for repetitions or dropping out. Even many of those who manage to complete, despite these handicaps, attain at best an incomplete mastery of the basic skills.

MLL at primary stage: Laying down minimum levels of learning should help to resolve some of these problems by identifying the irrelevant and excessive learning load in the existing curriculum. The MLL exercise should, therefore, be viewed as part of a larger curriculum reform endeavour attempting to move towards greater relevance and functionality in primary education. The implications of this exercise are:

- lightening the curriculum of its textual load and also the burden of memorizing unnecessary and irrelevant facts;
- leaving room for the teacher to relate textbook information and objective reality into a meaningful process of understanding and application;
- ensuring the acquisition of basic competencies and skills to such a level where they are sustainable, and would not easily allow for relapse into illiteracy;
- permitting mastery learning not only by the brighter students in the class but also by almost all children including the first generation learners.

Learner-centred Approaches To Curriculum Development

Learner-centred approaches to curriculum development is an alternative approach to curriculum development which indicates a close relationship between curriculum, planning goals, learning objectives, and implementation is the learner-centred approach (Nunan 1988). In a student-centred curriculum, although the teacher is the prime agent of curriculum development, both teachers and students share full responsibility for the learning process. A student-centred curriculum should include the principles and procedures for planning, imple-menting, and evaluating the curriculum and should consist of the following key elements:

- Initial and ongoing students' needs analysis;
- Content selection and setting priorities (including goals);
- Methodology (including the selection and gradation of learning activities and materials);
- Monitoring, assessment, and evaluation.

According to these elements the teacher's task can be de-scribed in terms of a cycle consisting of the following steps:

- Initial needs analysis for students;
- Setting goals and selecting contents;
- Selecting learning activities and materials;
- Assessing and evaluating the teaching outcome.

On the basis of the teaching outcome the teacher, who monitors the whole process, begins the cycle again and carries out a new needs analysis.

Traditional Curriculum Development versus Student-Centred Curriculum

A student-centred curriculum within an adult learning context contains many elements that are similar to those in traditional curriculum development, i.e. planning, implementing, and evaluating. The key difference between the two models is that, in the former, the curriculum is a collaborative effort of teachers and learners, since learners are closely involved in the decision-making process regarding the content of the curriculum and the way it is taught. As far as the curriculum process is concerned, a student-centred approach can be characterised and distinguished from traditional approaches by its initial planning procedures. These procedures include the collection of information about learners in order to diagnose their objective needs that are needs which are external to the learner.

This initial data collection, which is usually superficial, has to be supplemented by more subjective information on the preferred length and intensity of the course, the preferred learning arrangement and goals, as well as by information relating to the preferred methodology, the students' learning-style preferences, and so on. However, this sort of information, relating to the student's subjective needs as an individual in a learning situation can often only be obtained once a course has begun. Instruments have to be developed and used that help teachers and students to become aware of the individual objective and subjective needs.

Content Selection and Priority Setting

In a student-centred curriculum clear criteria for content selection give guidance on the selection of materials and learning activities and assist in assessment and evaluation. By making explicit the content objectives of a course and, eventually, by training learners to set their own objectives, the following benefits can be accrued:

- Students come to have a more realistic idea of what can be achieved in a given course.
- Learning comes to be seen as a process of gradually reaching achievable goals.
- Students develop greater sensitivity to their role as learners, and their rather vague notions of what it is to be a learner can become much sharper.
- Self-evaluation becomes more feasible.
- Classroom activities can be seen to relate to the learners' real-life needs.
- The development of competences can be seen as a gradual, rather than an all-or-nothing process.

A crucial distinction between traditional and student-centred curriculum development is that, in the latter, the structure is fluid and open to adaptations. It is, therefore, important that the contents selected at the beginning of a course are not seen as definite; they will vary, and will probably have to be modified as students experience different kinds of learning activities and as teachers obtain more information about the students' subjective needs. As most learners find it difficult to articulate their needs and preferences, the initial stages of a course can be spent in providing a range of learning experiences. Additionally, with low-level language learners, developing critical self-awareness can best be facilitated by the use of resources in the mother tongue. In some cases the use of bilingual assistants may be useful. Since contact hours often are limited, class time has to be used as effectively and productively as possible to achieve the following aims:

- To provide students with effective learning strategies;
- To assist students to identify their preferred ways of learning;
- To develop skills needed to negotiate the curriculum;
- To encourage students to set their own objectives;
- To encourage students to adopt realistic goals and time frames;
- To develop the students' skills of/by self-evaluation.

Teaching Methods : Teaching methods, which include learning activities and materials, are generally the area where there is the greatest potential for conflict between teacher and students. In a traditional curriculum this conflict would be ignored on the grounds that the "teacher knows best". In a student-centred curriculum it is imperative that conflicts be resolved by specific techniques and procedures for negotiation and consultation.

Evaluation : Traditionally, evaluation occurs at the final stage in the curriculum process. In a student-centred curriculum, however, evaluation is parallel with other curriculum activities and may occur at various times during the planning and implementation phases, as well as during a specified evaluation phase. In a traditional curriculum model, evaluation is identified with testing and is seen as an activity which is carried out at the end of the learning process, often by someone who is not connected with the course itself. (In other words, the emphasis is on "summative" rather than "formative" evaluation.) In a student-centred model, evaluation generally takes the form of an informal monitoring which is carried out alongside the teaching and learning processes, principally by the participants in that process, that is the teachers and learners.

By building evaluation into the teaching process, learners can evaluate learning materials, study activities, and their own achievement of objectives. By encouraging teachers to evaluate critically their own performance, evaluation becomes an integral part of both curriculum and teacher development. Any element within the curriculum may be evaluated. At the planning stage, needs analysis techniques and procedures may be evaluated, while, during implementation, elements to be evaluated may include materials, learning activities, sequencing, learning arrangements, teacher performance, and learner achievement.

Advantages of a Student-Centred Curriculum : The advantages of a student-centred approach to course curriculum planning are;

- A stronger bond between teaching and the curriculum;
- Greater emphasis on the students' needs, an aspect which could be especially helpful for students who attend courses that are not primarily intended for them;
- The research on teaching (e.g. action research) can concentrate on more relevant issues;
- A more realistic description of the role of teachers who have always been and will always be curriculum developers;
- The development of instruments which help teachers to do their jobs more efficiently;
- A stronger demand on schools and universities to define their requirements more thoroughly;

Constructivist Approaches To Curriculum Development

The term *constructivism* refers to the idea that learners construct knowledge for themselves-each learner individually (and socially) constructs meaning-as he or she learns. Constructing meaning is learning; there is no other kind. The dramatic consequences of this view are twofold;

- we have to focus on the learner in thinking about learning (not on the subject/lesson to be taught)
- There is no knowledge independent of the meaning attributed to experience (constructed) by the learner, or community of learners. Knowledge is dependent to the experiences/constructions of the learner.

If we accept the constructivist position we are inevitably required to follow a pedagogy which argues that we must provide learners with the opportunity to:

(a) interact with sensory data, and

(b) construct their own world.

This second point is a little harder for us to swallow, and most of us constantly think twice between faith that our learners will indeed construct meaning which we will find acceptable (whatever we mean by that) and our need to construct meaning for them; that is, to structure situations that are not free for learners to carry out their own mental actions, but "learning" situations which channel them into our ideas about the meaning of experience.

Constructivism is an epistemology, or a theory, used to explain how people know what they know. The basic idea is that problem solving is at the heart of learning, thinking, and development. As people solve problems and discover the consequences of their actions–through reflecting on past and immediate experiences–they construct their own understanding. Learning is thus an active process that requires a change in the learner. This is achieved through the activities the learner engages in, including the consequences of those activities, and through reflection. People only deeply understand what they have constructed.

A constructivist approach to learning and instruction has been proposed as an alternative to the objectivist model, which is implicit in all behaviourist and some cognitive approaches to education. Objectivism sees knowledge as a passive reflection of the external, objective reality. This implies a process of "instruction," ensuring that the learner gets correct information.

The psychological roots of constructivism began with the developmental work of **Jean Piaget** (1896–1980), who developed a theory (the theory of genetic epistemology) that analogized the development of the mind to evolutionary biological development and highlighted the adaptive function of cognition. The Russian psychologist **Lev Vygotsky**'s (1896–1934) relevance to constructivism derives from his theories about language, thought, and their mediation by society. For the American philosopher and educator **John Dewey** (1859–1952), education depended on action–knowledge and ideas emerge only from a situation in which learners have to draw out experiences that have meaning and importance to them. In short, Piaget contributed the idea of transformation in learning and development; Vygotsky contributed the idea that learning and development were integrally tied to communicative interactions with others; and Dewey contributed the idea that schools had to bring real world problems into the school curriculum.

Constructivist Processes and Education

There are a number of competing constructivist views in education. Constructivists tend to celebrate complexity and multiple perspectives, though they do share at least a few educational prescriptions.

- **Prior knowledge:** Constructivists believe that prior knowledge impacts the learning process. In trying to solve novel problems, perceptual or conceptual similarities between existing knowledge and a new problem can remind people of what they already know.

This is often one's first approach towards solving novel problems. Information not connected with a learner's prior experiences will be quickly forgotten. In short, the learner must actively construct new information into his or her existing mental framework for meaningful learning to occur.

- **Real and authentic problems:** Constructivist learning is based on the active participation of learners in problem-solving and critical thinking–given real and authentic problems.

Constructivist Principles of learning

What are some guiding principles of constructivist thinking that we must keep in mind when we consider our role as educators? Let us outline a few ideas, all predicated on the belief that learning consists of individuals' constructed meanings and then indicate how they influence education.

- Learning is an active process in which the *learner uses sensory input and constructs meaning out of it.* The more traditional formulation of this idea involves the terminology of the **active learner** (Dewey's term) stressing that the learner needs to do something; that learning is not the passive acceptance of knowledge which exists "out there" but that learning involves the learner's engaging with the world.
- *People learn to learn as they learn*: learning consists both of constructing meaning and constructing systems of meaning. For example, if we learn the chronology of dates of a series of historical events, we are simultaneously learning the meaning of a chronology. Each meaning we construct makes us better able to give meaning to other sensations which can fit a similar pattern.
- *The crucial action of constructing meaning is mental*: it happens in the mind. Physical actions, hands-on experience may be necessary for learning, especially for children, but it is not sufficient; we need to provide activities which engage the mind as well as the hands (Dewey called this reflective activity.)
- *Learning involves language*: the language we use influences learning. On the empirical level. researchers have noted that people talk to themselves as they learn. On a more general level. there is a collection of arguments, presented most forcefully by Vygotsky, that language and learning are inextricably intertwined. This point was clearly emphasized in Elaine Gurain's reference to the need to honour native language. The desire to have material

and programs in their own language was an important request of members of various native communities.

- *Learning is a social activity*: our learning is intimately associated with our connection with other human beings, our teachers, our peers, our family as well as casual acquaintances, including the people before us or next to us. We are more likely to be successful in our efforts to educate if we recognize this principle rather than try to avoid it. Much of traditional education, as Dewey pointed out, is directed towards isolating the learner from all social interaction, and towards seeing education as a one-on-one relationship between the learner and the objective material to be learned. In contrast, progressive education (to continue to use Dewey's formulation) recognizes the social aspect of learning and uses conversation, interaction with others, and the application of knowledge as an integral aspect of learning.
- *Learning is contextual*: we do not learn isolated facts and theories in some abstract ethereal land of the mind separate from the rest of our lives: we learn in relationship to what else we know, what we believe, our prejudices and our fears. On reflection, it becomes clear that this point is actually a corollary of the idea that learning is active and social. We cannot divorce our learning from our lives. As John Dewey sais;"Education is life itself, not a preparation for life".
- *One needs knowledge to learn*: it is not possible to assimilate new knowledge without having some structure developed from previous knowledge to build on. The more we know, the more we can learn. Therefore any effort to teach must be connected to the state of the learner, must provide a path into the subject for the learner based on that learner's previous knowledge.
- *It takes time to learn*: learning is not instantaneous. For significant learning we need to revisit ideas, ponder them try them out, play with them and use them. This cannot happen in the 5-10 minutes usually spent in a classroom. If you reflect on anything you have learned, you soon realize that it is the product of repeated exposure and thought. Even, or especially, moments of profound insight, can be traced back to longer periods of preparation.
- *Motivation is a key component in learning*. Not only is it the case that motivation helps learning, it is essential for learning. This ideas of motivation as described here is broadly conceived to include an understanding of ways in which the knowledge can be

used. Unless we know "the reasons why", we may not be very involved in using the knowledge that may be instilled in us. even by the most severe and direct teaching.

Constructivist curriculum

A constructively oriented curriculum presents an emerging agenda based on what children know, what they are puzzled by, and the teachers' learning goals. Thus, an important part of a constructivist-oriented curriculum should be the negotiation of meaning. Maggie Lampert, a mathematics teacher, guides students to make sense of mathematics by comparing and resolving discrepancies between what they know and what seems to be implied by new experience.

In constructivist classrooms, curriculum is generally a process of digging deeper and deeper into big ideas, rather than presenting a breadth of coverage. For example, in the Fostering Communities of Learners project where students learn how to learn, in knowledge-building classrooms where students seek to create new knowledge, or in Howard Gardner's classrooms where the focus is on learning for deep understanding, students might study endangered species, island biogeography, or the principles of gravity over several months. As students pursue questions, they derive new and more complex questions to be investigated. Building useful knowledge structures requires effortful and purposeful activity over an extended period.

This shift to Constructivism requires teachers to engage in what has been described in educational circles as "constructivist teaching." Constructivist teaching encompasses what good teachers have always done in their classrooms: reaching beyond the text and the blackboard to awaken, stimulate, and broaden students' minds. It is therefore a misnomer to label this philosophy as new. Interestingly, even Plato seemed to have been aware of multi-modal teaching when he wrote: "Do not use compulsion, but let early education be a sort of amusement: you will then be better able to find out the natural bent."

More recently, virtually all pioneers of modern education have developed systems of teaching based upon more than verbal pedagogy. The 18th century philosopher Jean-Jacques Rousseau declared in his treatise on education, ***Emile***, that the child must learn not through words but through experience; not through books but through the book of life. Others have emphasised an "integrated curriculum" that provides physical, moral, and intellectual training firmly based on concrete experiences. The curriculum of the modern-day kindergarten includes hands-on experiences with manipulative, games, songs, gardening, and caring for animals. Innovators like Marie Montessori, John Dewey, Lev Vygotsky, and Jean Piaget evolved systems of instruction based on constructivist approaches.

The influence of constructivism in teaching and learning is increasing. For example, the shift toward literature-based approaches to reading and the process approach to writing is founded on constructivism. In a sense, the increasing influence of constructivism can be seen across the school curriculum. The term "constructivism" means different things to different people, and advocates of this concept disagree on the nature of knowledge and the importance of different elements of the process.

Over the years, two mutually exclusive positions have emerged. The first position, based largely on **Jean Piaget**'s work, is called cognitive constructivism. It focuses on internal, individual constructions of knowledge. Within this framework, knowledge does not exist in the social environment as such, rather, social interaction is important primarily as a stimulus or catalyst for individual, internal cognitive conflict. Cognitive constructivists emphasise learning activities that are child determined and discovery oriented. For instance, mathematics educators taking this position would argue that children would learn maths more efficiently if mathematical knowledge was provided to them on the basis of what they already know, rather than have it presented by the teacher or other expert. The second position, which is strongly influenced by **Lev Vygotsky**, is called social constructivism. Social constructivists agree that knowledge exists in a social context and is, at least initially, shared with others rather than represented solely in the mind of an individual. As people interact, the process of sharing results in learning. Learners redefine their own ideas while, at the same time, helping to shape the ideas of others. Social constructivism acknowledges the contribution of others in the learning process. Unlike cognitive constructivism, which downplays the role of the social environment, social constructivism highlights that role and suggests that teachers consider all traditional questions of teaching: how to organize and implement learning activities, how to motivate students, and how to assess learning.

Despite their differing positions, most constructivists agree on four characteristics that permeate all learning. **First**, they agree that students develop knowledge through the process of active construction. Knowledge construction emphasises that learners develop their own understanding, which makes sense to them; they do not receive understanding from an outside source. Students should not passively receive or copy input from teachers, but instead actively mediate it by trying to make sense of it and relate it to what they already know. **Second**, they hold the view that new learning depends on current understanding. This view emphasises the role of background knowledge and current understanding in information processing. Constructivists emphasise the importance of students' current understanding, that is, seeing new learning interpreted in the immediate context of current understanding. **Third**, constructivists agree that learning is facilitated by social interaction. This view underscores the importance of social interaction in learning. Student interaction results in sharing, thinking, and decision making. Teachers play a critical role in this process. The creation of communities of learning in the classroom, in the school, and involving the larger community, is critical to learning. **Finally**, constructivists agree on the importance of dialogue in learning. The more knowledgeable makers of the culture—the teachers—should assist learning by encouraging dialogue: teacher–teacher and student–teacher.

A constructivist teacher can therefore be described as one who encourages and accepts students' autonomy and initiative. Constructivist teachers (1) frame questions using cognitive terminologies -clarify, analyse, predict, and create; (2) allow student responses to drive lessons, shift instructional strategies, and alter content; (3) enquire about students' understanding; (4) encourage students to engage in dialogue; (5) encourage student enquiry by asking thoughtful, open-ended questions and encourage students to ask questions of each other; and (6) engage students in experiments and nurture students' natural curiosity. These characteristics are certainly the hallmarks of a good teacher.

Process Of Curriculum Making

The curriculum development process systematically organizes what will be taught, who will be taught, and how it will be taught. Each component affects and interacts with other components. For example, what will be taught is affected by who is being taught (e.g., their stage of development in age, maturity, and education). Methods of how content is taught are affected by who is being taught, their characteristics, and the setting. In considering the above three essential components, the following are widely held to be essential considerations in education. The essential considerations for curriculum development are;

- issue/problem/need is identified (issue ! what),
- characteristics and needs of learners (target audience ! who),

- changes intended for learners (intended outcomes/objectives ! what the learners will be able to do),
- the important and relevant content ! (what),
- methods to accomplish intended outcomes ! (how),
- evaluation strategies for methods, content, and intended outcomes! (What works?).

Figure 6.1 shows how these components relate to each other and to the curriculum development process. It begins when an issue, concern, or problem needs to be addressed. If education or training a segment of the population will help solve the problem, then curriculum to support an educational effort becomes a priority with human and financial resources allocated. The next step is to form a curriculum development team. The team makes systematic decisions about the target audience (learner characteristics), intended out-comes (objectives), content, methods, and evaluation strategies. With input from the curriculum development team, draft curriculum products are developed, tested, evaluated, and redesigned - if necessary. When the final product is produced, volunteer training is conducted. The model shows a circular process where volunteer training provides feedback for new materials or revisions to the existing curriculum.

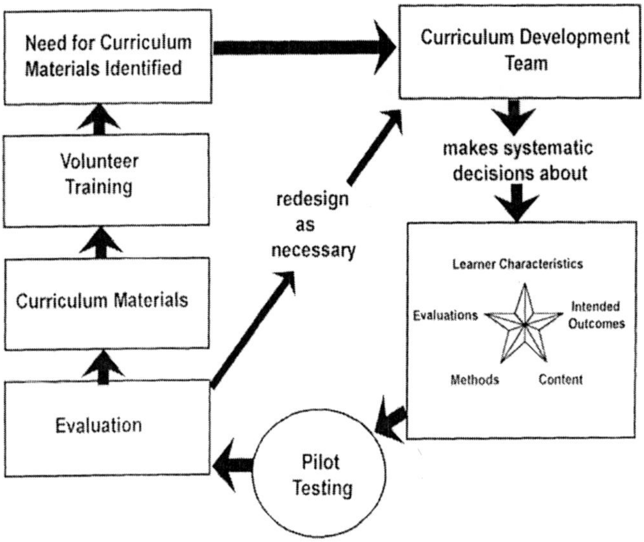

Figure 6.1 Curriculum Development Model

Phases and Steps in Curriculum Development

Figure 6. 2 further illustrates how the 12 essential steps progress from one to the next. It also shows the interaction and relationships of the four essential phases of the curriculum development process: (I) Planning, (II) Content and Methods, (III) Implementation, and (IV) Evaluation and Reporting.

It is important to acknowledge that things do not always work exactly as depicted in a model. Each phase has several steps or tasks to complete in logical sequence. These steps are not always separate and distinct, but may overlap and occur concurrently. For example, the curriculum development team is involved in all of the steps. Evaluations should occur in most of the steps to assess progress. The team learns what works and what does not and determines the impact of the curriculum on learners after it is implemented. Each step logically follows the previous. It would make no sense to design learning activities before learner outcomes and content are described and identified. Similarly, content cannot be determined before learner outcomes are described. These steps are essential to successful curriculum development and need to be emphasized.

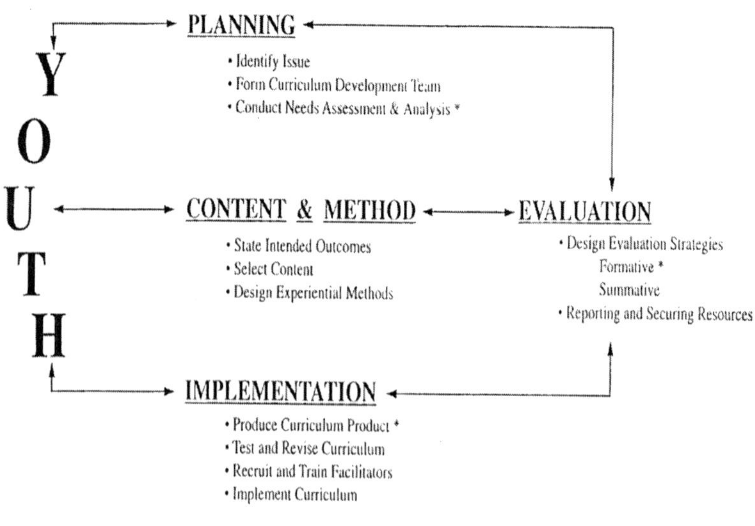

Figure 6.2: Phases and Steps in Curriculum Development

Essential Curriculum Development Steps Needing Emphasis

- **Needs assessment:** if not conducted, wonderful curriculum could be developed, but the appropriate needs of the target audience may not be met.
- **Involving youth:** the target audience and volunteers (or staff) who will be the implementers of the curriculum must be involved (i.e., they participate as full members of the curriculum development team).
- **Recruiting and training volunteer facilitators:** competent and skilled curriculum implementers are critical (the printed word cannot teach experiential group process, it does not provide feedback).
- **Evaluating and reporting on the impact of the curriculum:** is critical for securing human and financial support from key policy decision makers and for assessing whether the curriculum has achieved the intended outcome.

Two types of evaluation are included in the Phases and Steps illustration: (1) Formative provides feedback during the process of developing the curriculum, and (2) Summative answers questions about changes (impact) that have occurred in learners because of their learning experiences. Summative evaluation provides evidence for what works, what does not work, and what needs to be improved.

In every step of the curriculum development process, the most important task is to keep the learner (in this case, youth) in mind and involve them in process. For example, the curriculum team members, who have direct knowledge of the target audience, should be involved in conducting the needs assessment. From the needs assessment process, the problem areas are identified, gaps between what youth know and what they need to know are identified, and the scope of the problem is clarified and defined. The results may prompt decision makers to allocate resources for a curriculum development team to prepare curriculum materials. A brief description of each of the curriculum development steps is described below. After reviewing these descriptions, you should have a very clear idea of how the steps occur in each of the phases and what each step includes.

Phase I: Planning

The planning phase lays the foundation for all of the curriculum development steps. The steps in this phase include: (1) Identify Issue/Problem/Need (2) Form Curriculum Development Team (3) Conduct Needs Assessment and Analysis.

(1) Identify Issue/Problem/Need: The need for curriculum development usually emerges from a concern about a major issue or problem of one or more target audience. This section explores some of the questions that need to be addressed to define the issue and to develop a statement that will guide the selection of the members of a curriculum development team. The issue statement also serves to broadly identify, the scope (what will be included) of the curriculum content.

(2) Form Curriculum Development Team: Once the nature and scope of the issue has been broadly defined, the members of the curriculum development team can be selected. Topics covered in this section include: (1) the roles and functions of team members, (2) a process for selecting members of the curriculum development team, and (3) principles of collaboration and teamwork. The goal is to obtain expertise for the areas included in the scope of the curriculum content among the team members and develop an effective team.

(3) Conduct Needs Assessment and Analysis: There are two phases in the needs assessment process. The first is procedures for conducting a needs assessment. A number of techniques are aimed toward learning what is needed and by whom relative to the identified issue. Techniques covered in this section include: KAP - Knowledge, Attitude, and Practice Survey; focus groups; and environmental scanning.

Analysis, the second part of this needs assessment step, describes techniques on how to use the data and the results of the information gathered. Included are: ways to identify gaps between knowledge and practice; trends emerging from the data; a process to prioritize needs; and identification of the characteristics of the target audience.

Phase II: Content and Methods

Phase II determines intended outcomes (what learners will be able to do after participation in curriculum activities), the content (what will be taught), and the methods (how it will be taught). Steps include: (4) State Intended Outcomes (5) Select Content (6) Design Experiential Methods.

(4) State Intended Outcomes: Once the issue is defined, the curriculum team is formed, the needs assessed, analyzed and prioritized, the next step is to refine and restate the issue, if needed, and develop the intended outcomes or educational objectives. An intended outcome states what the learner will be able to do as a result of participating in the curriculum activities.

(5) Select Content: The next challenge in the curriculum development process is selecting content that will make a real difference in the lives of the learner and ultimately society as a whole. At this point, the primary questions are: "If the intended outcome is to be attained, what will the learner need to know? What knowledge, skills, attitudes, and behaviours will need to be acquired and practiced?"

(6) Design Experiential Methods: After the content is selected, the next step is to design activities (learning experiences) to help the learner achieve appropriate intended outcomes. An experiential learning model and it's components (i.e., experience, share, process, generalize, and apply) are discussed in this section.

Phase III: Implementation

(7) Produce Curriculum Product: Once the content and experiential methods have been agreed upon, the actual production of curriculum materials begins. This section includes: 1) suggestions for finding and evaluating existing materials; 2) evaluation criteria; and 3) suggestions for producing curriculum materials.

(8) Test and Revise Curriculum: This step includes suggestions to select test sites and conduct a formative evaluation of curriculum materials during the production phase. A sample evaluation form is provided.

(9) Recruit and Train Facilitators: It is a waste of resources to develop curriculum materials if adequate training is not provided for facilitators to implement it. Suggestions for recruiting appropriate facilitators are provided with a sample three-day training program.

(10) Implement Curriculum: Effective implementation of newly developed curriculum products is unlikely to occur without planning. Strategies to promote and use the curriculum are discussed in this step.

Phase IV: Evaluation and Reporting

(11) Design Evaluation Strategies: Evaluation is a phase in the curriculum development model as well as a specific step. Two types of evaluation, formative and summative, are used during curriculum development. Formative evaluations are used during the needs assessment, product development, and testing steps. Summative evaluations are undertaken to measure and report on the outcomes of the curriculum. This step reviews evaluation strategies and suggests simple procedures to produce valid and reliable information. A series of questions are posed to guide the summative evaluation process and a sample evaluation format is suggested.

(12) Reporting and Securing Resources: The final element in an evaluation strategy is "delivering the pay off (i.e., getting the results into the hands of people who can use them). In this step, suggestions for what and how to report to key shareholders, especially funding and policy decision makers, are provided and a brief discussion on how to secure resources for additional programming.

Formulating Aims And Objectives (Based On Overall Curricular Aims And Syllabus)

A teacher has certain goals or objectives in mind when planning a course. He/she wants students to learn certain things and decide what activities will achieve these objectives. Due to the need for accountability in education, curriculum and lesson planning are usually done in a more relevant approach through the use of behavioural objectives.

Behavioural objectives spell out specifically what students would have accomplished after implementing a teaching unit or programme. Thus, there are ways or methods of measuring observable behaviour by writing objectives in the following three domains:

- Cognitive (knowledge)
- Affective (feelings)
- Psycho motor (action)

Stenhouse (1975) wrote that the school is a purposeful institution, and the objectives of education must be formulated to reflect learners uniqueness, contemporary life, the nature of the subjects, the psychology of learning and a philosophy or a set of values. Aims are general expectations while objectives are more directional, specific in terms of curriculum study. Too often, educational objectives are stated so that only the coverage of the content is explicit without specifying what learners should do, or use the content for, to show that learning has taken place. Expected behaviour should be specified so that we can know whether learning has taken place or not.

Also specifying behaviour generally like, to think logically or to express oneself clearly is not adequate unless there is an indication of the kind of content in which the behaviour is to apply. The educational objectives provide an orientation to the main emphasis in educational programmes and they help to translate the needs and values of a society into an educational programme. They serve as a means for attaining goals of self realization at school and in later life and as a guide for assessing goals and achievement.

In the light of the aforementioned, we should have a fairly wide range of objectives clearly and precisely stated which can be used to plan the learning opportunities of the pupils as well as devise means of assessing the extent to which the pupils have achieved the pre-stated objectives.

The most useful and clearest statements of objectives are those which specify both the kind of behaviour, reaction that is expected and the content to which it applies such as the ability to interpret accurately data, on causes of anaemia, or the ability to differentiate between facts and opinions. If the behaviour denotes knowing and remembering, the statement of objectives should also indicate what is to be known or remembered. If the statement specifies attitude, then it should also state what the attitude is about. The objectives need to be stated in behavioural terms because the general purpose of all education is to change behaviour, therefore, course objectives must be stated in behavioural terms.

Major Characteristics of Behavioural Objectives

- Behavioural objectives indicate the intended behaviour of the learner as a result of his interaction with a particular curriculum. If for example a student is to name ten communicable diseases within a minute after instruction in a health education class, the behavioural objective may be stated in such a way that the learner will be able to name at this rate as a result of his/her exposure to a curriculum which emphasizes recollection of names and facts.
- In formulating behavioural objectives for a curriculum, care should be taken to: (i) Specify some form of performance (e.g. trace the mode of transmission of yellow fever). (ii) Set appropriate conditions of performances (iii) Indicate what should serve as evidence of satisfactory performance (e.g. drawing). (iv) Use action verbs – name, draw, sketch, list, describe, suggest, specify etc. The real goals and long term objectives of a curriculum are the real starting points for formulating objectives at a more specific level.
- Behavioural objectives specify what is expected to be performed, so that they are often called performance objectives. Since the performance has to be observable, verbs like to understand, to know, to love, to appreciate are not normally used, they are not action verbs.

Below a behavioural objectives is stated as an example. (Curriculum for Senior Secondary, Course : Health Education, Unit 1: Growth and Development)

Behavioural Objectives:- At the end of the lesson, the students should be able to:

- Explain the meaning of growth and development
- Distinguish between the terms growth and development
- Explain the different types of cell division
- Distinguish between mitosis and meiosis
- State the stages of cell division

Cognitive Objectives (Knowledge and Information) sets to see ability of students in recalling facts and ideas during instructional programme which is one of the major objectives of education. Knowledge of facts must also include understanding of principles, concepts, trends and generalizations which will serve as basis for doing well in affective and psychomotor domains. The affective objectives emphasise feelings and attitudes, so that they are usually difficult to define and even more difficult to measure or evaluate e.g. when and how does a student prove that he "appreciates" a desirable health "attitude". Psychomotor objectives are interested in a learner being able to coordinate his/her brain and physical powers (e.g. skills in studying, using the library, handling data, manipulate things, playing soccer etc). It is mainly concerned with motor skills so that in instructional objectives, performance skills are prominent. Most psychomotor tasks reside in the human organism that develop naturally.

Generally, objective s are necessary as they are guides to: (a) specific content to be studied by the learner in a specific learning programme (b) specific changes in behaviour that are sought in the learner with respect to content (c) selection of learning opportunities that best enable the learner to achieve and or promote the desired behavioural outcomes (d) what to evaluate in terms of the content studied and the behaviours sought in the learner.

Criteria For Selecting Knowledge And Representing Knowledge In The Form Of Thematic Questions In Different Subjects

What goes into the curriculum in terms of content needs to be well built in especially in this time of knowledge explosion. Content areas that are relevant to the socio-economic and cultural needs of the society need to be given a pride of place in the curriculum. The specified or stated objectives are always the determinant of what should be presented to the learner to learn as well as the psychological makeup of the learner, the nature of the society, the necessary teaching materials and so on.

The defining of objectives that makes clearer the area of curriculum design which enables both educational planners and researcher to bring their practical knowledge to bear on the matter. It is therefore necessary to look at the curriculum as a sequence of content units that may be accomplished as a single act provided the capabilities described by specified prior units (in the sequence) have already been mastered by the learner. Therefore we say that a curriculum may be of any length, that it may contain any number of units. A curriculum is specified when: (1) the terminal objectives are stated (2) the sequence of prerequisite capabilities is described and (3) the initial capabilities assumed to be processed by the student are identified.

The World Confederation of Organization of the Teaching Profession (1987) wrote that: "The content element in a curriculum refers to that aspect of the package which deals with the body of knowledge which is to be absorbed by the learner. Curriculum content can be seen in different forms:

- **a concept**: a particular principle to be learnt e.g. the concept of heat, wind direction number, etc.
- **a topic**: a body of knowledge made up of a body of related concepts, and the links between them, e.g. how rains are formed, how an internal combustion engine works.
- **a discipline**: a traditional distinct area of scientific inquiry, e.g. history, geography, mathematics, science.
- **survival Kits**: a body of knowledge drawing on the orthodox disciplines but designed to tackle specific life problems, e.g. family life education, population education, drug education, road traffic education.
- **a set of skills**: activities to be carried out, using a set of scientific principles, e.g. swimming, typewriting, cookery.

The curriculum content should represent an appropriate balance and depth (sequence) and should provide for a wide range of objectives which leads to scope. Scope delimits the content to be taught and also involves the depth and breadth of the subject matter to be taught at a given class. Level or Maturity level is important. Also important are needs, interests and concerns of the students.

The term curriculum is viewed in two different ways: the **micro** and the **macro**. The **micro curriculum** refers to subjects while the **macro curriculum** refers to curricular programs. For example, the subject biology is a micro curriculum while B.Tech. in Civil Engineering is a macro curriculum. What do the micro and the macro curriculum contain? The following criteria discusses the content of these two levels of the curriculum. The selection of subject matter for micro curriculum employs the seven criteria below. For the macro curriculum, the subjects needed for the curricular program or course.

1. Self-sufficiency: To help learners attain maximum self-sufficiency in the most economical manner is the main guiding principle of subject matter or content selection (Scheffler, 1970) as cited by Bilbao et al. (2008). Although the economy of learning implies less teaching effort and less use of educational resources, students gain more results. They can cope up with the learning outcomes effectively. This criterion means that students should be given a chance to experiment, observe, and do field study. This system allows them to learn independently. With this principle in mind, It is suggest that for a high school curriculum or preparatory year, there should be a one-day independent learning activity each week. However, this should be carefully planned by the teacher. When the students return, they should present outputs from the activity.

2. Significance: The subject matter or content is significant if it is selected and organized for the development of learning activities, skills, processes, and attitude. It also develops the three domains of learning namely the cognitive, affective and psychomotor skills and considers the cultural aspects of the learners. Particularly, if your students come from different cultural backgrounds and races, the subject matter must be culture-sensitive. In short, select content or subject matter that can achieve the overall aim of the curriculum.

3. Validity: Validity refers to the authenticity of the subject matter or content you selected. Make sure that the topics are not obsolete. For example, do not include typewriting as a skill to be learned by college students. It should be about the computer or Information Technology (IT). Thus, there is a need to check regularly the subject matter or contents of the curriculum, and replace it if necessary. Do not wait for another 5 years to change it. Modern curriculum experts are after current trends, relevance and authenticity of the curriculum; otherwise, the school or the country becomes obsolete.

4. Interest: This criterion is true to the learner-centred curriculum. Students learn best if the subject matter is meaningful to them. It becomes meaningful if they are interested in it. However, if the curriculum is subject-centred, teachers have no choice but to finish the pacing schedule religiously and only teach what is in the book. This approach explains why many fail in the subject.

5. Utility: Another criterion is the usefulness of the content or subject matter. Students think that a subject matter or some subjects are not important to them. They view it useless. As a result, they do not study. Here are the questions that students often ask: Will I need the subject in my job? Will it give meaning to my life? Will it develop my potentials? Will it solve my problem? Will it be part of the test? Will I have a passing mark if I learn it? Students only value the subject matter or content if it is useful to them.

6. Learnability : The subject matter or content must be within the schema of the learners. It should be within their experiences. Teachers should apply theories in the psychology of learning to know how subjects are presented, sequenced, and organized to maximize the learning capacity of the students.

7. Feasibility: Feasibility means full implementation of the subject matter. It should consider the real situation of the school, the government, and the society, in general. Students must learn within the allowable time and the use of resources available. Do not give them a topic that is impossible to finish. For example, you have only one week left to finish the unit but then, the activities may take a month for the students to complete. Thus, this requirement is not feasible. Do not offer a computer subject if there is no even electricity in the area, or there are no computers at all. Further, feasibility means that there should be teachers who are experts in that area. For example, do not offer *English for Business Communication* if there is no teacher to handle it. Also, there is a need to consider the nature of the learners. The organization and design of the subject matter or content must be appropriate to the nature of students. So, it would be better if students in a subject-centered curriculum (with pacing schedule that must be religiously implemented every week) shall be grouped homogeneously; otherwise, many will flunk in that subject.

In conclusion, teachers in elementary and high school are not directly involved in the selection of subject-matter because there are already lesson plans made by the Department of Education. All they have to do is to follow it. However, they can also customize the lessons if their department heads or principals allows them. The selection of the subject matter or content of the micro and macro curriculum is only one of the considerations in designing the curriculum.

Organising Fundamental Concepts And Themes Vertically Across Levels And Integrating Themes Within (And Across) Different Subjects

Continuity refers to the repetition of concepts and generalizations of principles as they are continuously revisited throughout the curriculum.

This simply means that a given concept permeates the learning of students as they move to higher classes, but what is also important is that each higher level must have something new to be learnt. In other words, the composition of a specific lesson/curriculum must have order as well as progress. With increasing complexity or depth, this plan makes provision for vertical organizations.

Sequence is more than the ordering of the subject matter to be taught and also beyond continuity to which it is very closely related. The latter centres on repetitions of concepts, but the former emphasizes succeeding higher levels or complexity. That is, at each class level, concepts and behaviours sought are considered in greater depth and breadth. The application o f this criterion of sequence is the planning, for example, health instruction allows for vertical organization.

Integration is the relationship which subject matter or concept has with another. The implementation of this criterion of integration provides for horizontal organization of the curriculum. This also presents a subject in a unified view as against segmented one e.g. it relates learning in nutrition to learning in disease prevention and learning in health education to learning in related subject fields such as science, physical education, social studies, home economics and even mathematics.

Integration of Subjects (A) and Topics (B)

A	Physical Education	Health Education	Science
B	Nutrition	Growth & Development	Disease prevention

The selection of content also limited by an essential criterion – "**utility**" which means the content selected must be useful to students both in and out of the subject matter area. Utility has generally been viewed as the usefulness of concepts and skills in solving "real world" problems (called transfer of training)" by psychologists. Nevertheless, we must ensure that contents are organized and sequenced behavioural outcomes specified for each element of content. Translation of content into behavioural objectives is very essential as it gives direction to the development of measuring instruments that are needed to evaluate students' progress. Therefore content must be related to pre-stated objectives of the curriculum, reflect on the knowledge of the past, deal essentially with the current knowledge in a discipline and also stimulate thinking in teachable form for utilization and advancement of the learner and his/her society.

Fundamental Concepts and Themes

There are several concepts that can guide the development and review of all types of curricula at both the program and course level.

- **Alignment and Coherence** - all parts of the curriculum must be logically consistent with each other. There must be a "match" or a fit between parts.
- **Scope** - the range or extent of "content" (whether information to be learned, skills to be acquired etc.) that will be included in a course or program. It must be sufficient to lead learners to achieve the program or course outcomes. However, there is a constant tension between breadth and depth when considering scope. In general, when deep learning is required, "lean" is best.
- **Sequence** - is the ordering of learning experiences so that learners build on previous experiences and move to broader, deeper or more complex understandings and applications. Common ways of sequencing content within courses include simple to complex, wholes to parts (or part to wholes), prerequisite abilities, and chronological.
- **Continuity** - refers to the vertical repetition of major curriculum elements in different courses over time (also known as vertical organization or articulation). It is important to identify the themes or skills that need to run through a program and to map how they will be addressed at each level.
- **Integration** - refers to the horizontal relationship among major curriculum components at any given point in time (also known as horizontal organization). Integration fosters reinforcement of key learning and is needed to promote application of learning across course boundaries.

Gordon Cawelt (1990) of The Association for Supervision and Curriculum Development (ASCD) offered these principles to guide course planning.

- Offer a balanced core of learning in each course.
- Adopt the belief that in-depth study of a limited number of important topics will have a more lasting effect than a course that tries to cover too many disconnected bits and pieces of information.
- Design course outcomes to focus on results, with multiple indicators (assessments) of performance.

- Design authentic assessments that will encourage originality, insightfulness, and problem-solving, along with master of important information.
- Design courses to encourage active involvement.
- Get students "doing" early in the course rather than studying all the principles and basics prior to performing.

Some Common Curriculum Frameworks

There are several different patterns frequently used to organize programs. Some of those more commonly found in college programs are listed here.

- **Subject or Discipline-Centered** - the curriculum is organized around separate, specific subjects or disciplines. For example anatomy (subject) or life sciences (discipline)
- **Broad Fields** - the curriculum is organized to cut across subject lines and to emphasize relationships between subjects. It usually if organized into a 3 to 5 fields. For example, fields for technical career learning, professional and personal growth, supporting sciences, etc.
- **Spiral** - the curriculum is organized around key concepts/skills that are introduced and revisited for deeper understanding as the learner moves through the program of study
- **Inquiry or Problem-Based** - the curriculum is organized around a set of problems or areas of inquiry.
- **Experiential** - learners engage is a set of experiences and then are helped to process and draw meaning from them.

Outcome-Based Curriculum

All teaching learning programs leading to a Degree or Certification are guided by standards that are expressed as learning outcomes. Students need to be able to "show what they know"—to demonstrate achievement of these learning outcomes. The curricula that we develop for these programs can be very different across different colleges but all must lead to the achievement of these program level learning outcomes. In this context, some of the concepts and principles linked to outcomes-based curriculum design can guide our work.

What is Outcomes-Based Education (OBE)?

The High Success Network (1992) defines Outcomes-Based Education as "...defining, organizing, focusing, and directing all aspects of a curriculum on the things we want all learners to demonstrate successfully when they complete the program". Outcomes-based education is a student-centered, results oriented design premised on the belief that all individuals can learn. The strategy of OBE implies the following:

- What students are to learn is clearly identified
- Each student's progress is based on demonstrated achievement
- Each student's learning needs are addressed through multiple instructional strategies and assessment tools
- Each student is provided time and assistance to realize his/her potential. (Boschee & Baron 1993)

Selection And Organisation Of Learning Situations

Much debate on curriculum organization is now guided largely by rules of thumb and by opinions arrived at without sufficient basis in research. It is not possible for the curriculum to be maximally effective without careful planning and appropriate organization. The practice of curriculum construction needs to be guided by a theory which has been carefully developed, utilizing an acceptable philosophy of education, based upon known principles of learning, and taking into account the results of school experience and experimentation. Our educational institutions have more serious responsibilities than they have ever had before. The sheer existence of our society depends upon an educated citizenship that must have knowledge, ideals, habits, and intelligence far greater than has been required in any other age. The only possibility of meeting these imperative demands for an educated citizenship, with all that this implies, is an efficient curriculum that produces the maximum cumulative effect in the time which schools can devote to education. Sound theory is needed to guide the making of this effective organization.

When learning experiences are to be organized, the question that arises early in the planning is this: For a given learner or group of learners, which of all the learning experiences are to be included in the plan of organization? If one considers a pupil's total learning experiences over a period of time, there will be experiences within the school's course of study and in extra-curriculum activities. There will also be learning outside the school at home, at play, and at work. There will be not only the experiences the pupil has today but those of tomorrow, next week, next month, next year, and so on. In practice, no plan of organization could expect to relate effectively all the experiences of the learner during the years he is attending school. Too many of these experiences are completely outside the control of the school and even beyond the control of parents, churches, and youth agencies or other social organizations. An effective theory of organization should indicate the extent of these experiences that need to be organized for practical, efficient, and effective learning.

The method by which the teacher presents his/her material to learners may promote or hinder learning. It may also sharpen mental activities which are the basis of social power or else it may hinder initiative and curiosity thereby making self reliance and survival difficult. The importance of using appropriate teaching - learning situation is so important. For effective teaching to take place the skilful teacher needs to use the many different methods and techniques at his/her command.

Even though there is a great diversity in teaching methods and techniques, there is no one of them that can be regarded as the best for every teaching situation. A carefully planned teaching method can work wonders in making learning effective. The success in the use of the methods depends on an intelligent analysis of the educational purpose, the pupils in the class, and the curriculum content of the moment or the type of subject matter being taught. Since we want to facilitate learning and see that learners gained knowledge, attitude, practices are better than when learning was initiated, appropriate methods need to be specified for each subject teacher to choose from (but it is not mandatory for the teacher that he/she must use any of them) to facilitate learning. Methods to be chosen by teachers must take the age, interest, cultural background, experience, extent of content areas to be learnt, pre-stated objectives, evaluation techniques to be used, into consideration. This implies that the methods must blend well with other tasks the teacher needs to perform in the course of teaching learning process.

In addition, methods to be used need not be teacher domineering but making the learners to be active through talking, demonstrating, explaining and not passive or aggressive. It should also enable the learners to pay attention, listen and think in problem solving or learning situations. One thing we must know is that no method is either absolutely right or wrong and the best is to combine some or all, depending on the learners and teachers' competencies.

Evaluation can be regarded as a series of processes which entails a systematic processing of looking analytically into educational problems through the asking of appropriate questions, examining the answers correctly and using them as a basis for further decision-making. It is in-built into every process of systematic curriculum development. Since curriculum work involves conceptualizations, planning, development of materials and monitoring, at each stage, necessary questions need to be asked and critically examined so as to know what step to take next. The success or failure of any programme, in education or any other sphere of human endeavour, to achieve a particular set of objectives may be judged in many ways. These include; the amount of activity expended towards the accomplishment of the objectives and the magnitude of the outcome or the effect produced by the programme activity.

Since evaluation is a process of determining programme performance for the purpose of improving service delivery, the process should be a continuous one. The evaluation process must enable us to see whether our objectives are being met, help us to diagnose and give guidance at every stage of curriculum development, see the need for curriculum reform or change as well as promote further curriculum research.

An effective learning experience can only be had in well structured and skilfully executed learning situation. Teaching consists basically or arranging situations that promote desired learning. The essential role of a teacher is to create learning situations that stimulates and guide the learning activity. The effective extension worker is one who can create and manage learning situations in which learners have effective learning experience. A learning situation is the condition or environment in which all the elements necessary for promoting learning are present. An effective learning situation consists of following five essential elements:

- An effective Instructor or Leader.
- Learners who want and need to learn.
- Content or subject matter that is useful to learners.
- Appropriate teaching equipments and material.
- An appropriate physical environment

Characteristics of a Learning Situation in a Pre-School

- Comes from the interest/concern /need of a child (appropriate to child development)
- Respects the play context of the kindergarten classroom
- Promotes exploration, inquiry, problem based learning
- Linked to the attitudes, behaviours, strategies, process and product(s)
- Respects the Preschool Education mandate.
- Respects the trans-disciplinary nature of the Preschool Education Program

- Encourages the child to be active (kinaesthetic sensory), reflective and meta-cognitive
- Provides different avenues for children to demonstrate the same learning goal (not necessarily concrete measures)
- Purposeful and meaningful for the child with respect to the contexts of the development of the competencies.
- Is process driven
- Respects the global nature of the competency(ies) being targeted.
- Respects the child's Zone of Proximal Development.

Conclusion

The development of an effective curriculum is a multi-step, on-going and cyclical process. There are many approaches to curriculum development as presented in this Unit. No matter the choice of approach, the curriculum developer must be guided by the following principles. The curriculum developer must establish a clear philosophy and set overarching goals that guide the entire curriculum and the decisions that affect each aspect of the curriculum. S/he should establish sequences both within and between levels and assure a coherent and articulated progression from one level to another. A basic framework must be outlined for what to do, how to do it, when to do it and how to know if it has been achieved. S/he must allow for flexibility and encourage experimentation and innovation within an overall structure. The curriculum must promote interdisciplinary approaches and the integration when appropriate. Methods of assessing the achievement of the curriculum goals and objectives must be suggested and a means for revision and improvement provided.

The direction for procurement of human, material and fiscal resources to implement the curriculum should also be provided. There is no perfect approach. However, to be effective, an approach must attract acceptance of the teachers and other stakeholders in the education of the learners. This acceptance will be far easier to attain when the curriculum approach reflects child growth and development, the philosophy of the society, principles of teaching and learning, needs and varying abilities of the learners, ease of implementation; and cooperatively developed by a broad-based committee of teachers and relevant experts. The approaches presented here resemble each other. The difference, one can rightly claim is in the semantics (terminology), because they emphasize the same process.

Model Questions

1. What are different approaches to curriculum development? Which one you like more? Why?
2. How we can incorporate local concerns in to the curriculum?
3. Are you in favour of Constructivist approach of curriculum Development? Why?
4. What you mean by Competency Based Curriculum? Illustrate.

References

Alvior, Mary G. (February 7, 2015). Seven Criteria for the Selection of Subject-Matter or Content of the Curriculum. In *Simply Educate Me*. retrieved on 03-07-2016 from http://simplyeducate.me/2015/02/07/7-criteria-for-the-selection-of-subject-matter-or-content-of-the-curriculum/

Approaches to Curriculum., retrieved on 02-07-2016 from https://educational researchtechniques.wordpress.com/2014/05/15/approaches-to-curriculum/

Bellack, A.A. & Kliebard, H.M. (Ed.). *Curriculum and Evaluation*. California: McCutchan Publishing Corporation. retrieved on 03-07-2016 from http://www.project2061.org/publications/designs/dod/dsl_text/Reprints/1_Tyler.pdf

Burton, L.D. *Subject-Centered Curriculum*. retrieved on 14-05-2016 from http://sk.sagepub.com/reference/curriculumstudies/n436.xml

Competency-based learning. retrieved on 02-07-2016 from https://en.wikipedia.org/wiki/Competency-based_learning

Curriculum Overview. retrieved on 03-07-2016 from http://gototheexchange.ca/index.php/curriculum-overview/curriculum-models-and-design-principles

Dagalea, C.R. *Curriculum Approaches*. retrieved on 02-07-2016 from http://www.slideshare.net/CarlRichardDagalea/curriculum-approachers

Darrin (2014). *Types of Curriculum Design: Subject Centered*. retrieved on 14-05-2016 from https://educationalresearchtechniques.wordpress.com/2014/06/19/types-of-curriculum-design-subject-centered/

Delajane. *Curriculum Approaches*. retrieved on 02-07-2016 from http://delajane.blogspot.in/2012/08/curriculum-approaches.html

Directorate of State Education, Research and Training, Bengaluru. (2012). *Teaching –Learning of Environmental Studies (EVS) at the Primary School Level: A Position Paper*. retrieved on 02-07-2016 from http://dsert.kar.nic.in/circulars/position/EVS-positionPaper.pdf

European Centre for Modern Languages of the Council of Europe. *Student-Centred Course Curriculum Development*. retrieved on 02-07-2016 from http://archive.ecml.at/mtp2/chagal_setup/en/student_centredness/student_centred_course_curriculum_development.htm

Everhart, D. (Oct 2, 2014). *3 Key Characteristics of Competency Based Learning*. retrieved on 02-07-2016 from http://blog.blackboard.com/3-key-characteristics-of-competency-based-learning/

Farooq, U. (2013). *What is Subject Centered Curriculum*. retrieved on 14-05-2016 from http://www.studylecturenotes.com/curriculum-instructions/what-are-the-characteristics-of-subject-centered-curriculum

G.V.Gopal and V.V. Anand, *Environmental Education in school Curriculum an overall perspective.,* Regional institute of education, Mysore-6., retrieved on 02-07-2016 from http://www.ces.iisc.ernet.in/biodiversity/sahyadri_enews/newsletter/issue22/art5.htm

International Bureau of Education. *What Makes a Quality Curriculum?*. retrieved on 02-07-2016 from http://www.ibe.unesco.org/en/document/what-makes-quality-curriculum

Kallon, M. *What Good Teachers Do*. School of Education, UWI, St. Augustine. retrieved on 03-07-2016 from http://uwispace.sta.uwi.edu/ dspace/bitstream/handle/2139/ 7181/Michael%20Kallon1. pdf?sequence=1

Learning Situation. retrieved on 03-07-2016 from http://agriinfo.in/?page=topic &superid=7&topicid=628

Learning Situations in Kindergarten. retrieved on 03-07-2016 from http://www.learnquebec.ca/en/content/curriculum_elem/kinder/learnSits/

Learning Theory - Constructivist Approach. retrieved on 03-07-2016 from http://education.stateuniversity.com/pages/2174/Learning-Theory-CONSTRUCTIVIST-APPROACH.html

Lewy, A. (1991). *National and school-based development*. Paris: UNESCO; International Institute for Educational Planning. retrieved on 24-04-2016 from http://unesdoc.unesco.org/images/0009/000901/090127eo.pdf

Minimum Levels of Learning at primary stage. retrieved on 02-07-2016 from http://www.teindia.nic.in/mhrd/50yrsedu/r/2S/99/2S990101.htm

Minimum Levels of Learning: Some important features. retrieved on 02-07-2016 from http://www.teindia.nic.in/mhrd/50yrsedu/r/2S/99/2S990201.htm

MOEF, 2002: Empowering People for Sustainable Development, Ministry of Environment & Forests, Government of India, India. http://envfor.nic.in

Mylona, E. *Developing a Competency Based Curriculum*. retrieved on 02-07-2016 from http://www.dent.uoa.gr/fileadmin/dent.uoa.gr/uploads/curriculum-competency/mylona-march-2013.pdf

Natural Resources Management and Environment Department. *Overview of the Curriculum Development Process*. retrieved on 03-07-2016 from http://www.fao.org/docrep/009/ah650e/ah650e03.htm#Figure 2

NCERT, 2004: *Environmental Education in Schools*, National Council for Education Research and Training, New Delhi

NCF 2005: *National Curriculum Framework*, National Council for Education Research and Training, New Delhi

NPE, 1986: *National Policy on Education (1986)*, Ministry of Human Resource Development, Government of India, India.

Offorma, G.C. (2014). Approaches to Curriculum Development. retrieved on 02-07-2016 from https://www.researchgate.net/publication/280554159_APPROACHES_TO_CURRICULUM_DEVELOPMENT

Ornstein, A. C., & Hunkins, F. P. (2009). Curriculum: Foundation, principles, and issues (5th ed.). Boston, MA: Allyn & Bacon.

Stages of Curriculum development. retrieved on 03-07-2016 from https://www.yaaka.cc/unit/stages-of-curriculum-development/#sthash.HpWOfLuN.dpbs

Thamarasseri, I. (2016). *Psychology of Learning.* New Delhi: Dominant Publishers & Distributors (P) Ltd.

The Behavioural Approach to Curriculum., retrieved on 02-07-2016 from https://educ-7220-group-3-understanding-by-design.wikispaces.com/The+Behavioral+Approach+to+Curriculum

Unesco, 1997: Educating for a Sustainable Future: A Transdiciplinary Vision for Concerted Action, Paris

UNESCO-UNEP IEEP, 1996: Teaching for Sustainable World, UNESCO, Paris

Writ Petition (Civil) No 860 0f 1991, M.C.Mehta, Hon'ble Supreme Court of India.

Chapter - 7

Curriculum Implementation and Renewal

Introduction

The curriculum renewal process is done inclusively, collaboratively, and participative when: (1) a shared vision is developed, (2) a variety of perspectives are shared and taken into account, and (3) decision making and planning are open to broad engagement. To ensure success the process needs: (1) leadership, (2) effective and ongoing communication, (3) to be planned, (4) to be resourced and supported, (5) to be monitored, and (6) to be evaluated.

Throughout this curriculum renewal process 3 key questions are asked.

- Why? (1) to validate decisions and actions (2) to engage stakeholders (3) to provide a context for decision making, goal setting and evaluation.
- How? (1) to determine the process (2) to develop agreed criteria for success for review and evaluation.
- What? (1) What is the intent and purpose of the program? (2) What skills and knowledge do students need to develop: (for the program?, for the main / major? for the specialisation? for the course?)
- What courses will be needed (core) and which can help (electives) to achieve the intent and purpose of the program?
- What will students do to develop the expected knowledge, skills and application (learning activities)?

- What will students need to do to demonstrate they have achieved program and course learning outcomes (assessment)?

Many of these questions will be answered through the curriculum mapping process. Curriculum development and renewal is a multi-phase process as depicted in Figure 5.1 below:

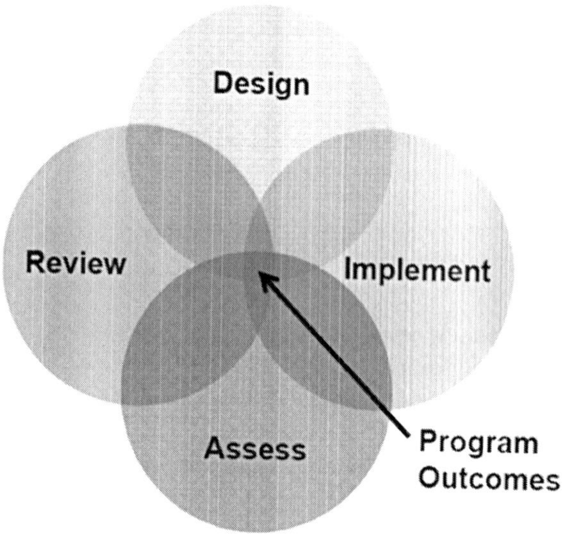

Figure 7.1: Curriculum design and development process

Curriculum development and renewal might start at any of these four phases. For some Schools/ Departments / Centres, change is initiated following a program review; for others, their interest stems from the recognition that a new program is needed. Curriculum work might relate to a suite of courses, an entire program, or to faculty-wide initiatives. The curriculum renewal process has included retreat facilitation, consultations, specialized course design workshops, and dedicated support for curriculum committees.

Operationalising Curriculum Into Learning Situations

Curriculum Transaction is the effective and desired implementation of the curriculum contents on the basis of aims and objectives listed in the curriculum. Children will benefit only if the implementation is effective.

A teacher's effort should be to reach out effectively to each child in the group. Lesson plans should be prepared much in advance. If there is a gap between planning and implementation, changes could be required before implementing the plan. A teacher should meaningfully engage children and stimulate their thought processes. Children listen to some teachers and are receptive, while the same group of children could respond differently to another teacher. Some of the requirements of effective curriculum transaction are:

- Planning
- Clarity of thought
- Organising
- Knowing how we will transact
- Review of the work
- Clarity of communication
- Addressing different levels of children
- Knowing, observing and understanding children at all times
- Time management
- Alertness
- Material organisation
- Room set up
- The way we reach out to the children
- Ready alternatives

The **National Curriculum Framework (NCF 2005)** aims to guide the development and transaction of curriculum in schools and to address the problems of transmission of information and rote learning. It includes guidelines for curriculum transaction to make learning active, social and meaningful. Schools are supposed to adopt these guidelines and the current five-year plan of the Indian government reiterates this. The guidelines are as follows:

- **Connecting knowledge to life outside the school**: The first guideline aims to contextualize learning and ensure that the content gets a broader perspective as it is linked to the life of the learners during the instructional process.
- **Ensuring that learning shifts away from rote methods :** The second guideline intends that learners are enabled to link new and old learning so that they develop conceptual clarity and are encouraged to think critically and apply learning.

- **Enriching the curriculum so that it goes beyond textbooks:** The third guideline aims to address the problem of considering textbooks as the sole and final source of knowledge. It is in fact an extension of the first guideline and requires that learners be introduced to various sources of knowledge. This will introduce learners to various views, sometimes even contradictory ones and help them to build a perspective that may accommodate diverse opinions.
- **Making examinations more flexible and integrating them with classroom life:** The fourth guideline seeks to make assessment a formative process so that teaching and assessment determine each other and the meaningfulness of learning can be ascertained on a continuous basis.
- **Nurturing an overriding identity informed by caring concerns within the democratic polity of the country:** The fifth guideline underscores the need to raise awareness, nurture a sense of identity and the ability for critical thinking on socio-political realities. It also intends that learners are helped in internalizing India's constitutional values of equality, justice, liberty and fraternity so that democracy does not remain only as a form of governance but becomes a way of life for them. Thus, while making learning an active process to be carried out through group activities, it seeks to impart training in citizenship for India.

Academic curriculum designs tend to focus on a body of knowledge which is grouped into disciplines, subject matter, or broad fields. It is a familiar pattern of organization that is evident in the way in which knowledge is organized for course work in most schools. Besides being a means of designing curriculum, the academic design carries with it the message that knowledge is organized into logical categories and that values can be attached to those categories. For example, the academic rationalism conception of curriculum created by Eisner and Vallance (1974) illustrates this design. Selected content, such as the basic subjects in the liberal arts, is held to be the central purpose of schooling and the curriculum. These subjects, through a disciplinary organization of content, focus the curriculum. Often, academic rationalism as an ideology influences issues in education such as the "back to the basics" movement. Those who promote these designs identify particular subject matter which is designed to transmit the heritage of a culture through literature, history, science, and other fundamental disciplines.

The least frequently represented curriculum design deals with the development of **Intellectual / cognitive processes**. This design makes the development of either cognitive processes such as critical thinking and problem solving or human processes and traits such as creativity and self-confidence the focus of curriculum, rather than a structured discipline or a sequenced task. The goal of this design is to increase learning efficiency and the transfer of problem solving abilities to all areas of the curriculum and life. Emphasis on processes has recently been increased through current research on students' cognition and meta-cognition. The emphasis in this design is on such processes as problem solving, first, and then on the context and content of the learning situation. Current research about cognition reveals the importance of the context and content of the activity, in addition to factors associated with the student such as prior knowledge with respect to intellectual processes. Clear-cut examples of process curricula are difficult to identify. Recent thinking skills curricula which have been developed as separate courses or as subject-matter-specific programs in the social studies and language arts are the best examples of curriculum which are designed with a clear focus on intellectual processes to the exclusion (or relegation to lesser consideration) of content. In **technology education**, examples of intellectual processes curriculum designs often appear in design courses. In these courses, the instructor identifies a problem solving model as the basis of subject matter and particular activities related to industry and technology for improving or teaching about critical thinking and problem solving. These activities, similar to the activities one would find in an Odyssey of the Mind competition, are examples of an emphasis of intellectual processes within a subject matter.

Social design curriculum focuses on the application of knowledge in realistic or real world situations. A variety of assumptions may contribute to this design with some mutual exclusivity to the assumptions. In brief, there are two distinct and opposite sides to this design. For example, one variation of the design could focus on social reconstruction with the assumption that the future of society can be changed as a result of the educational activities of the current generation. This assumption leads to a curriculum plan which would focus on providing students with opportunities to work on social projects for the purposes of changing their environment. On the other hand, the social design could also focus on social adaptation with the assumption that students are the raw material of society, and they need to be shaped to conform to existing social values. In this variation, a social design takes the opposite direction with respect to students, society, and the future by focusing on the information students need in order to fit into adult society.

Examples of **social reconstruction** (changing society) assumptions are in the work of **Dewey**, Counts, and others of the Reconstructionist Era during the beginning and middle of this century, and in the work of the contemporary reconceptualists such as **Apple**, **Giroux**, and **Anyon**. Adaptation (conforming to society) assumptions are present in the early curriculum work of **Bobbitt**. These same assumptions are often a part of technical designs of vocational curriculum when the goal is to prepare students to fill selected roles in an occupation. Vocational education curricula often involve social adaptation by preparing students for occupations.

Personal curriculum designs are learner-centered with a focus on the individual needs and interests of the student. Students help or totally create curriculum by expressing interests and investigating those interests. Teachers serve as diagnosticians and facilitators for this effort. It is the teacher's role to help students to identify interests and guide them to appropriate resources and connections to other knowledge. The autobiographical nature of curriculum as currere, a personal experience, and the desire to de-school society because of the rigidity of schools fit into personal curriculum designs. The curriculum writing of **Paulo Freire** illustrates the nature of personal involvement in curriculum. The goals of the personal design are to put the control and choice of the curriculum into the hands of the students instead of subject matter specialists and to allow students to personally integrate the information which they choose. This curriculum design is associated with the progressive education movement, and more recently, open schools.

Teachers' Role In Generating Dynamic Curricular Experiences

Among the greatest of all services that can be rendered by men to Almighty God or Nature, is the education and training of children, so that they can foster by grace in the way of salvation, growing like pearls of divine bounty in the shell of education and will be one day the jewel in the crown of abiding glory.

Henry Von Dyke has said about teachers and teaching. "Ah! There you have the worst paid and the best rewarded of vocations. Do not enter it unless you love it. For the vast majority of men and women it has no promise of wealth and fame, but they to whom it is dear for its own sake are among the nobility of mankind. I sing the praise of the unknown teacher, king of himself and leader of the mankind, This, we may say is the philosophical meaning of teaching, but is very relevant and meaning also".

The teacher is the yardstick that measures the achievements and aspirations of the nation. The worth and potentialities of a country get evaluated in and through the work of the teacher, The people of a country are the enlarged replica of their teacher. They are the real nation builders.

It needs no description that the teacher is the pivot of any educational system of the younger students. On him rests the failure or the success of the system. If the teachers are well educated and if they are intellectually alive and take keen interest in their job, then only, success is ensured. But, if on the other hand, they lack training in education and if they cannot give their heart to their profession, the system is destined to fail. Hence, the teacher is another vital component of the school.

The teacher is a dynamic force of the school. A school without teacher is just like a body without the soul, a skeleton without flesh and blood, a shadow without substance. There is no greater need for the cause of education today than the need for strong manly men and motherly women as teachers for the young. As social engineers, the teachers can socialize and humanize the young by their man-like qualities. Students tend to copy the behaviour and mannerism of the teachers. The teachers entire personality is a reflection on the minds of the students. If the teacher is honest, leads a balanced and disciplined life, the children adopt these virtues as a ideal conduct unconsciously. The ideal teachers one who through his thoughts, words and deeds, gives and an impression of an honest upright life which can serve as a model for the students to copy, follow and emulate.

A flower in bloom is loved by all and in this lies its glory. Similarly, man may be viewed as having achieved everything in life when he becomes perfect in character. If the best flowers among mankind take to teaching, society is abundantly enriched, their fragrance and beauty are then made the best use of. If the teacher becomes an embodiment of right conduct in thought, word and deed, the students by their association will learn virtue and develop manly qualities. They can be humanized and can live and act like normal human beings. They can become thoughtful, concerned and courageous.

Every teacher must have a good personality. Radiant, pleasing and impressive personal appearance, refinement, pleasant manners, industry, enthusiasm, drive, initiative, open mindedness etc., are some of the essential traits of an ideal teacher. External appearance has a psychological effect upon the students. By attractive appearance, he/she can win the love and affection of his students and can command respect. He/she should be frank, tolerant, kind, fair and straight-forward so that he/she can stimulate learning.

Engagement is regarded as an important component of interactive teaching. Thus, there is an emphasis on the importance of maintaining pupils' interest in language learning and providing an enjoyable and engaging classroom environment. Early studies identified student engagement through observable behaviours such as participation and time on the task. Some researchers focused on the emotional or affective aspects of engagement such as Connell (1990) and Finn (1989) who identified it as feelings of belonging, enjoyment and attachment. Other researchers such as Fredricks, Blumenfeld and Paris (2004) studied aspects of cognitive engagement such as students' investment in learning, perseverance in the face of challenges and use of deep rather than superficial strategies. Another group of researchers included self-regulation, referred to as the extent to which students demonstrate control over their learning actions, as a component of cognitive engagement.

One of the challenges facing schools and teachers today is **how to provide an engaging curriculum**. Such a curriculum should be relevant to the actual world in which the child is living as well as allowing the opportunity for hands-on activities, child's questioning, curiosity, exploration, discussion and reflection. Children need to have tasks suited to their age level, language ability and interests. They need to feel included as valued members of the learning community, to have an access to success and recognition and to enjoy learning.

Meaningful engagement in classroom activities is a key protective factor in children's cognitive and social development. It helps them make a psychological investment in learning. They incorporate the new material in their lives. Teachers should engage the pupils through experiential, authentic activities relevant to the pupils' lives and suited to their levels and interests. They should reach out to all pupils and provide support when needed.

Authentic, experiential and enjoyable learning experiences help children become more interested and motivated and consequently, more engaged in the learning process. These experiences satisfy some of the fundamental psychological needs of children, namely the need for competence, success and fun. Engaging learners' emotions helps better retention and more enjoyment. Geake and Cooper (2003) emphasized that the strongest connections in our brains occur when we are emotionally engaged in concrete, meaningful learning experiences.

The most effective learning experiences are engaging. Teaching should be tailored to students' needs. Many children commence their schooling without the language skills and the supportive background to assist their learning. They may fail to achieve satisfactory results. In the past, such students could leave early and join unskilled work. The restructuring of work eliminated such opportunities and called for specialized skills.

Learning is more effective if it attracts the attention and interest of the learner. It should also be relevant and contextualized. It should require an action on the part of the learner. Relevance is an important variable in the in the teaching/learning process. If something is important or relevant to students, they are more likely to actively participate and experience long-term learning. Authentic methods of instruction require learners to produce, rather than reproduce knowledge that is relevant to their own lives and to achieve tasks in ways that are of value to themselves and to society.

Whenever children are allowed to take risks, apply learning in different contexts and express their opinions in a non-threatening atmosphere, they are highly engaged in the learning activities. Children are more engaged when they understand the learning objectives and try to review their learning and improve it. They are capable of entering into many roles and having different identities. Both teachers and learners bring their knowledge, skills, attitudes and creative capabilities to the learning process. Consequently, having balanced roles and responsibilities for both teachers and pupils can help engagement. An indication of that engagement is when learners participate, attend classes, pay attention to the teacher, respond to teacher's directions and questions, show enthusiasm and engage in a range of peer or group interactions and develop longer attention spans. Whenever pupils and teachers share decision-making through discussion, recursive role taking and co-construction of learning activities, they engage in a joint exploration of learning and teaching.

Children are not simply learners; they are individuals who have psycho cognitive make up, personal history, prior experiences and life goals. These factors combine to influence their attitude to the process of language learning itself and the way they define the goals of learning. Each learner has his/her personal perspective on language teaching/learning. Effective teaching depends crucially on teachers being able to tune in to the meaning which language learning has for their students, both as individuals and as members of a learning group.

Learners' willingness to join in as collaborators in the teaching/learning process determines their success. Learners have a shared set of expectations, interests and needs. These shared aspects have roots in their cultural background or may emerge from the interpersonal dynamics of a given class group. An explicit culture of success where there are high expectations, high aspirations and an explicit celebration of that success can create an optimism and hope which are fundamental to engagement, commitment and motivation. Teachers' acceptance of learners, respect for their comments and opinions and listening attentively to their answers are all motivating factors that lead learners to be engaged. Assessing children's growing commitments is also motivating. In addition, implementing a sense of humour and relating information to children' culture and background lead to engaging and meaningful learning experiences.

Teachers, like learners, are individuals and their actions in the classroom reflect their individuality and their own personal philosophy of teaching. Each teacher defines the nature and goals of teaching according to his own rationality of teaching. This affects what teachers do in the class and how they interact with the actions and expectations of other participants. Teachers need to examine their own expectations and assumptions and how these contribute to the dynamics of their teaching. It is, therefore, necessary to explore what the classroom means to the different participants involved, and how these various rationalities influence participants' choices and decisions.

Humour and laughter help relieve tension, make learning more human, increase students' interaction and participation, and make the learning environment more enjoyable. It is also important for emotional health and well-being. It can help capture and keep students' attention. People tend to remember humorous incidents better than others do, so it can maximize students' recall in instructional situations, particularly when the humour is spontaneous and relevant to the topic being taught.

Teachers are crucial to the presence of humour in the classroom. They can promote appropriate uses of humour by using a variety of strategies to foster enjoyable and humorous approaches to the teaching/learning process. Teachers can display playfulness, take risks, be open to learners' ideas and communicate the message that learning can be fun, even though it requires hard work and persistence.

Teaching should expand beyond school building into the society. Media can be used not only as a source of information and entertainment but also as a form of public education. Because the mass media constitutes a powerful and pervasive force, educators must guide students in review of the electronic media and their effects on individuals and society. Students should be trained to show their own products on the school website, to design and work on e-games, caricatures and language comic strips, which tune in their local dynamics.

Teachers must inform their decisions about which teaching tools and techniques to use with knowledge related to individual learners and diverse learning needs. They also must consider learners' prior knowledge and experiences so they can effectively connect what learners already know and can do with the new knowledge and skills they are learning. Effective instructional approaches are culturally responsive and culturally relevant. Culturally inclusive approaches promote harmony among different groups and increase students' knowledge of their cultural heritage. In addition, culturally responsive instructional strategies create connections between different curricular components, are authentic, are learner-centred, and are relevant to learners' real lives. Such relevance and connections can be achieved in part by using materials from learners' cultures and history to illustrate specific principles and concepts.

Teachers need to be trained to structure the learning environment, both the physical environment and the affective one, to promote and encourage more active learner participation and more student responses to teachers' questions. Students' learning goals and needs influenced proactive decisions about tasks and materials; students' affective states had an impact on interactive decisions.

Project-based learning, is a dynamic approach to teaching in which students explore real-world problems and challenges, simultaneously developing cross-curriculum skills while working in small collaborative groups. Because project-based learning is filled with active and engaged learning, it inspires students to obtain a deeper knowledge of the subjects they're studying. Research also indicates that students are more likely to retain the knowledge gained through this approach far more readily than through traditional textbook-centred learning. In addition, students develop confidence and self-direction as they move through both team-based and independent work.

Teachers' Role In Flexible Interpretation Of Curricular Aims

When asking students to explore issues of personal and social identity, teachers must provide safe spaces where students are seen, valued, cared for and respected. It is also important that students have opportunities to learn from one another's varied experiences and perspectives. To create this learning environment, teachers need to skilfully draw on student experiences to enrich the curriculum.

Teachers can show they value students' lives and identities in a variety of ways. Some are small, like taking the time to learn the proper pronunciation of every student's name or getting to know young people's families. Others require more time and investment, like building curriculum around personal narratives or incorporating identity-based responses into the study of texts. At the community level, it is important to understand neighbourhood demographics, strengths, concerns, conflicts and challenges. Like students themselves, these dynamics may change frequently.

For teachers whose experiences differ from those of their students, it is critical to exercise sensitivity. Honouring student experience supports three of the four anti-bias domains: Identity, Diversity and Action. Students who feel their experiences are unwelcome, judged, stereotyped, disrespected or invisible find it extremely difficult to engage in meaningful discussion of identity and justice issues. Those whose stories and voices are heard and reflected in the classroom are more likely to engage with anti-bias curriculum and translate their learning into action.

Simple curriculum maintenance at the school level is not easy, and can be a full-time job if done correctly. Any number of recurring tasks will determine the readiness of the school to deliver the planned curriculum as intended. Without tip-top maintenance, the curriculum can become distorted and even inefficient. In fact, in some schools, there is no overview of what the curriculum should be and no plan for maintaining the existing programme.

Among the most important maintenance functions for the school-based curriculum leader is serving as a conduit for information about classroom instruction. School leaders attend numerous meetings at the district level, and may also attend informational conferences at the state level where rules and regulations are promulgated. Getting this information to the teachers in their classrooms is vital for any modern curriculum. Most recently, for example, we are witnessing states changing their mathematics and science standards, and this activity has direct implication for what teachers do with students in their classrooms. The school curriculum leader serves as a bridge for both the upward flow of inquiry and the downward flow of information. Another very important maintenance task in any school is to ensure compliance with changing laws that govern education. Such laws may address the subjects in school, monitoring student achievement, class size requirements, or even the required resources for specific student populations.

Exceptional students, for example, must be placed in classrooms under very specific conditions and this, in turn, can affect related decisions about hiring staff, building use, recordkeeping, and other items on a day-to-day basis. Today, almost every state in the nation has achievement tests to measure the attainment of minimal curriculum standards. The curriculum leader has to ensure that what is tested is, in fact, also being taught. Working backwards from test results, the curriculum leader can localize areas of low achievement using curriculum maps of each subject. In curriculum maintenance, where the school is deficient in achievement, corrections will have to be planned and implemented. Keeping the school supplied with adopted texts and appropriate instructional materials is another task of curriculum maintenance leadership. In most states, textbooks are first cleared by a state textbook committee that assesses the text by a number of criteria. For example, the committee will want to know whether the content of the text matches the curriculum standards required by law in that state. The committee will also try to determine if the text is relevant, supported by research, developmentally appropriate for that grade level, and so forth. Once adopted by the state committee, each district, and sometimes even each school, can select a text from the approved state list.

At the school level, the curriculum leader must help teachers replicate this adoption process by looking at things such as the alignment of the text with school curriculum requirements; the difficulty of the content level; the degree of reading difficulty; the accuracy, relevance, and authenticity of the content; and the multicultural representation as found in the school population. It is worth noting here that research has shown that the most common criterion for text selection at all levels of schooling is the physical appearance of the textbook. Curriculum leaders must work diligently to raise the level of sophistication by the teaching staff in dealing with such important matters.

Curriculum leaders providing a "maintenance function" in the school will also be responsible for all accreditation requirements. In most states, the school and the district is re-accredited every 10 years with an interim visit every 5 years. The importance of being and remaining accredited cannot be overstated. Parents and community members recognize accreditation as the single best measure of instructional quality. The workload to prepare for an accreditation visit can be unpleasantly burdensome for a new school curriculum leader unfamiliar with the process.

Reviewing student achievement and maintaining summary records of such achievement requires the curriculum leader to have strong organization skills. In most schools, such records (state reports, district records, and test results) are kept by the head of the institution who is guided by the curriculum leader. Setting up a system of recordkeeping, and a schedule of such requirements, is an important maintenance task in every school. It is equally important for the curriculum leader to develop a way to monitor how students are being assessed in the classroom. In most schools, the grading patterns vary widely from teacher to teacher. In-service sessions on this topic, and the expectations for student achievement, will contribute to a more manageable procedure in this area. Parents, in particular, will appreciate a fair system of assessment.

In all schools, staff development programs can help connect curriculum plans with classroom instruction. Assessing student achievement gains, for example, may identify some learning skills that are not being taught well. Once the weak areas of the curriculum are identified, the curriculum leader can schedule training sessions to improve faculty knowledge in those areas. It is inappropriate, and wasteful, for the curriculum leader to schedule regular in-service sessions without connecting them to school needs. Teachers and parents can be used to help identify areas of greatest need for additional training.

One of the most important curriculum maintenance tasks is to assess the deployment of staff positions. Faculty salaries and the physical facility account for 80 percent of any school budget. Vacated faculty lines are often simply replaced without thought about the changing needs of the curriculum. A long-range plan for any future vacancies is useful to develop as time allows. Part of this overall task is to develop clear and realistic job descriptions for the instructional positions at the school.

Finally, an important curriculum maintenance function is to try to keep abreast of existing research in the district and beyond. Knowledge of current research will help the curriculum leader make instructional materials decisions, help identify new ways of doing things, and help answer instructional questions from faculty and parents in an authoritative way. Together, these maintenance tasks keep the school curriculum rolling along and out of trouble. Obviously, the completion of such tasks will make the school curriculum more efficient and a great deal more effective. But the premise of such a maintenance orientation in curriculum leadership is that schools just do not change much year to year. In today's schools, maintenance will never be enough. A more dynamic role is required for successful school curriculum leadership.

Teachers' Role In Contextualisation Of Learning

Contextual learning is based on a constructivist theory of teaching and learning. Learning takes place when teachers are able to present information in a way that students are able to construct meaning based on their own experiences. Contextual learning experiences include internships, service learning, and study abroad programs, among others. Contextual learning has the following characteristics:

- emphasizing problem solving
- recognizing that teaching and learning need to occur in multiple contexts
- assisting students in learning how to monitor their learning and thereby become self-regulated learners
- anchoring teaching in the diverse life context of students[clarification needed]
- encouraging students to learn from each other
- employing authentic assessment

Current perspectives on what it means for learning to be contextualized include;

- situated cognition- all learning is applied knowledge
- social cognition- intrapersonal constructs
- distributed cognition- constructs that are continually shaped by other people and things outside the individual

Constructivist learning theory maintains that learning is a process of constructing meaning from experience. Contextual learning may be useful for child development if it provides learning experiences in a context in which children are interested and motivated. Various experiential learning theorists have contributed to an understanding of contextual learning.

Rationale for contextualisation of learning: Skills in reading, writing, and mathematics are key to academic learning, but conventionally, these skills are taught separately from the discipline areas to which they must be applied. For example, students may be taught writing skills in the morning in an English course and then be expected to apply them to writing an essay in a history class in the afternoon. Several problems arise with this structure. First, for reasons still to be determined (Barnett & Ceci, 2002), students do not necessarily transfer their morning writing skills to the afternoon history assignment. Second, students may not be motivated to learn writing skills in the English class because they do not consider such skills to be relevant to their personal goals (Cavazos, Johnson, & Sparrow, 2010). Third, weaknesses in essay-writing skills may not be addressed by the afternoon content-area teacher, who aims to teach subject knowledge rather than basic skills (Fisher & Ivy, 2005). These problems have serious implications for the academic trajectory of the many underprepared students who enter postsecondary education. Despite the allocation of considerable resources to providing developmental education courses that intend to bring the reading, writing, and math skills of underprepared students to the college level (Boylan, Bliss, & Bonham, 1997), many students in college-credit courses display continuing difficulties in applying these foundational skills to the learning of subject matter (Perin & Charron, 2006). A growing literature, especially in the field of adolescent literacy, suggests that bringing basic skills and subject-area instruction closer together may be a solution to this problem (Heller & Greenleaf, 2007; Lee & Spratley, 2010). One way to create this relationship is through contextualization, or the teaching of basic skills in the context of disciplinary topic areas.

Postsecondary developmental educators have recommended that pre-college academic skills instruction be directly related to the content of college-level courses (Simpson, Hynd, Nist, & Burrell, 1997). Contextualization, which achieves this purpose, can be seen as a form of "deep learning" that comes about through linking ideas and concepts across courses (Moltz, 2010). For example, Simpson et al. (1997) suggested that instruction to improve outcomes for low-skilled college students "would probably use authentic materials like the textbooks used in college courses such as Psychology or Biology". Drawing on research on the transfer of learning, Simpson et al. (1997) contrasted such "embedded" instruction with the predominant "generic" instruction, where technical aspects of literacy or math are taught apart from content, such as when students are taught to analyze text structure or find main ideas using short reading passages that have no obvious relation to each other, to content area courses, or to students' goals. In the generic writing approach, language is fragmented into decontextualized segments such as sentence- and paragraph-writing skills, with no connection to authentic uses. Accordingly, generic instruction has been criticized as uninteresting and ineffective (Grubb, 1999).

As E. Baker, Hope, and Karandjeff (2009) point out, contextualization has been defined in numerous ways. The definition proposed by Mazzeo, Rab, and Alssid (2003) is that; "A diverse family of instructional strategies designed to more seamlessly link the learning of foundational skills and academic or occupational content by focusing teaching and learning squarely on concrete applications in a specific context that is of interest to the student".

In any one program, contextualization of basic skills instruction contains one or more of the following components: interdisciplinary learning (Berns & Erickson, 2001), use of students' informal, out-of-school knowledge (Goldman & Hasselbring, 1997), active, student centred learning (Dirkx & Prenger, 1997; Dowden, 2007), student collaboration (Johnson, 2002), use of explicit literacy strategies (Paquette & Kaufman, 2008), authentic assessment (Johnson, 2002), and teacher collaboration to identify real world examples (Orpwood, 2010). Professional development may be given (Stone, 2006) but seems rare. Guidelines for contextualization have been provided for workplace and transition programs, and instructions for integrating literacy instruction in high school science courses have also been offered (Krajcik & Sutherland, 2010). Workplace literacy focuses on a broader range of skill than do other forms of contextualization; oral language, problem solving, teamwork, research skills, and basic computer operations are taught in addition to reading, writing, and math (Jurmo, 2004). Some programs have a vocational English language component where oral language is taught to English language learners using the content of specific jobs for which they are preparing (Mazzeo, 2003). Contextualization is implemented using many different instructional techniques, and over the years a fairly large number of program descriptions have accumulated, although many are not accompanied by student outcome data.

Implications of contextualisation for the Curriculum

The curriculum of primary schools in most developing countries is centralised and inflexible with an urban, western, middle-class bias. In these situations, decentralisation of the curriculum development process seems unlikely to happen in the near future. There are different approaches to curriculum development, however. Some educationalists advocate the creation of integrated curricula. Such an approach to curriculum development is certainly conducive to the use of contextualisation in schools, since there is much greater potential for teachers to develop the content themselves within certain topic areas. This means that they can relate learning much more closely to the local environment.

Bacchus (1982) defines integration as "the combination of the several components of an object, organisation or a system into a whole in order to render it entire or complete". A curriculum developed on this basis may have a core, which is identified as essential learning for all primary pupils throughout a country, but the way in which this core is handled is not prescribed by central policy makers. In order to render the curriculum complete, additional, optional areas will be included, depending on the locality of the school and the background of the pupils and teachers.

There are strong arguments in favour of this approach. As Krogh (1990) states: "Most of the learning in our lives is along the lines of an integrated curriculum". Following this idea, Krogh suggests ways that integrated learning, which prevails in everyday life, could be incorporated in the school programme. The teacher can choose a theme, create a topic web which relates and links a range of sub-themes or topics, and then add or subtract activities as it becomes apparent that there is too much or too little emphasis in some areas. This flexible method of teaching is an extension to natural teaching which takes place outside the school. It can build on a child's experiences, covering the whole curriculum whilst developing skills in a meaningful context, as opposed to breaking learning down into categories by subject area, which is less natural, more forced, and less interesting or exciting. Through a learning web, academic, social and emotional needs can be met. This approach was supported strongly at a recent conference held in Ethiopia (PEAP, 1996):

"Children see the world holistically, that is they make meaning of their surroundings by making connections. Learning takes place through the introduction of new information which meets prior knowledge and experiences of the learners. Learners come to school with knowledge from their home, friends, environments, radio, etc. This knowledge is not necessarily broken up into maths, mother tongue, natural science, social studies, etc. They come with knowledge and experiences that have meaning to them. In helping children to learn new concepts and processes it is important to make connections to the knowledge and experience that they already have. These connections between new knowledge and their existing knowledge are best make in a holistic manner which is facilitated by the integration of fragmented subjects into one or two areas (such as is being done with natural science, social studies, agriculture, home economics and handicraft)".

Most primary school curricula in use at present are not topic-based, but are organised according to the study of separate, specific subject areas or disciplines, such as language, mathematics, science, history, etc. Contextualisation still allows teachers to relate the content, however rigid, to the local environment. There are elements of all subject areas which can be contextualised. In this way, a centrally produced curriculum can be "localised" because teachers adapt the way in which they deal with the prescribed content by using the experience of the learners as a basis for teaching and learning. This is one way of addressing the problem of rigid "relevant" basic education programmes produced on a national scale, as curriculum flexibility is encouraged at a local level. The process of contextualisation will, necessarily, involve a range of stakeholders, not only school, government and community representatives, but also the learners themselves as they contribute actively to the learning process. An important impact of contextualisation, therefore, is, "curriculum empowerment".

Contextualisation can achieve the difficult task of linking "school knowledge" and "home knowledge". The Report of the National Advisory Committee of India (1993), gives an example: "one teacher who tried to make such a bridge in a lesson about letter-writing was asked by a class VI child: "madam, shall we write it the way we write at home or in the school way?"

The report continues to state: "this kind of perception results in the confinement of classroom life to a narrow orbit. Classroom knowledge assumes total independence from the child's own experience and knowledge of the world. As a consequence of this de-coupling, children begin to compartmentalise knowledge into two categories: that which has currency in the school and classroom, and the other which has uses and relevance outside the school." An aim of contextualisation is to put an end to this de-coupling by de-compartmentalising knowledge, and allowing all those involved in the learning process to recognise that learning is in fact a common currency to all learning environments.

Teachers' Role In Generating Varied Learning Experiences

To be a great teacher and role model to the students, teachers must adapt to the changing times and keep themselves updated with changes in social outlook and technology. If you are new in the teaching field or want to become an educationist, equipping yourself with modern teaching methods and improving your skill set is critical to your success as a teacher. Most teachers enter the profession right after their university degree and subsequent teacher training programs. Seldom do they have the experience to establish and manage an effective learning atmosphere for the students.

This makes it imperative for them to learn effective teaching skills on their own. After all, a good teach would not want students to learn through a disorganized or haphazard process of teaching that may use outdated approaches and curriculum standards. Teachers and educationists who take their responsibilities seriously endeavour to provide high-quality education to students from every strata of the society. Let us look in to the popular teaching skills that are relevant today and how teachers can keep up with the latest social media and mobile technologies to keep up with the demands of this competitive age. If you aspire to be a good teacher, learn more about this noble profession in our course on how to master **teaching skills**.

Teaching is a tough job and teachers need to be on their toes constantly to keep up with the rapidly changing pace of education in our society. With the advent of the internet and social media tools, the power of information is enabling people to learn about anything and everything. In today's challenging education atmosphere, how can teachers motivate their students to get interested, think differently and sharpen their curiosity? Here are some important teaching skills that every modern teacher must be equipped with to bring about significant development in their individual teaching styles:

- **Commitment and Passion** – If you are truly passionate about teaching, then nothing can stop you from achieving the highest standards in quality education. If a teacher is committed to his or her profession and strives to nurture students with an innovative learning platform, then half of the work is already done; the rest gets taken care of automatically!
- **Innovate and make it Interesting** – If a teacher thinks that he or she knows it all, then it's very difficult for them to adopt new teaching practices that can improve their instructional strategies. Teachers must look for innovative ways to teach children, stimulate their thinking process while developing their own teaching style to make a greater impact. At the end of the day, you have to capture the child's imagination, and heart, for them to truly learn well.
- **Planning Makes Perfect** – You might be a primary school teacher or a professor at a reputed university; students look up to you to learn new things and be shown the right path to attaining good education. So, prepare your lessons well in advance and organize them to manage your teaching schedules effectively so that students can learn in a holistic manner.
- **Be Impartial and Tolerant** – While discussing topics in class ensure that you don't thrust upon your views on the students; instead allow them to speak their minds freely and encourage different perspectives. It's important for a teacher to treat her students equally and stay away from favouritism or prejudices.
- **Communicate Effectively** – You have been a student yourself at some point of time; think from the student's perspective while introducing them to new topics. Young minds will have several questions that need to be answered properly; it's possible that at times you may not have the right answers but make sure that you communicate this to your students and come back with the solutions. Build a good rapport with your students, encourage them to discuss amongst themselves and enable them to look for answers.
- **Adopt Latest Technologies** – Students are constantly exposed to the never-ending stream of latest gadgets like mobiles and smart phones or iPads and Notebooks, acquiring a wealth of knowledge

even outside the classroom. Similarly, their teachers must also bring themselves up-to-date with technologies like the social media, mobile apps and online education so as to draw the positives from them and ramp up the teaching process to more effective levels. Our course on teaching online will give you more insights on how to use technology to reach out to more students, effectively.

- **Planning and Organizing Lessons for Effective Teaching -** Planning makes perfect; this is not just true for developing a lesson plan but also for executing them effectively in the classroom so that the course is covered in its entirety. There are several strategies to organize your lesson or course so as to master the art of effective teaching. If you are a young teacher, you will have to do your homework well so that you are not caught off-guard in the classroom. You must plan your lessons keeping in mind your audience, the objectives of the lesson and the methods of instruction. Teachers must ask themselves questions like "Who are my students?", "What should the students learn from this course?" and "Shall I use the standard whiteboard approach to teaching or bring in practical examples and case studies?" Planning helps teachers prepare for the class better and be ready to answer the most difficult of questions too. While planning your lesson, also factor in the assessment needs to understand if your audience has grasped the subject the way you intended it to. You may want to incorporate Learning Management Systems like Canvas to help organize your material better.
- **Managing the Classroom** – It's very easy for distractions to creep into students' minds and therefore a teacher's primary objective should also be to manage the classroom effectively and hold the audience's interest. Whether the learners are young students or college grads, the key to classroom management is to make your teaching sessions exciting and lively. Bring in the surprise element from time to time with tools such as practical examples, discussions, projects or workshops, debates and storytelling etc. Encourage an environment of interactive and cooperative learning to keep the flow of thought running in the young minds. Students not only learn more through such innovative classroom sessions but also start admiring and respecting the teacher better.
- **Student Assessment** – It is not enough to deliver your lessons or courses to the students; you must also make efforts to understand

how much the students have learnt during the class or term. Plan assessment strategies like multiple-choice papers, short essays on a topic, group discussions etc. to evaluate the learning process as well as the effectiveness of your teaching methods.

Developing skills to be a good teacher can be very intensive and exhausting, especially if the teacher is new to the field or has shifted gears from being a hard core professional to an academician. Therefore, it is important to build teaching skills in a structured manner so as to not be overwhelmed by the whole experience of teaching. While establishing good communication skills and adopting new practices are essential to succeed as a modern teacher, you must also accept failures as opportunities for improvement. Do not hesitate to try out new things in your class and do not be afraid to fail in the process. It is important to move ahead with conviction and carve out a niche for yourself in the world of teaching.

Modern teachers not only need to be competent technically but also be equipped to meet the emotional needs of their students in today's highly mechanized life. Often parents are unable to give attention to their kids due to their hectic work schedules; at times like these, teachers have to go the extra mile to look after the well-being of their students by assuming the role of a mentor or a guide.

Today teachers are not just seen as disciplinarians or educationists but are also regarded as friends and well-wishers; then isn't it the duty of a teacher to take his or her job seriously and work for the betterment of their students? Don't wait any longer. If you want to develop your teaching skills and make a difference to the society, then assess your strengths and weaknesses and work on them with dedication to establish yourself as a good teacher!

Selection And Development Of Learning Resources

The term "learning resources" will refer to any person(s) or any material with instructional content or function that is used for formal or informal teaching/learning purposes. Some examples of learning resources would include but are not limited to:

- teaching-learning materials and resources outside the school – local environment, community and media, etc
- print materials (e.g. textbooks, printed teaching materials)
- electronic media (e.g. computer software and programs, websites, movies and other multi-media)
- library resources

- guest speakers and presenters
- field trip sites
- other teaching and resources chosen to support student learning

When developing or reviewing curriculum we need to ensure that learning resources support the learning activities and/or the evaluation and assessment planned for the course. They also need to align with the needs, interests and abilities of the learners. Learning materials may be developed or selected from existing resources. As developments in cognitive science have helped us understand more about how learners construct knowledge, there has been a growing trend towards the greater use of raw data, primary sources and manipulative and interactive learning resource materials.

The primary objective of learning resources is to support, enrich, and help to implement the educational program of the school through the interaction of professional personnel and other members of the school community. It is the duty of professional staff to provide students with a wide range of materials at varying levels of difficulty, with diversity of appeal, and the presentation of different points of view.

Choosing the right textbook: For a long time textbooks were the major learning resource in most educational institutions. With the growth of multimedia and other resource materials teachers need to decide what place textbooks will have in the teaching of a course.

Evaluating websites: More and more students (and teachers too) are turning to the Internet as a source of information. However, as we know, not all sites are created equal. Here are some tips for evaluating websites.

Finding and Using Multimedia Resources: With a greater number if "digital natives" in our classrooms, the expectation for interactive and multimedia learning resources is growing.

Questions to consider when choosing, developing or assessing learning materials

- Are there sufficient learning resources identified to help learners achieve the expected learning?
- Are the learning materials appropriate to the learners' needs, interests and abilities?
- Do learners have an opportunity to work with primary sources and authentic (real world) materials?
- Are learning materials focused? Do they target the key concepts

and skills to be learned?

- Are the learning materials available at a reasonable cost?

Responsibility for Selection of Learning Resources: While selection of learning resources involves many people (administrators, teachers, students, community persons, resource centre personnel), the responsibility for co-ordinating the selection of school learning resources and making the recommendation for purchase rests with the principal and professional personnel. Educational personnel employed by the concerned authority have responsibility for selecting and issuing learning resources in accordance with the norms and regulations prescribed. The Superintendent of Schools and school principals have general responsibility for ensuring that the approved criteria are known and appropriately applied.

Procedures for Selection of Learning Resources

- Selection of learning resources shall be in accordance with prescribed criteria.
- Those charged with responsibility for selecting learning resources shall place principle above personal opinion and reason above prejudice in the selection of materials in order to assure a comprehensive collection appropriate to the school community.
- To every extent possible, the learning resource will be reviewed fully before selection and use.
- It is understood that in situations such as library resource centres, it is impossible to review all materials in entirety.
- Selection is an ongoing process which includes the removal of materials which are no longer appropriate according to the prescribed criteria.

Criteria for Selection of Learning Resources: The following criteria will be used as they apply:

- Learning resources shall support and be consistent with the educational goals of the province and district, as well as the needs of individual schools and specific courses.
- Learning resources shall be chosen in order to support and enrich the curriculum, taking into consideration the varied needs of the students.
- Learning resources shall be chosen in order to help students gain an awareness of our pluralistic society.
- Learning resources shall be selected to present various sides of controversial issues so that students may have an opportunity to

develop, under guidance, the practice of critical analysis and making informed judgment in their daily lives.

- Biased or slanted learning resources may be provided to meet specific learning objectives; for example, to recognize propaganda and its purposes in a given context.
- Emphasis will be placed on the selection of indigenous learning resources where appropriate.

Supplementary Learning Resources: Educational personnel shall not recommend the purchase of supplementary learning resources to families or students, unless a parent or student makes a specific request for information.

Parent Requests: Individual parents/guardians can request in writing to the school principal that specific learning resources not be used with their children. No parents/guardians have the right to restrict access to instructional materials for students other than their own children.

Reconsideration of Learning Resources: Anyone with a concern shall be provided with a copy of the National / State policy and procedures regarding learning resources. The first attempt to resolve the learning resource issue shall be at the school level. Should the concern not be resolved at the school level, the complaint shall be referred to a Learning Resource Reconsideration Committee (LRRC). The LRRC shall prepare a written report recommending that action should be taken regarding the challenged learning resource. This report will be communicated to the Board, school principals, and the complainant The LLRC shall be a broadly representative ad-hoc committee with members appointed by the Board and Superintendent. Members would includes Trustee, National representative, State representative, Teacher-Librarian representative, Student (where appropriate), School-based administrator and Superintendent or designate.

The complainant will have the right to attend and present at an LRRC meeting convened to discuss the learning resource being reconsidered. The complainant can appeal this decision to the Board as per Board Policy. All challenges to learning resources shall be dealt with as expeditiously as possible. Access to challenged material shall not be restricted during the reconsideration process unless otherwise determined by the Superintendent.

Procedures for Selection of Learning Resources

In selecting learning resources, professional personnel will evaluate available resources and curriculum needs and will consult reputable, professionally prepared aids to selection and other appropriate sources.

The actual resource will be examined whenever possible. Recommendations for purchase involve administrators, teachers, students, district personnel, and community persons, as appropriate. Gift materials shall be judged by the criteria outlined and shall be accepted or rejected by those criteria. Selection is an on-going process that should include the removal of materials no longer appropriate and the replacement of lost and worn materials still of educational value.

Controversial topics: Controversial topics will often be appropriate and important subjects of study in schools and, at times, cannot be avoided in the context of teaching and learning. However, the contexts of controversial topics or themes about which objections can be anticipated include:

- themes related to magic or fantasy
- racial and religious themes
- sexual activity, nudity and related themes
- drug misuse or addiction
- crime, violence and cruelty
- suicide and excessively bleak scenarios
- the depiction of revolting or abhorrent phenomena
- satirical or comparative perspectives on race, religion or gender.

The resource-based learning approach supports, enriches, and helps to implement the educational program of the school through the interaction of professional personnel, students, and parents/guardians in the school community. It is the duty of professional staff to provide students with a wide range of materials at varying levels of difficulty, with a diversity of appeal, and representative of different points of view.

References

Contextual learning. retrieved on 06-07-2016 from https://en.wikipedia.org/wiki/Contextual_learning

Curriculum Transaction-Operationalizing Curriculum into Learning Situations (17 February 2016). retrieved on 03-07-2016 from http://englishmylacompu.blogspot.in/2016/02/operationalizing-curriculum-into.html

Defining Effective Curriculum Leadership. retrieved on 06-07-2016 from https://us.corwin.com/sites/default/files/upm- binaries/25972_Chapter_1_ Defining_ Effective_ Curriculum_Leadership.pdf

Edutopia. *Why Teach with Project-Based Learning*?. retrieved on 06-07-2016 from http://www.edutopia.org/project-learning-introduction

Eisner, E. W., & Vallance, E. (1974). Conflicting conceptions of curriculum. Berkeley, CA: McCutchan.

Kootenay Columbia School District. *Selection and Challenge of Learning Resources*. retrieved on 11-06-2017 from https://www.sd20.bc.ca/tl_files/Policy/Section%201%20REVISED/1.14%20Selection%20and%20 Challenge%20of%20Learning%20Resources.pdf

Perin, D. (February 2011). *Facilitating Student Learning Through Contextualization*. CCRC Working Paper No. 29. retrieved on 06-07-2016 from http://ccrc.tc.columbia.edu/media/k2/attachments/facilitating-learning-contextualization-working-paper.pdf

Prince Edward Island, Canada. Dept of Education. *Evaluation and Selection of Learning Resources - A Guide*. retrieved on 11-06-2017 from http://www.gov.pe.ca/photos/original/ed_ESLR_08.pdf

Richa (June 6, 2014). *Teaching Skills: Create a Dynamic Learning Environment*. retrieved on 06-07-2016 from https://blog.udemy.com/teaching-skills/

Selecting Learning Resource Materials. retrieved on 11-06-2017 from http://gototheexchange.ca/index.php/curriculum-at-course-level/selecting-learning-resource-materials

Singh, N. *Role of teacher in a school*. retrieved on 06-07-2016 from http://www.navodaya.nic.in/Role%20of%20Teacher.htm

Soliman, R.A. The Role of a Learner Engagement Manual in the Dynamics of the Language Classroom. *American Journal of Educational Research*. Vol. 4, No. 3, 2016, pp 234-247. retrieved on 05-07-2016 from http://pubs.sciepub.com/education/4/3/3/

Southern Poverty Law Centre (2016). *Classroom Culture*. retrieved on 06-07-2016 from http://www.tolerance.org/publication/classroom-culture

The Academic Senate for California Community Colleges (2009). *Contextualized Teaching & Learning: A Faculty Primer*. retrieved on 06-07-2016 from http://www.cccbsi.org/websites/basicskills/images/ctl.pdf

The Centre for Teaching Excellence. *Curriculum design and renewal*. retrieved on 03-07-2016 from https://uwaterloo.ca/centre-for-teaching-excellence/support-faculty-and-staff/curriculum-renewal

The University of Adelaide. *Curriculum Renewal Process*. retrieved on 03-07-2016 from https://www.adelaide.edu.au/professions/pedagogical-possibilities/change/curriculum/process/

Vancouver School Board. *Instructional Materials (Selection of Learning Resources)*. retrieved on 11-06-2017 from https://www.vsb.bc.ca/district-policy/iia-instructional-materials-selection-learning-resources

Victoria State Government. *Selecting Teaching and Learning Resources*. retrieved on 11-06-2017 http://www.education.vic.gov.au/school/principals/spag/curriculum/Pages/selection.aspx

Zuga, K.F. *Relating Technology Education Goals to Curriculum Planning*. retrieved on 03-07-2016 from http://scholar.lib.vt.edu/ejournals/JTE/v1n1/backup/zuga.jte-v1n1.html

Index

G

H

I